Rocks and Minerals of California
THIRD REVISED EDITION

By
Vinson Brown
David Allan
James Stark

Illustrations
Robert Edison
Kay Brown

D0963310

Maps
George Andrews
John Hinkel

Color Photographs
W. Scott Lewis

Acknowledgements

The pictures on pages 6, 41, 44, and 47 were originally done by Don Greame Kelley for the book, *The Amateur Naturalist's Handbook*, by Vinson Brown. These pictures are reproduced by permission of the publishers (Little, Brown & Co.) and the artist.

We are greatly indebted to Dr. Gordon Oakeshott of the California State Division of Mines for his kind examination of our book and his criticisms and suggestions. We appreciate all the help and suggestions received from the staff of the Geology Department of San Jose State College. We wish also to acknowledge and express our appreciation for Richard Hartesveldt checking over the key. In preparing all the paste-ups we were aided by the careful work of Mrs. W.B. Sheldon, Mrs. Bertha B. Brown, and Mrs. Stella Ford Walker. For our revised edition we wish to acknowledge and express our appreciation to Mrs. Eleanor M. Learned, who worked for the California Division of Mines and Geology, for looking over the added supplementary Quadrangle Map information.

Naturegraph Publishers, Inc.
3543 Indian Creek Road
Happy Camp, CA 96039
U.S.A.

Books for a better world

Table of Contents

Topographical Map Information

The quadrangle map supplement, pages 115 to 195 , will provide the hobbyist, mineral collector (or rock hound), and prospector with a condensed guide to many mineral localities. Quadrangle maps are not included in this publication because of their large size. Reducing their size for this book would destroy their usefulness and clarity. Furthermore, the large quantity of maps required would make the book unnecessarily bulky. These maps are available at a reasonable price and you may obtain one or several at a time as you choose the area to cover. To order maps see page 195 for addresses.

A few areas can be located by using a standard road map. Most of the localities are listed by section, township and range. Several types of maps may be used to locate an area listed by section, township and range. Probably the best ones are the topographic maps published by the U.S. Geological Survey. The unit of survey for this map is a quadrangle bounded by parallels of latitude and meridians of longitude. Each quadrangle is designated by the name of a city, town or prominent natural feature within it. Quadrangles covering 7½ minutes of latitude and longitude are published at the scale of 1:24,000 (1 inch = 2,000 feet). Quadrangles covering 15' of latitude and longitude have a scale of 1:62,500 (1 inch = approximately 1 mile). An index map showing the location of the quadrangle maps is available free for any state upon application to the U.S. Geological Survey.

Some areas in the U.S. are unmapped or unsurveyed. If the area is within a National Forest use the U.S. Forest Service maps, otherwise utilize the AMS (Army Map Series) maps published by the U.S. Geological Survey. These maps have a scale of 1 inch equals approximately 4 miles and indicate the approximate topography with either a 100 or 200' contour interval. The maps cover rather large areas, 1 degree of latitude and 2 degrees of longitude (32, 15' quadrangle maps would fit within their boundaries), or about 7,000 square miles. Sections can be located approximately by scaling from the Township and Range lines, i.e., ¼ inch equals 1 mile approximately (1 mile being the width of a section).

Chemical Abbreviations
To assist you in using the Mineral Key

In chemistry and mineralogy each element in a compound is given an arbitrary sign, such as Au for gold and Ag for silver. Thus the rare mineral calaverite has the symbol of $AuTe_2$, and this means that one atom of gold is united to two atoms of tellurium. Both $2O$ and O_2 signify two atoms of oxygen, but only the second of these symbols means the two atoms are closely united. The abbreviations explained below are used in this book.

Al	aluminum	**O**	oxygen
Sb	antimony	**P**	phosphorus
As	arsenic	**Pt**	platinum
Ba	barium	**K**	potassium
Bi	bismuth	**Si**	silicon
B	boron	**Ag**	silver
Ca	calcium	**Na**	sodium
C	carbon	**Sr**	strontium
Cl	chlorine	**S**	sulfur
Cr	chromium	**Te**	tellurium
Co	cobalt	**Sn**	tin
Cu	copper	**Ti**	titanium
F	fluorine	**W**	tungsten
Au	gold	**U**	uranium
H	hydrogen	**V**	vanadium
Fe	iron	**Zn**	zinc
Pb	lead	**Zr**	zirconium
Li	lithium		
Mg	magnesium		
Mn	manganese		
Hg	mercury		
Mo	molybdenum		
Ni	nickel		
N	nitrogen		

Introduction: A Glorious State

The state of California is blessed with probably the most wonderful variety of rocks and minerals of any state in the Union. The geologic history of California shows us this region on the edge of the great hollow of the Pacific Ocean has been subject to unusual stresses and strains. The constant mountain building, due to the folding of the earth's crust near a great ocean, has again and again brought the forces of pressure and heat to play on the rocks and minerals. Volcanic action, hot springs and fumaroles (hot gas holes), as well as the leaching and weathering action of water on new rock layers exposed by mountain building has produced a veritable fairyland of rock and mineral forms.

With a rock pick (purchasable at most hardware stores), a seeking eye and a pair of good legs you are prepared for the adventure of exploring one of the most interesting worlds of nature. Anywhere where there are hills or mountains or stream beds you are likely to make surprising discoveries. Look always for fresh exposures of rock layers, such as road cuts, stream cuts, places where landslides have occurred, quarries and localities where there has been volcanic action. Take specimens of rocks and minerals that are about 2 x 2 x 2 inches in size. Put all specimens from one locality in a single cloth bag, marked with the date and locality. At home paint a small strip of white enamel on each specimen, and on this enamel write a number with India ink. In a notebook write these numbers and opposite each number write the date and locality where collected. Also write any other information about the specimen you may have noticed.

This book is only a very simple beginning to a very complex subject. If it whets your interest, shows you in simple language how to be a good rock and mineral collector, and identify some of the commoner species you encounter, then it will have done its main job. The bibliography in the back of this book lists several more advanced publications that will take you much farther along the trail. Learn to use them. It is suggested that as you use the maps in this book, you mark on them new discoveries.

Warning: Collect rocks and minerals only where you have a right to go and collect sparingly. Hogs, wasters and trespassers give rock hounds everywhere a bad name.

How To Use This Book

Take time to turn the pages and, at least briefly, investigate the whole book. Notice that we have divided the book into two major parts, one on minerals and one on rocks, with the mineral division first because rocks are usually made up of different minerals. To understand rocks and how to identify them, you should first study the minerals that make them. The rock-making minerals are in bold capital letters in the mineral key, as is **CALCITE.**

Observe that the map key on page 74 shows you by page number where all the maps in the book are located in relation to the whole state. Study the maps of areas near you to see in general what minerals and rocks are likely to be found in your neighborhood. We have mapped in detail only the more important mineral areas of the state, as our space is limited.

As you begin to collect specimens of rocks and minerals, you will find that there are several kinds of keys in this book that will help you unlock the secrets of their identity. The general mineral key (on page 6) and the general rock key (on page 55) are first in importance. Second, there are the maps, starting on page 74, which show where many of the minerals and the more interesting rocks are found. Third, there are the charts of mineral habitats, starting on page 38, which show which minerals are likely to be found together, and fourth, there are the full color pictures of rocks and minerals starting on page 65. Pictures, both those in color and those not, should be used with considerable caution because of the wide variation in appearance.

The whole idea of using keys is to narrow your choices down by eliminating kinds that cannot be the specimen you hold in your hand. You notice where on the map your mineral was found. It is likely to be one of the minerals shown as being found in that part of the country. You notice what kind of a habitat or environment it was found in, whether in a limestone quarry, an ore vein, a stream bed, and so on. Only certain kinds of minerals are found in each mineral habitat. Last, you start using the general key, keeping your eyes open for a mineral name that fits both the map and the habitat, but realizing it could possibly be a different mineral. Because this book deals only with California rocks and minerals you have already eliminated many kinds talked about in general books but not found in this state.

3

THE MINERALS OF CALIFORNIA

There is a very good reason for studying minerals before we study rocks. Rocks are made up of minerals, often several of them mixed together. Many rocks are almost impossible to identify without knowing at least something about the minerals of which they are formed. In the following descriptions of minerals we have set in bold captials each mineral which is commonly found in rocks. Before you ever start to learn the names of rocks it would be worth your while to make a special study of rock-forming minerals so you will know how to recognize them.

Here we had better plunge right in to the identification of minerals, followed by some interesting facts about a number of the commoner and more spectacular minerals of California. The marvelously complex history of mineral development in this state can only be briefly touched on in a small book of this kind.

To identify minerals you must test them. This testing of minerals to determine their names is comparable to an exciting puzzle or game. But you must remember that like all really good puzzles or games, to do them requires real skill and patience. It is very easy to make a mistake and to hurry almost guarantees you will make an error. The major means of testing a mineral are listed below.

Physical Tests

Hardness is very important in identifying minerals, as they differ greatly in hardness. Ten different minerals have been chosen to soft) to 10 (extremely hard). There are:

1 Talc	4 Fluorite	7 Quartz	9 Corundum
2 Gypsum	5 Apatite	8 Topaz	10 Diamond
3 Calcite	6 Feldspar (Orthoclase)		

There are four common objects, available anywhere, that we can use for judging hardness. These are a *fingernail,* with a hardness of 2.5, a *copper coin,* with a hardness of 3, a *knife blade,* with a hardness of 5.5, and a piece of sharp *quartz,* with a hardness of 7. You know, for example, that what quartz will scratch has a hardness of 7 or less. What it won't scratch has a hardness of more than 7. Have these tools with you when identifying minerals, as they will help you in using the keys.

Streak. The color of a powdered mineral may be different than its apparent color. This streak is obtained by rubbing the mineral on a piece of unglazed porcelain as shown.

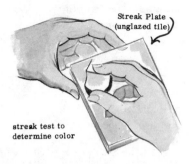

Streak Plate (unglazed tile)

streak test to determine color

Color. Most minerals have so many different colors that this is not a good physical test. However, certain metallic minerals have very distinctive colors. Unfortunately the metallic luster of these minerals appears poorly in color plates.

Luster. The reflection of light on the surface of a mineral gives it its luster. The big division is into metallic and non-metallic luster in minerals. Silver, for example, has a typical metallic luster; quartz a typical non-metallic luster. Non-metallic lusters include vitreous (glassy), pearly, adamantine (diamond sparkling), resinous (like resin in a tree), silky and greasy.

Cleavage. Most minerals have a tendency to break in certain definite directions. This is called cleavage.

Cubic

Rhombic

Orthorhombic

CLEAVAGE EXAMPLES

Octahedral

The more or less smooth surfaces left are called the cleavage planes, which are always planes of the crystal structure and thus are parallel to the possible crystal faces. The exact angle and type of cleavage is often important in identification. So far as possible these cleavages are illustrated in the key (see index also).

Fracture. If a mineral breaks irregularly rather than in smooth planes, it is said to fracture. See illustration for kinds of fracture.

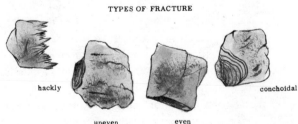

TYPES OF FRACTURE

hackly

uneven

even

conchoidal

Specific gravity (sp. gr.) is the weight of a mineral compared to the weight of an equal volume of water. To find the specific gravity of a

5

mineral, get a pure
specimen and weigh
it as shown, first in
air and then in water.
The specific gravity
will be the weight in
the air divided by the
difference between
the weight in the air
and the weight in

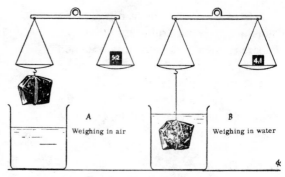

A — Weighing in air

B — Weighing in water

the water. In the example shown, 4.73 would be the specific gravity of the mineral, which would make it likely to be pyrrhotite, which has a specific gravity of about 4.7.

Crystal form. Most minerals have a definite crystal structure on which is based their outward appearance or form. So far as possible, in the illustrations of the minerals, we show their crystal form when it is useful in their identification. The index lists all the crystal forms shown in this book.

Chemical Tests

There are numerous complex chemical tests for aid in identifying minerals, but most of these are too advanced for this book. Certain minerals, however, can be identified by simple chemical tests, such as heating them in a gas flame or touching them with dilute hydrochloric acid to see if they will fizz. Whenever these simple tests are mentioned in the mineral key, use them.

Key to Common California Minerals

Note that if a mineral does not fit this key it will probably be because it is a rare kind, since at least 99 out of 100 minerals you find will be found in this key. The black and white illustrations used in this key are designed almost entirely to emphasize certain definite characteristics about a mineral, such as streakiness or type of cleavage, and are to be considered only partially realistic. Each number in the key gives you 2 to 4 choices (a, b, c, d). Carefully test your mineral against each choice and then move on to the new number your choice leads to. Thus, if you have a metallic mineral that is scratched with a fingernail, you turn to number 3 in the key and so on until identified. (Mineral formulas are explained on page 115 to 117.)

1a. Mineral with a metallic or sub-metallic luster. **2**
1b. Mineral with a non-metallic luster **25**

2. Metallic and Sub-metallic Minerals

2a. Mineral can be scratched by a fingernail (hardness less than 2.5), and will usually leave a mark on paper. **3**
2b. Mineral can't be scratched by a fingernail, but can be scratched with a knife (hardness between 2.5 and 5.5) **10**
2c. Mineral cannot be scratched by knife (hardness more than 5.5) **20**

3. Metallic Minerals Scratched with Fingernail

3a. Streak red or red-brown, color reddish or red **4**
3b. Streak and color otherwise. **5**

4a. Scarlet streak; luster part adamantine (sparkling); a very heavy mineral with sp. gr. of 8.1. (see 12 a.). . . . . **cinnabar**
4b. Streak reddish-brown; luster part earthy; sp. gr. 5.2. A chief ore of iron. (see full description at 24a.) . . . . **HEMATITE**

5a. Color yellow-brown; streak yellow-brown; earthy appearance and feel; sp. gr. 3.6—4. (see 24b.). . . . . **LIMONITE**
5b. Color & streak black, gray-black or blue-black, not earthy. **6**

GALENA (lead gray; metallic luster)
cubic cleavage — step-like layers

6a. Good cleavage **7**
6b. Cleavage poor or not evident. **9**

7a. Good cleavage in 3 directions, forming what look like steps and cubes; streak gray-black; a heavy mineral with a sp. gr. of 7.6; color black; hardness 2.5. An important ore of lead. . . . PbS **galena**
7b. Good cleavage in one direction; sp. gravity about 4.5 . . . . **8**

MOLYBDENITE (Molly) bluish-gray
hexagonal crystals often misshapen flakes

8a. Hardness 1—1.5; color blue-black or lead gray with bluish tinge; shaves with knife; has platy cleavage; easily marks paper. An ore of molybdenum. . . . . . MoS$_2$ (see p. 68) **molybdenite**
8b. Hardness 2; color blue-black or dark gray; streak gray-black; melts in match flame; marks paper. Ore of antimony. . . . . Sb$_2$S$_3$ **stibnite**

7

black, bluish
black or
steel gray

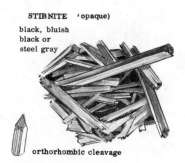

orthorhombic cleavage

GRAPHITE (hexagonal scales, opaque)

dark gray
to black

soils fingers

9a. Specific gravity 4.7; often fibrous (with radiating fibers), but usually massive; luster often dull; brittle; soils fingers; hardness 1–2.5; color & streak black; often is splintery; found with psilomelane and limonite. Chief ore of manganese.............. MnO_2 **pyrolusite**

9b. Very light mineral, sp. gr. 2.3; feels greasy; soils fingers; hardness 1–1.5; color and streak black; often fibrous; cleavage 1 direction and scaly with flexible scales; is used in lead pencils. ...... C **GRAPHITE**

10. Minerals of Metallic and Sub-metallic Luster that can be scratched with Knife, but not Fingernail.

10a. Red or copper red color & streak **11**
10b. Otherwise **13**

11a. Red color and streak, but not copper red.............. **12**
11b. Copper red color and streak; tarnishes black; is easily shaped and twisted with tools; hardness 2.5–3; sp. gr. 8.9 (very heavy); often with green spots. .... Cu **copper**

12a. Scarlet streak; hardness 2.5; very heavy with an 8.1 sp. gr.; luster partly adamantine (diamond glittering); usually granular with perfect prismatic cleavage (see p. 23); turns into mercury gas under hot flame (see p. 66)................................... HgS **cinnabar**

12b. Streak browish-red; hardness 3.5–4; sp. gr. 6; massive or in isometric crystals; brittle; luster often adamantine or sub-metallic; often has green or blue spots and bits of copper... Cu_2O **cuprite**

CUPRITE (red to dark red)

green or blue
spots

octahedral
cleavage

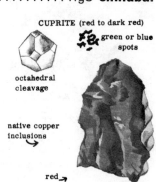

native copper
inclusions

red

13a. Color and streak black, gray, brown, red-brown, yellow-brown **14**
13b. Color otherwise; streak sometimes black **19**

8

14a. Good cleavage............ **15**
14b. Cleavage not important **16**

SPHALERITE (yellow to red-brown or black)

typical tetrahedral crystal

15a. Color brown to black; sp. gr. 3.9–4.1; luster part resinous; the 6 cleavages usually appear cubic (so called "false galena"); streak brown; hardness 3.5–4. An ore of zinc........ ZnS **sphalerite**
15b. Color gray to black; streak is black; good cubic cleavage in 3 directions at right angles; sp. gr. 7.5 (see 7a) **galena**

(See 7a.)   GALENA

WOLFRAMITE (black to brown)

granular surface

curved plates

15c. Color brown; black or gray; cleavage in 1 direction along length with the plates curved; luster is sometimes resinous; hardness 5–5.5; in thick tabular crystals and massive forms with thin splinters; sometimes deep red; brittle; very heavy, sp. gr. 7–7.5; streak dark brown to black. A tungsten ore.
.... (FE,Mn)WO$_4$ **wolframite**

perfect cleavage on fracture face

16a. Color black, brownish black, yellowish or red brown **17**
16b. Color golden or silverish; extremely heavy metals with specific gravity greater than 10..................................... **18**
16c. Color bronze-brown to brass-yellow; not so heavy **19**

17a. Streak brown to black; hardness 5.5 (very hard to scratch with a knife and can scratch glass); a luster sometimes like that of pitch; usually granular; uneven fracture; sp. gr. 4.6; sometimes slightly magnetic............................... FeCr$_2$O$_4$ **chromite**
17b. Streak red-brown; hardness 5.5–6.5; sp. gr. 4.8–5.3; usually massive or kidney-shaped; sometimes sparklng like mica (specular hematite); uneven fracture .... (24a) **HEMATITE**
17c. Streak yellow-brown; hardness 5–5.5; sp. gr. 3.6–4.0; color brown to black; cleavage in 1 direction when present; usually massive in form, sometimes fibrous with radiating plates, stalactites and dark and light bands; usually becomes magnetic when heated. Iron ore
.... Fe O(OH)nH$_2$O **LIMONITE**
17d. Streak black-brown; hardness 5–7; color black; sp. gr. 3.6–4; appears like bunch of grapes (botryoidal) (p. 68), or massive or in stalactites; luster sub-metallic to dull; conchoidal fracture))) prominent (see 24c).. **psilomelane**

9

18a. Color and streak silvery white; specific gravity 10.5 hardness 2.5–3; tarnishes black on exposure to air, can be worked with tools; found in veins in rocks. . . . . Ag **silver**

18b. Color and streak golden yellow; sp. gr. 19.3; hardness 2.5–3; can be worked with tools; found in quartz veins and as loose nuggets and flakes in streams. (see p. 67) . . . . Au **gold**

19a. Color brownish-bronze, but tarnishes purple and often with iridescent colors (so-called "peacock ore"); usually in compact masses; streak black; specific gravity 5.1; hardness 3. A common copper ore. . . . . Cu_5FeS_4 **bornite**

19b. Color a peculiar reddish-bronze; usually magnetic when powdered; commonly either massive or granular or compact; sp. gr. 4.61; hardness 3.5–4; streak gray-black; often found with chalcopyrite, gabbro, peridotite . . . . FeS **pyrrhotite**

19c. Color brass-yellow; streak greenish-black; hardness 3.5–4; sp. gr. 4.1–4.3; often has iridescent tarnish; becomes magnetic after heating; commonly in massive forms, less often in wedge-shaped crystals . . . . $CuFeS_2$ **chalcopyrite**

20. Metallic or Sub-metallic Luster; Minerals cannot be scratched with a knife.

20a. Color whitish, yellow, or steel gray. **21**

20b. Color brown, black or gray . . . **22**

21a. Color brass yellow; streak is greenish-black; hardness 6–6.5; sp. gr. 5.0; the crystals often in cubic form with striated (grooved) faces; often in massive form. Sometimes called "fool's gold." . . . . FeS_2 **pyrite**

21b. Color pale yellow; streak dark greenish; hardness 6–6.5; sp. gr. 4.9; the crystals often take cockscomb shape; also in radiating masses, which take dark tarnish; dissolves in concentrated nitric acid when powdered (pyrite does not); may be fibrous . . . . FeS_2 **marcasite**

21c. Color silver-white to steel gray; streak black; hardness 5.5; common in striated crystals (with grooved lines), or in granular or compact masses; sp. gr.

PYRITE (often called fool's gold)
(brass yellow, opaque)

Pyritohedron sometimes

usually striated cubes

ARSENOPYRITE (tin white to black)

common crystals

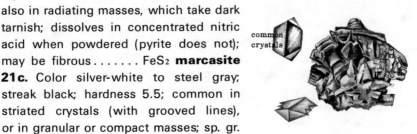

10

5.9–6.2; strong garlic odor when mineral is heated in gas flame. Often found with gold.......................... FeAsS **arsenopyrite**

22a. Streak black or dark brown   **23**

22b. Streak red-or yellow-brown **24**

MAGNETITE
(Black metallic luster)
Octahedral (striations)

23a. Strongly magnetic; color and streak black; hardness 5.5–6; sp. gr. 5.1–5.2; even fracture; form usually compact or granular massive, sometimes with octahedral crystals. Dissolves in hydrochloric acid. .... Fe_3O_4 **magnetite**

23b. Magnetic only when heated; sometimes gray or black color; uneven fracture; striations on crystal faces; also in granular & compact masses; garlic odor in heat .... (21c) **arsenopyrite**

23c. Never magnetic; streak black-brown; hardness 5–7; sp. gr. 3.3–4.7; opaque in appearance; luster sub-metallic or dull; & has prominent conchoidal))) fracture. Found in massive forms, with rounded, grape-cluster-like surfaces, or in stalactites or seams.

.... $BaMnMn_8O_{16}(OH)_4$ **psilomelane**

24a. Streak red-brown; color black, red, gray & reddish-brown; hardness 1–6.5; sp. gr. 4.9–5.3; found in California mainly in earthy (soft) or granular form; more rarely in crystals or micaceous masses (specular hematite) that sparkle and appear to cut with knife between crystals; rarely kidney shape; uneven fracture; magnetic on heating. A chief ore of iron. .... Fe_2O_3 **HEMATITE**

HEMATITE (black, gray, reddish–brown)
common earthy mass (soft)
rare crystals (hard)

24b. Streak yellow-brown; color brown, black or yellow; hardness 5–5.5; sp. gr. 3–4.3; fracture mainly conchoidal))) when this hard. Usually in massive form or appearing in grapelike clusters, stalactites or kidney-shaped crusts. It is a lesser ore of iron caused by weathering of other iron ores such as hematite. It usually becomes magnetic when heated. Also called goethite. (see 17c)..... $FeO(OH) \cdot nH_2O$ **LIMONITE**

24c. Streak pale brown; color reddish-brown to brownish-black; hardness 6–7; specific gravity 4.1–4.3; luster adamantine to metallic; brittle; crystals in long, vertically striated prisms; sometimes in grains. An ore of titanium. .... TiO_2 **rutile**

11

25. Minerals with Non-metallic Luster

25a. Mineral can be scratched by a fingernail (hardness 1–2.5)

25b. Mineral cannot be scratched by fingernail, but can be scratched by a copper coin (2.5–3)

25c. Mineral cannot be scratched by a copper coin, but can be scratched by a good knife blade (hardness 3.5–5)

25d. Mineral cannot be scratched by a knife blade, but can be scratched by quartz (hardness 5.5–7)

25e. Mineral cannot be scratched by quartz (hardness 7.1 +)...

RUTILE (red–orange, brown)

uneven fracture

hairlike striations

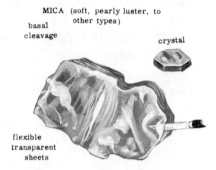

MICA (soft, pearly luster, to other types)

basal cleavage

crystal

flexible transparent sheets

26. Non-metallic Minerals Scratched by Fingernail

26a. The mineral has good cleavage

26b. The mineral has poor or no cleavage

27a. Cleavage flakes elastic, which means they snap back into place when sharply bent

27b. Cleavage flakes flexible, but not elastic

28a. Color brown, yellow or clear (the common light-colored mica); hardness 2–2.5; sp. gr. 2.76–3.0; luster glassy; crystals in tabular form in 6-sided plates; highly basal cleavage, permitting it to be split into thin, transparent leaves. . . . . $KAl_3Si_3O_{10}(OH)_2$ **MUSCOVITE**

28b. Color dark brown to black (the common dark mica); hardness 2.5–3; sp. gr. 2.95–3.0; luster glassy to pearly; perfect basal cleavage. In tabular or short, prismatic crystals, 6-sided plates, leaf-like, scaly or micaceous masses; often a main part of granite.

. . . . $K(Mg,Fe)_3AlSi_3O_{10}(OH)_2$ **BIOTITE**

28c. Color apple green; otherwise like muscovite. Common in the Mother Lode country. . . . . **mariposite**

28d. Color lilac, lavendar, violet-blue, pink & colorless; luster glassy or pearly; hardness 2.5; common in scaly masses or groups of short

prismatic crystals; fuses in flame to bubbly, fluorescent glass.
. . . . $K_2Li_3Al_4Si_7O_{21}(OH,F)_3$ **lepidolite**

29a. Greasy feel; in leaf-like, granular or compact masses, a perfect basal cleavage; luster pearly; extremely soft and easily powdered; color white to dark green; sp. gr. 2.7–2.8. Often forms talc schist.
. . . . $Mg_3Si_4O_{10}(OH)_2$ **TALC**

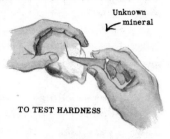

Unknown mineral

TO TEST HARDNESS

29b. No greasy feel; hardness is at least 2. . . . . **30**

30a. Color green, rarely white, pale yellow or rose red; the cleavage flakes curved; hardness 2–2.5; sp. gr. 2.6–2.9; luster pearly; often makes schist.
$(Mg,Fe,Al)_6(Si,Al)_4O_{10}(OH)_8$ **CHLORITE**

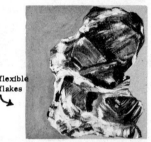

CHLORITE (glassy to pearly; green, rose, yellow to black)

30b. Colorless or white, also tints of yellow, red or brown; hardness 2; sp. gr. 2.32; when heated, it turns dense white in color, peels off in flakes and fuses to a round globule; the soft cleavage flakes

flexible flakes ↘

are barely flexible (some massive forms have no cleavage). Forms transparent selenite, snowy-white alabaster, and silky satin-spar. (see p. 67). . . . . $CaSO_4 \cdot 2H_2O$ **GYPSUM**

31. Minerals with Poor Cleavage
31a. Usually massive **33**
31b. In bunches of long slender fibers or fibrous crusts **32**

GYPSUM (translucent gray–white)

white patches of → powder

32a. Luster silky; color usually whitish or greenish, but may be brown, red, yellow or black. This is the fibrous or asbestos form of serpentine (see 40a). . . . . . . **chrysotile**
32b. Luster glassy to dull or earthy; color white; has a bitter salty taste; hardness 2–2.5; sp. gr. 1.7–1.8; found in fibrous bunches or crusts; soluble in water. . . . . $MgSO_4 \cdot 7H_2O$ **epsomite**

33a. Colorless or white, rarely shades of red, yellow or brown; luster glassy, pearly or silky; massive form (poor in cleavage) called alabaster. (see 30b, and p. 67) . . . . **GYPSUM**

33b. Pale yellow color; luster resinous; burns easily with a blue flame and acrid smell; hardness 1.5–2.5; specific gravity 2.05–2.09. In massive form, thick tabular crystals, pyramidal crystals, crusts or powdery form . . . . S **sulphur**

33c. Colorless or white; luster earthy; sticks to your tongue and smells and tastes like clay when wet; hardness 2–2.5. One of the basic clay minerals . . . . $Al_2Si_2O_5 (OH)_4$ **KAOLINITE**

33d. Color steel-gray to iron-black; soils fingers; luster dull; sp. gr. 4.7; hardness 1–6.5; fibrous or prismatic . . . . **pyrolusite**

33e. Greasy feel; extremely soft (see 29a) . . . . **TALC**

33f. Earthy, yellowish masses (see 24b) . . . . **LIMONITE**

34. Mineral of Non-metallic Luster, Scratched by Copper Coin, but not by Fingernail.

34a. The mineral has good cleavage **35**

34b. The mineral has poor or no cleavage **40**

35a. One cleavage; color lilac, lavender, violet-blue, pink to color-less; usually in scaly masses, broad plates or irregular sheets; hard-ness 2.5–4. (see 28d & p. 68) . . . . **lepidolite**

35b. Cleavage in 3 directions **36**

35c. Cleavage tabular ⬭ or prismatic △ **37**

36a. Salty taste; colorless, white or occasionally red or blue; 3 cleavages at right angles; hardness 2.5; sp. gr. 2.1–2.3; easily soluble in water. (sylvite & epsomite also have salty taste, but are very bitter) Salt . . . . NaCl (see p. 67) **halite**

36b. No salty taste; fizzes in cold dilute hydrochloric or acetic acid; colorless, white or with various shades; rhombic cleavage; a hardness of 3; sp. gr. 2.72; luster glassy; common in crystals or in more massive forms, also fibrous granular, chalky & in stalactites ᵛᵛ; turns flame a bright red. (see p. 65) $CaCO_3$ **CALCITE**

CALCITE (white, colorless)

typical crystals

37a. Heavy mineral, gr. 3.9+ **38**

37b. Lighter mineral; gr. 3.9– **39**

38a. When heated, colors flame a deep crimson (of strontium); sp. gr. 3.96; usually colorless, white or light shades of red or blue; hardness of 3–3.5; glassy luster; usually in tabular or prismatic crystals, or in fibrous or radiating masses; the cleavage basal . . . . $SrSO_4$ **celestite**

38b. When intensely heated, turns flame yellowish-green; sp. gr. 4.5; colorless, white or light shades of yellow, red or blue; luster glassy; usually found in tabular or prismatic crystals, granular, massive forms or in nodules within rocks; cleavage perfect and basal; brittle; called heavy spar.. . . . . BaSO₄ **barite**

38c. Sp. gr. 8.1; streak scarlet; red color; sparkles. (12a) **cinnabar**

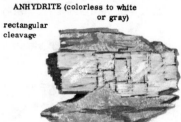

ANHYDRITE (colorless to white or gray)

rectangular cleavage

CERUSSITE (light yellow, white, gray) (white lead)

⬈ fibrous white crust

⬉ loose needles

39a. Cleaves into rectangular blocks; colorless, white gray, blue or red; commonly massive, granular or leaf-like, but once in a while in thick tabular or prismatic crystals; brittle; luster glassy or pearly; sp. gr. 2.89–2.98; turns a hot flame reddish-yellow and may break apart. . . . . CaSO₄ **anhydrite**

39b. Cleavage basal & also prismatic splintery, producing long splinters; usually colorless, but turns white or streaky white; sp. gr. 1.9; hardness 2.5–3; luster glassy; in solid veins of large crystals or in large masses like gypsum; common beneath many dry lake beds in Kern County. . . . . Na₂B₄O₇·4H₂O **kernite**

40. Cleavage Poor or None

40a. Luster greasy, wax-like or silky; usually appears mottled dark green and white in the massive form, but may be greenish brown, whitish or yellow; hardness 2.5–4; sp. gr. 2.2; in fibrous form it is chrysotile asbestos. (see 60a.) . . . . **SERPENTINE**

40b. Luster glassy; sp. gr. 6.4–6.6 (very heavy); color white, gray or brown; hardness 3–3.5; fracture conchoidal (shell-like); very brittle; effervesces in nitric acid; fuses in hot flame to metallic balls of lead. . . . . PbCO₃ **cerussite**

BARITE (glassy, transparent, colorless to bluish)

tabular crystals (heavy)

40c. Luster glassy, dull or earthy; color sky blue, greenish-blue or green and usually streaked with black; often sticks to tongue; sp. gr.2.0–2.4; fracture conchoidal (shell-like); usually in solid veins or grape-like masses. (see 62b) . . . . **chrysocolla**

41. Minerals with Non-metallic Luster that cannot be Scratched with Copper Coin, but can be Scratched by Knife.

41a. Mineral has good cleavage **42**
41b. Mineral has poor or no cleavage **54**

42a. Fizzes or foams in cold hydrochloric or acetic acid, at least along a scratch. **43**
42b. Does not fizz or foam when touched with cold acid even along a scratch. **44**

43a. Fizzes or foams in cold hydrochloric acid only along a scratch; colorless, white, pink, green, gray, brown or black; hardness 3.5–4; sp. gr. 2.85; 3 cleavages not at right angles (rhombohedral). Found with peculiar, curved crystals or in massive forms; luster glassy; white to pink crystal intergrowths often easy to see. $CaMg(CO_3)_2$ **DOLOMITE**

DOLOMITE (transparent to translucent, glassy-white to pearly tints)

rocky ball (geode)

curved crystals

43b. Fizzes or foams in cold acid on mineral surface; 3 cleavages not at right angles (rhombic); colorless, white or variously shaded; hardness 3; sp. gr. 2.72. (see 36b) **CALCITE**
43c. Fizzes or foams in cold acid on mineral surface; usually found in colorless or white clusters of radiating, slender, pointed crystals only one cleavage face of 3 is ever good and it not frequently; hardness 3.5–4; sp. gr. 3.7. (Closely related to calcite, but powdered aragonite boiled in a solution of cobalt nitrate turns violet.) (see 57b) **aragonite**

44a. Luster silky, pearly, adamantine, glassy or greasy. **45**
44b. Luster resinous or adamantine; color yellow, brown, black or red, often iridescent; cubic cleavage. (15a) . . . . **sphalerite**

45a. Quite heavy minerals with specific gravity of higher than 4; usually with adamantine, greasy or pearly luster. **46**
45b. Specific gravity below 4; luster glassy, pearly, silky. **47**

46a. Sp. gr. 6–6.4 (very heavy); luster adamantine to greasy; color white, gray or colorless; hardness 3–3.5; streak white; difficultly soluble in nitric acid; brittle; found in prismatic ⊖ and in tabular crystals ⬠ also massive and granular forms; 3 good cleavages. A lead ore . . . . $PbSO_4$ **anglesite**

46b. Sp. gr. 5.9–6.1 (very heavy); luster adamantine; hardness 4.5–5; color white, light brown or light green, crystals look like double pyramids ◈ ◍; also found as grains in rock; fluoresces in ultraviolet light . . . . $CaWO_4$ **scheelite**

46c. Sp. gr. 4.5; luster pearly; colorless, white, yellow, blue or red; hardness 3–3.5; usually in plate-like masses, also in granular or massive forms and nodules in rocks; cleavage is basal. (see 38b) . . . . $BaSO_4$ **barite**

46d. Sp. Gr. 4.3–4.4; luster sub-adamantine to glassy; cleavage rhombohedral; fizzes in hot dilute hydrochloric acid; hardness 5; common in grape-cluster or nipple-like crusts; also in small, round crystals . . . . $ZnCO_3$ **smithsonite**

SMITHSONITE (white, yellow, bluish, greenish, or pink)

47a. Hardness of 5 or more; hard to scratch with a knife **53**

white dry-bone ore ↙

47b. Hardness of 5 or less; easy to scratch with a knife **48**

dull ←brown crust

WOLLASTONITE (white, pink, gray)

48a. Dissolves slowly in cold hydro-chloric acid **49**

48b. Does not dissolve in cold hydro-chloric acid **50**

49a. Usually found in fine collections of tiny crystals, showing what looks like rectangular cleavage ◈ ; but also found in tabular ◍ crystals and in massive, leaf-like & granular forms; colorless, white, blue, gray or red; hardness 3–3.5; sp. gr.

often fibrous ↗

2.89–2.98; luster glassy, but pearly on cleavage faces. (see 39a.) . . . . $CaSO_4$ **anhydrite**

49b. Usually found in fibrous or compact masses or in tabular or short prismatic crystals; luster glassy; two good cleavages; brittle; color white, gray or rose, fuses easily in hot flame to a clear glass; hardness 4.5–5; sp. gr. 2.8–2.9; fluoresces yellow or orange. $CaSiO_3$ **wollastonite**

49c. Usually tinged with rose-red rarely brown or pink; fizzes in hot hydrochloric acid; in cleavable masses or in small crystals; brittle; luster glassy; sp.gr. 3.45–3.60; hardness 3.5–4.5. $MnCO_3$ **rhodochrosite**

50a. Cleavage usually in only one direction **51**
50b. Cleavage usually in two or more directions **52**

51a. Cleavage basal and with elastic plates (micaceous); color lilac, gray-green and yellow; luster pearly and glassy; hardness 2.5–4; sp. gr. 2.8–3.3; in flame begins to bubble, turns flame red, & becomes fluorescent (blue and pinkish). An ore of lithium. (see 28d) **lepidolite**

51b. Has a peculiar double hardness, with hardness of 5 parallel to the length and hardness of 7 across; color blue, white, gray or green; sp. gr. 3.5–3.7; usually in slender, blade-like crystals. Luster glassy. .... $AlSiO_5$ **kyanite**

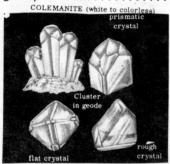

COLEMANITE (white to colorless) prismatic crystal

Cluster in geode

flat crystal

rough crystal

KYANITE (greenish, bluish, to colorless)

bladed crystal in quartz

51c. Color white or colorless; sp. gr. 2.2–2.4; hardness 4–4.5; it breaks apart violently when put in hot flame; luster glassy; streak is white; subconchoidal to uneven fracture; found usually in short crystals, or in massive, granular and compact forms. In deserts. .... $Ca_2B_6O_{11} \cdot 5H_2O$ **colemanite**

52a. A piece held in forceps colors flame a deep red; colorless, white or red or blue; 3 cleavages (one perfect basal, giving diamond appearance ✧; hard. 3–3.5; sp. gr. 3.95; crystals tabular ▱ or prismatic ▱; also radiating fibrous.

FLUORITE (pink, purple, light-green or yellow)

octahedral crystal

.... $SrSO_4$ **celestite**

52b. Usually appears in perfect cubic crystals, more rarely in fibers or columns in masses; colorless, violet, green, yellow and brown; hardness always 4; sp. gr. 3.8; luster glassy; cleavage is perfect octahedral; sometimes in granular form; usually fluoresces blue .... CaF_2 **fluorite**

53a. Crystals generally slender ⌒; 2 cleavage directions at 54 degrees and perfect prismatic; luster glassy to pearly; color white, gray, green, brown, or black; hardness 5–6; sp. gr. 3–3.3. Found also in fibrous, columnar, granular and massive forms. Several of the kinds are described on page 22 .... **AMPHIBOLES**

53b. Crystals generally short and stout ⌂ ; 2 cleavage directions at about 90 degrees making perfect prisms; found in granular and massive forms; color black, green and white; sp. gr. 3.2–3.4; hardness 5.5. (see 68a & b) . . . . **PYROXENES**

53c. Usually massive or fine-grained, sometimes with short, prismatic crystals ⬭ ; prismatic cleavage at 92 and 88 degrees; color pink, brown-pink to grayish, turning black on weathering; luster glassy; sp. gr. 3.4–3.7; hardness 5.5–6 (very hard to scratch with knife) . . . . $MnSiO_3$ **rhodonite**

54. Minerals with Poor or No Cleavage

54a. Fizzes when touched with cold hydrocholic acid (see 63d) **55**
54b. Does not fizz or foam when touched with cold acid **58**

55a. Usually green or blue **56**
55b. Not green or blue **57**

56a. Bright green color; in fibrous or grape-like (botryoidal) masses or coatings; usually found with azurite; hardness 3.5–4; sp. gr. 3.9–4.0. Important ore of copper . . . . $Cu_2CO_3(OH)_2$ **malachite**

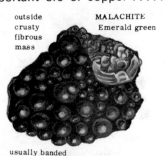

outside
crusty
fibrous
mass

MALACHITE
Emerald green

usually banded

AZURITE (deep azure blue)

crystalline
agregates

conchoidal
fracture

vitreous
or glassy
luster

56b. Color blue; usually in crystal coatings or as small crystals, associated with malachite; may be in massive or earthy forms; luster glassy to adamantine (sparkling); conchoidal))) fracture; often velvety to feel; streak light blue; sp. gr. 3.9–4; hardness 3.5–4 brittle.
. . . . $Cu_3(OH)_2(CO_3)_2$ **azurite**

57a. Usually found in fibrous masses or granular; colorless, white, red, or brown; sp. gr. 2.72; hardness 3; often forms stalactites in caves (see 36b) . . . . **CALCITE**
57b. Usually found in clusters of radiating, slender, & pointed crystals; sometimes fibrous in structure; colorless or white or gray; conchoidal))) fracture; hardness 3.5–4; sp. gr. 2.95. Closely related to calcite,

19

but powdered aragonite boiled in a solution of colbalt nitrate turns violet.
. . . . CaCO₃ **aragonite**

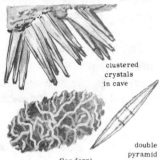

ARAGONITE (colorless, white, yellow)

clustered crystals in cave

double pyramid

flos ferri

58a. Very heavy minerals **59**
58b. Less heavy; under 3.6 sp. gr. **60**

59a. Usually found in isolated pyramidal crystals ⬡ and massive patches; sp. gr. 5.9–6.1; luster adamantine (sparkling) or greasy; color gray, white or yellowish; streak white; hardness 4.5; even fracture; fluoresces blue; sometimes has pyramidal ⬙ cleavage (see 46b). . . . . CaWO₄ **scheelite**
59b. Found in massive forms or platy crystals ▱ ; sp. gr. 6.4–6.6; luster adamantine (sparkling); fracture conchoidal))); crystals often in hollow network ⬙ ; color gray, creamy or brown; hardness 3–3.5; very brittle. A secondary lead mineral formed from galena. (see 40b)
. . . . PbCO₃ **cerussite**

60a. Luster greasy or waxy or sometimes silky; usually appears mottled green and white in the massive form; when colored a pure, light green, called antigorite; in the fibrous form makes chrysotile asbestos; color dark green, yellow-green or whitish; hardness 2–5; sp. gr. 2.2. (see illustration p. 69) . . . . . . Mg₃Si₂O₅(OH)₄ **SERPENTINE**
60b. Luster glassy, resinous, adamantine (sparkling), pearly or dull, rarely greasy and then it is opal. **61**

SERPENTINE (green, brown, black, yellow, red, white)

waxy appearance

61a. With conchoidal (curved) fracture
. . . . **62**
61b. No conchoidal fracture or breaking into curved chips. **63**

greasy feel

often banded with asbestos

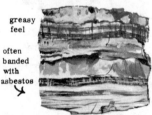

62a. Luster glassy, greasy or dull; streak white; color is very variable, sometimes with fire-like flashes (fire opal); it often shows patches of different colors; glassy opal (hylatite) lines the inside of rock cavities; hardness 5.5–6.5; sp. gr. 1.9–2.2 (very light); moss opal shows moss-like forms inside it made of chlorite or pyrolusite. Opal is often fluorescent. Found in volcanic localities. (see 74b) . . . . SiO₂·nH₂O **opal**

SPHENE (brown gray, green
(Titanite)   yellow)

envelope-
type
crystals

CHRYSOCOLLA (sky blue to green)

glassy to   blue
opaque   conchoidal
                          fracture

brown
veins

green

62b. Luster glassy to dull: streak pale green or blue; hardness 2–4; color usually greenish-blue; sp. gr. 2–2.2; usually found as opal-like incrustations in veins in rock. Fracture))); sticks to the tongue.
. . . . $CuSiO_3 \cdot 2H_2O$ **chrysocolla**

62c. Luster resinous to adamantine (sparkling); color greenish-yellow, brown, yellow, gray or black; usually in wedge-shaped & flattened crystals, but sometimes massive and compact; streak white; hardness 5–5.5; sp. gr. 3.4–3.5. Insoluble . . . . $CaTiSiO_5$ **sphene**

62d. Luster earthy or dull; usually found as snow-white to light brown veins in serpentine rock; hardness 3.5–4.5; sp. gr. 3–3.2; fizzes in hot hydrochloric acid. A magnesium ore . . . . $MgCO_3$ **magnesite**

63a. Luster glassy; color brownish-red, rose-pink or brown; streak reddish-white; in compact or granular masses; hardness 5–6; sp. gr. 3.4–3.7. (see 53c. & p. 69) . . . . **rhodonite**

63b. Luster dull; color ocher-yellow, brown or black; streak yellowish-brown; usually in massive, stalactitic, grape-cluster shaped, columnar, fibrous or earthy forms; hardness 5–5.5; sp. gr. 3.6–4; often gets magnetic when heated; soluble in hydrochloric acid. (see 17c)
. . . . $FeO(OH) \cdot nH_2O$ **LIMONITE**

63c. Luster glassy; colorless, white, greenish or reddish; usually found as a sprinkling of tiny even-sided crystals ⊕ in zeolitic cavities in lava; hardness 5–5.5; sp.gr. 2.3; luster glassy (appearing shiny); clear crystals become cloudy when heated. (Analcime.) . . . . $NaAlSi_2O_6H_2O$ **analcite**

63d. Luster glassy to greasy; found in prismatic and tabular (6-sided) crystals; also massive, granular and compact; color-

APATITE (mixed colors)

6-sided

patch-like
colors

looks melted

21

less, green, yellow and brown; streak white; hardness 5; sp. gr. 3.1–3.2; colors often appear in patches, looking as if melted; fracture even; soluable in hydrochloric acid . . . . $Ca_5(Cl,F)(PO_4)_3$ **apatite**

64. Minerals with Non-metallic Luster that cannot be scratched with Knife, but can be scratched by Quartz.

64a. Mineral with good cleavage **65**
64b. Mineral with poor or no cleavage **69**

65a. Has a peculiar variation in hardness, with hardness of 7 across width and hardness of 5 parallel to length; usually found in blade-like clusters; color blue, gray, green or white; sp. gr. 3.5–3.6 (see 51b)
. . . . Al_2SiO_5 **kyanite**
65b. No peculiar hardness **66**

66a. Mineral usually a peculiar yellow green or pistachio green in color (quite distinctive); hardness 6–7; sp. gr. 3.3–3.5; one cleavage; luster glassy; parallel striations (grooves) on crystals; streak white; fuses easily in flame to a black slag; crystals prismatic . . . .
$\qquad$ $Ca_2(Al,Fe)_3(SiO_4)_3(OH)$ **epidote**

AMPHIBOLE (black, green, white)

luster
glassy

good
cleavage

66b. Mineral not of above color **67**

EPIDOTE (pale yellow-green to dark brown-green)

end
view

parallel
grooves

67a. Color deep blue, bluish-black or grayish; streak grayish-blue; usually fibrous; cleavage similar to amphiboles; luster glassy to pearly; fracture conchoidal to uneven; hardness 6–6.5; gr. 3.04-3.11.
$Na_4Mg_6Al_4Si_{16}O_{44}(OH,F)_4$ **GLAUCOPHANE**
67b. Cleavages 2 at 90 degrees $\llcorner$ **68**
67c. Cleavage in 2 directions at 56 $\angle$
and 124 degrees $\diagdown$; crystals often slender and fibrous, forming asbestos; hardness 5–6; sp.gr. 3–3.3; luster glassy, silky or pearly; found also in granular masses and as scattered grains among igneous and metamorphic rocks. Color is white to light green in **tremolite** $Ca_2Mg_5Si_8O_{22}(OH)_2$; a light green to dark green in **actinolite** $Ca_2(Mg, Fe)_5Si_8O_{22}(OH)_2$; and dark green to black in **HORNBLENDE** $CaNa(Mg,Fe)_4(Al,Fe,Ti)_3Si_6O_{22}(O,OH)_2$ Mountain cork and mountain leather

22

are white to gray leather and cork-like masses of tremolite. Common in
rocks. . . . . **AMPHIBOLES**

68a. Found in stout prisms and irregular grains in rocks; color
white, gray, red, brown, black & green; hardness 5–6; sp. gr. 3.2–3.5;
has glassy luster; brittle. The white to deep grass green form is
diopside $CaMgSi_2O_6$; the violet colored is **violan** (same formula); the
dark green to black is **AUGITE** $Ca(Mg,Fe,Al)(Si,Al)_2O_6$. These are the
most important of the group . . . . **PYROXENES**

68b. Prismatic crystals ◈ often flattened
and may be large; in massive form has
perfect prismatic L cleavage; brittle; color
grayish and greenish-white to emerald-
green, lilac or light blue; luster glassy;
hardness 6.5–7; sp. gr. 3.13–3.20; in a hot
flame gives red lithium color. This is
another pyroxene, usually in pegmatites.
. . . . LiAlSi_2O_6 **SPODUMENE**

PYROXENE (green, black, white, pink, violet)

68c. Found in cleavable masses and
irregular grains in rocks; color white, gray,
red or green; hardness 6; sp. gr. 2.5–2.6.
(Note: feldspars can be told by the 2
prominent cleavages at right angles visible
even in rock grains when looked at under
magnifying glass.) $KAlSi_3O_8$ **ORTHOCLASE**
& MICROCLINE FELDSPARS

FELDSPAR (white, pink)

has striations

plagioclase

blocky
cleavage
orthoclase

(clear crystal)

68d. Color white, tan or gray; the mineral
shows striations (tiny grooves) on 1
cleavage face; otherwise like above 2 minerals.
. . . . Ca or $NaAlSi_3O_8$ **PLAGIOCLASE FELDSPARS**

69. Mineral with Poor or No Cleavage

69a. Color some shade of green **70**
69b. Color red-brown or brown. **71**
69c. Color violet, dark blue or pink violet (bright color distinctive);
usually in fibrous collections, but also in small prisms and massive and
granular forms; luster glassy to dull; hardness 7; sp.gr. 3.2–3.4.
. . . . $Al_8BSi_3O_{19}(OH)$ **dumortierite**
69d. Color usually otherwise, or does not fit descriptions as given
under 70 or 71 (rarely green or brown). **72**

23

70a. Color olive green to grayish or yellowish-green; usually found as scattered grains in dark igneous rocks; the crystals flattened and lengthened ⬠ ; sometimes in massive & granular forms; hardness 6.5–7; sp. gr. 3.2–3.5; luster is glassy; fracture conchoidal; texture often looks like granular sugar, soluble in hydrochloric acid.
. . . . (Mg,Fe)$_2$ SiO$_4$ **OLIVINE**

70b. Greenish or blackish color; in compact, tough mass that is easily carved with tools; hardness 6–6.5; sp. gr. 2.9–3.1 luster glassy. A jade . . . . Ca$_2$(Mg,Fe)$_5$ Si$_8$O$_{22}$(OH)$_2$ **nephrite**

70c. Color blue, bluish-green or green; fracture conchoidal; luster waxy to dull; hardness 6; sp. gr. 2.6–2.8; found in massive forms, also in thin seams and incrustations; becomes brown or black when heated and flies to pieces; soluble in hydrochloric acid. (see p. 70)
. . . . CuAl$_6$(PO$_4$)$_4$(OH)$_8$•4H$_2$O **turquoise**

71a. Color commonly red, rarely brown, green, yellow, black or white; luster glassy; fracture even; hardness 6.5–7.5; sp. gr. 3.0–3.3; usually found as scattered or massed crystals, each crystal rounded and equal-sided ⬡ ; sometimes in massive form. (see 77a. and p. 67). . . **garnet**

71b. Color reddish-brown or orange to brownish-black; luster adamantine (glittering); fracture uneven or almost conchoidal; hardness 6–6.5; sp. gr. 4.2–4.3; brittle; has long needle-like crystals with striations (grooves). (see 24d) . . . . **rutile**

71c. Color usually brown, rarely red, gray, white or yellow; a very heavy mineral; sp. gr. 7; fracture uneven; luster adamantine (sparkling); streak pale brown; hardness 6–7; crystals low pyramidal ⬡ ; often in twins ⬡ . A principal ore of tin. (see pic p. 66.) . . . . SnO$_2$ **cassiterite**

CHALCEDONY (white, green, brown, gray or black)

72a. Luster waxy or glassy; sp. gr. 2.65; waxy appearance hardness 6.5–7; in dense masses or layers (often banded) as deposited from springs; or in linings of cavities and fissures of a volcanic rock mass (often making geodes); color white, gray, blue, red, brown and black; conchoidal fracture))). (Note: **agate** is chalcedony made of concentric rings or bands of many colors; **moss agate** has

often banded or spotted

brown or black moss-like inclusions; when red called **jasper**; green with red spots **bloodstone**.) (see p. 67) . . . . . SiO$_2$ **CHALCEDONY**

72b. Luster greasy, dull or glassy; often found in veins, seams or lining the inside of rock cavities (glassy opal or hyalite); can be almost any color, sometimes with fire-like flashes (fire opal); chrysopal or prase opal is green; also in kidney-shaped, grape-cluster shaped and stalactitic forms; sp. gr. 1.9–2.2 (very light); hardness 5–6; fracture conchoidal, and often has patches of different colors. $SiO_2 \cdot nH_2O$ **opal**

72c. Luster glassy; hardness 6.5–7.5. (see 78b.) . . . . **garnet**

73. Minerals of Nonmetallic Luster not scratched by Quartz.

73a. Mineral with good cleavage (basal); hardness 8; usually found in prismatic crystals 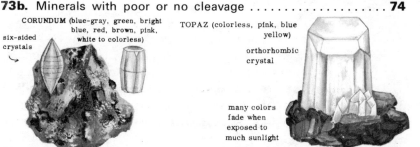 ; colorless, yellow, pink, blue or green; sp.gr. 3.4–3.6; luster glassy; also found in coarse or fine granular masses
. . . . $Al_2SiO_4(F,OH)_2$ **topaz**

73b. Minerals with poor or no cleavage **74**

CORUNDUM (blue-gray, green, bright blue, red, brown, pink, white to colorless)

six-sided crystals

TOPAZ (colorless, pink, blue yellow)

orthorhombic crystal

many colors fade when exposed to much sunlight

74a. Hardness 9 (scratches quartz with ease); luster glassy to dull; color bluish-gray, brown or pink or blue; sp. gr. 4; usually found in prismatic six-sided crystals with triangle markings on top, or in massive forms and granular. As precious gems, blue is **sapphire,** and red is **ruby.** (see page 66) . . . . Al_2O_3 **corundum**

74b. Hardness of 8 or less (scratches quartz with less ease) **75**

75a. Found in 6-sided prisms or in crystals with triangular cross-sections or in massive forms. **76**

75b. Not as above, except Andalusite may appear massive (77c) **77**

76a. Found in typical six-sided prismatic crystals that can scratch quartz; hardness 7.5–8; sp. gr. 2.6–2.8; fracture is conchoidal))); more rarely found in tabular crystals (usually pink), or in masses, grains or columns; color is blue-green in **aquamarine,** deep green in **emerald,** pale pink to deep rose **morganite,** a clear yellow in **golden beryl** and colorless; luster glassy; whitens in heat; usually found in granite pegmatites . . . . $Be_3Al_2Si_6O_{18}$ **beryl**

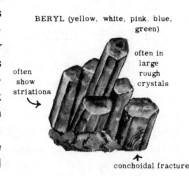

BERYL (yellow, white, pink, blue, green)

often in large rough crystals

often show striations

conchoidal fracture

QUARTZ (colorless, rose, violet, brown)

six-sided crystals

TOURMALINE (black, white, pink, red, blue, green, brown and colorless) colors often zoned

common prismatic crystal

76b. Luster glassy; crystals in six-sided prisms with horizontal striations; also in massive forms with conchoidal))) fracture; hardness 7; sp. gr. 2.65; colorless, white or many colors. **Rock crystal** is the clear kind; **amethyst** is purple; **smoky quartz** is smoky brown; **milky quartz** is milky white (two pieces of milky quartz rubbed together at night become illuminated); **rose quartz** is pink (see p. 69), while **prase** is green................................. SiO_2 **QUARTZ**

76c. In slender, prismatic crystals with triangular cross section; hardness 7–7.5; color black and various colors (often pink, green and red); sp. gr. 3–3.3; luster glassy to resinous; the bunched crystals in radiation groups, usually striated (grooved); crystals sometimes banded or zoned in color; fracture conchoidal))). **Lithia tourmaline** (red, green or blue) is $Na(Al,Fe,Li,Mg)_3B_3Al_3(Al_3Si_6O_{27})(O,Oh,F)_4$, while **black tourmaline** is .... $NaFe_3B_3Al_3(Al_3Si_6O_{27})(OH)_4$ **tourmaline**

Special Note: Careful attention to hardness is important in this group of minerals. While quartz can be scratched by quartz this is only with great difficulty. Thus a mineral that can scratch quartz without too much difficulty is obviously not quartz. Notice that some minerals soften under weathering (Andalusite).

77a. Usually found as scattered crystals in rocks, each crystal rounded and equal-sided with numerous faces (called dodecahedrons and trapezohedrons), but sometimes in massive form; hardness 6.5-7.5; sp. gr. 3.0–3.3; fracture even; color yellow-red (**pyrope** $Mg_3Al_2Si_3O_{12}$), dark violet red (**almandite** $Fe_2Al_2Si_3O_{12}$), black to dark brown or reddish-pink (**spessartite** $Mn_3Al_2Si_3O_{12}$), bright green (**uvarovite** $Ca_3Cr_2Si_3O_{12}$), pale yellow, brown or green (**grossularite** $Ca_3Al_2Si_3O_{12}$

—see p. 67), & pale yellow, brown or black (**andradite** — $Ca_3Fe_2Si_3O_{12}$). Often an important gem stone . . . . **garnet**

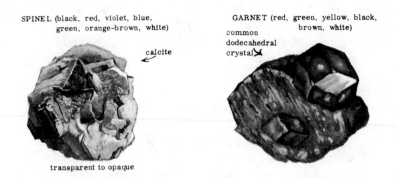

SPINEL (black, red, violet, blue, green, orange-brown, white)

calcite

transparent to opaque

GARNET (red, green, yellow, black, brown, white)

common dodecahedral crystal

77b. Commonly in eight-sided crystals or in rounded grains; hardness 8; sp. gr. 3.5–4.1; fracture conchoidal))); luster glassy; color is ruby red, black, blue, green, violet, orange-brown, lilac or white; will not melt in intense heat as will garnet. . . . . $MgAl_2O_4$ **spinel**

77c. Commonly in square, prismatic crystals; luster adamantine (glittering) or glassy; color is usually brown, red, green, gray or whitish; streak white; hardness 7.5; sp. gr. 4.6–4.7; often shows black cross in cross-section (chiastolite variety); found in coarse, prismatic crystals; also in massive and columnar forms; fracture uneven; often has mica scales and rough edges. . . . . Al_2SiO_5 **andalusite**

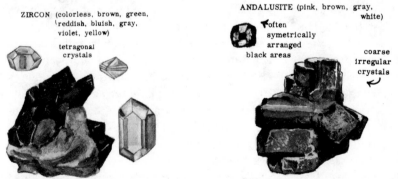

ZIRCON (colorless, brown, green, reddish, bluish, gray, violet, yellow)

tetragonal crystals

ANDALUSITE (pink, brown, gray, white)

often symetrically arranged black areas

coarse irregular crystals

77d. Usually in small but distinct crystals of prismatic or double pyramid form; luster adamantine (sparkling); color usually reddish brown or brown, pink, grayish, yellowish or colorless; hardness 7.5; sp. gr. 4.6–4.7; often fluoresces yellow-orange; most often is found in sands and gravels . . . . $ZrSiO_4$ **zircon**

27

Some Rarer Minerals of Special Interest

The minerals given in the above key are by far the most likely ones to be found by the California collector. We could have put the many rare minerals of the state also in the key, but for the majority, this would have been too confusing. However, a few of the rare minerals merit special mention and their qualities should be learned so they may be recognized in the field.

bauxite Al$(OH)_2$ + Al & H_2O, chief ore of aluminum. It looks like clay; color dark red-brown to white; massive or pisolitic (p. 65) in form; blue color when moistened with $CoNO_3$ and heated.

benitoite $BaTaSi_3O_9$ is a beautiful blue to white mineral found in tabular, 6-sided crystals (see p. 65) in white natrolite in serpentine in San Benito County. Hardness 6–6.5.

calaverite $AuTe_2$ appears as deeply striated crystals or massive granular; color pale-yellow to silvery-white; very heavy.

chalcocite Cu_2S is dark lead-gray or soft brown-black, sp. gr. 5.5–5.8; H. 2.5–3; in massive forms, usually in copper ore.

natrolite $Na_2Al_2Si_3O_{10}$ $2H_2O$ In white, granular veins often surrounding benitoite & neptunite; melts easily to a bubbly glass.

tetrahedrite $CuFe_{12}Sb_4 S_{13}$ A gray to iron-black copper ore with distinctive crystals $\Diamond$ & brilliant, conchoidal fracture.

Uranium Ores: autunite $Ca(UO_2)_2(PO_4)_2 \cdot 10–12$ H_2O and **torbernite** $Cu(UO_2)(PO_4)_2$ 8—12(H_2O) are the most commonly met uranium ores in California, found in seams of pegmatites & weathered zones of copper and vanadium ores; with crystals in very thin plates $\Diamond$ or are found in flaky, mica-like deposits. The first is yellowish-green or lemon yellow in color, the second emerald or yellowish-green; hardness of both 2–2.5; sp. gr. 3.1, but only autunite has a brilliant green fluorescence in ultraviolet light. **Uraninite** (pitchblende) UO_2, **gummite** U oxides + H_2O and **carnotite** $K_2(UO_2)_2(VO_4)_2 \cdot 3H_2O$ are rarer ores in this state. The first is steely to brownish-black, often with a velvety touch and grape-cluster form, hardness of 5–6 and sp. gr. of 6.4–9.7, but it is usually hard to detect without a geiger counter or careful chemical tests. **Gummite** has a distinctive orange-red to grayish-yellow color and a waxy to greasy luster, usually is not fluorescent. Found in pegmatites and with uraninite in medium temperature veins (see p. 29). **Carnotite** (see p. 66) is a very soft, powdery and crumbly bright yellow mineral that often takes the place of other minerals (making pseudomorphs) or materials (such as wood or bone) in sedimentary rocks. It does not fluoresce.

28

STORIES OF CALIFORNIA MINERALS

The physical characteristics of minerals have already been described in the chapter before this. In this chapter we want to discuss some of the more interesting minerals of California and their stories. Each mineral is the product of different earth forces. Different amounts of heat, pressure, and various chemical actions and reactions have placed the mark of distinctive character on each element or compound found in a mineral.

The story of rock-forming minerals will be taken up in more detail in the next chapter, which covers the story of the rocks. This chapter covers mainly the non-rock forming minerals, but actually both chapters should be read almost simultaneously for full understanding. It is customary in most books to divide both kinds of minerals into Oxides, Sulphides, Silicates, and other mineral families. For those who wish to go more deeply into the study of minerals, books are listed in the bibliography at the end of this book that take up this technical subject. Here we think it is a matter of greater interest to the amateur rock and mineral enthusiast to take the minerals according to how they are formed in the earth of our state. This will lead also to a knowledge of the best places in which to look for these minerals.

Certain minerals are usually associated together because they are formed at about the same temperature and under the same conditions. Thus, when we find one mineral of one of these associations, we know the chances are good of finding other members of the same association near. In the pages that follow these types of mineral formations or associations are first discussed and then a chart is given that lists the actual minerals in association. Use this chart as a guide to mineral associates when collecting and identifying minerals.

Minerals of Primary Ore Veins

A large number of minerals are deposited or developed as a result of the gradual cooling of a large body of hot, semi-liquid rock, called magma, under the surface of the earth. Hot liquids bearing mineral solutions are forced up cracks and fissures

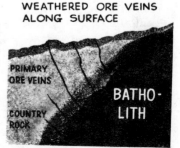

ORE VEINS

WEATHERED ORE VEINS ALONG SURFACE

PRIMARY ORE VEINS

COUNTRY ROCK

BATHO-LITH

29

towards the earth's surface. As the liquid cools, the minerals are deposited along the walls of the cracks forming what are called *primary ore veins.* Some minerals, such as gold and the metallic sulphide ores, can be carried in solution only when under great heat and pressure, so they are usually deposited deep in the earth near the source of the heat. They are only exposed after many centuries of erosion or by deep rock mining. Other minerals, such as cinnabar (the ore of mercury), and realgar and orpiment (the ores of arsenic), can be carried a long way by cooling solutions before they are deposited. Thus we can divide our primary ore veins into two general types, high temperature and low temperature veins. There are also *weathered* or *secondary* veins, but these will be taken up in the next section.

a. Minerals of High Temperature Ore Veins

Almost all rocks develop planes of weakness when placed under great stress. At such points cracks and crevices are formed and up these cracks and crevices hot liquid from under the earth is forced. In the mountains of California we have much evidence of tremendous earth forces twisting and lifting the layers of rocks. Immense bodies of semi-liquid rock pressed up under these twisted rock layers, sometimes becoming gradually cool to form underground masses of granite, and other times they burst through the surface as volcanoes that spew forth andesite, rhyolite and basalt lavas over the countryside.

Gold and its associates. Over one hundred million years ago a vast body of semi-liquid rock rose up under the region that we now call the Sierra Nevada. The region at that time was very low and covered with thick layers of sedimentary rock. Up into the cracks that changing pressures had developed in this rock the magma carried extremely hot water bearing many minerals in solution. The pressure that forced this liquid up must have been truly tremendous, because the existing quartz veins we find today are often several feet wide.

Along the walls of rock the liquid, as it cooled, began to deposit quartz and with it gold and the gold telluride minerals. The green mica mineral mariposite, and the metallic sulphides, such as sphalerite, chalcopyrite, pyrite and galena, were also deposited in certain localities. Often the quartz alone was deposited, especially when it had moved far from the magma.

30

These many and varied quartz and gold veins that today we call *The Mother Lode,* were in the beginning completely hidden under the surface of the earth. But, as the ancestral mountains of the Sierra Nevada rose, the rock layers above the quartz veins began to be washed away by erosion and at last the rich veins were exposed. How the veins themselves were gradually and partly washed down as gravels into the streams and later formed the rich placer gold deposits so avidly sought by the forty-niners is told on page 37.

The gold-bearing quartz veins of the foothills of the Sierra today represent only part of the vast matrix of veins that existed in California a hundred million years ago hidden under the earth. These veins generally come up from the depths at very steep angles, from 60 to 80 degrees, though a few of lower angles have been found. The miners had to drive their shafts down at these steep angles into the earth, and the amount of ore they took out depended on the cost of moving it up to the surface from far under the earth. As new and better equipment was developed deeper and deeper shafts were put down until such mines as the Kennedy and Argonaut near Jackson, California reached depths of greater than a mile. Millions upon millions of dollars were taken from such mines—possibly two billion altogether—but finally a point was reached where it was economically unprofitable to continue digging. On top of this most of the mines were stopped from production by governmental order during World War II and this, through the inevitable deterioration of equipment and caving in of shafts, put a severe crimp on future production.

The High Temperature Sulphide Ores. Most of the high and medium temperature sulphide ores of California are found in the copper mining districts, though smaller quantities are found in the gold mining districts and galena (a sulphide) is common as the chief ore of lead. As the hot sulphide solution rises from the magma deep under the earth, the most typical high temperature minerals, pyrrhotite and arseno-pyrite, are deposited in the lower part of the vein. But such minerals as pyrite, chalcopyrite, sphalerite and bornite may be carried to higher levels, while galena is usually carried in solution still higher.

Chalcopyrite, a beautiful golden and iridescent color, is the chief ore of copper. It is most often found in California as part of a mass of pyrite (an iron sulphide), which has been deposited in a wide crack or crevice. Over a long period of time the pyrite begins to oxidize near the surface and forms an earthy coating of hematite or limonite (both oxides of iron) over the deeper copper ore. Such caps in Plumas, Shasta and Calaveras counties have helped in the discovery of large copper ore bodies. The action of water solutions under the earth may gradually change (alter) chalcopyrite ($CuFeS_2$) to bornite (Cu_5FeS_4, then to covellite (CuS), then chalcocite (Cu_2S), and finally to native copper (Cu) as the copper content increases.

b. Minerals of Low Temperature Ore Veins

Long after such minerals as chalcopyrite, pyrrhotite and gold have been dropped out of solution in deep veins, other minerals, such as cinnabar, orpiment, realgar, galena, pyrite, stibnite, sphalerite and bornite are carried higher and in cooler solutions to veins near the surface. Of these pyrite and sphalerite are not typical, as they are found as often in high temperature veins as in low, while galena and bornite are deposited also in veins of medium temperature.

Cinnabar is the commonest and most typical low temperature ore mineral in the state. It was the first metal ore mined in California and was in production long before the discovery of gold in 1848. The proper conditions for the formation of this ore of mercury are found in a few places in the Coast Ranges of California, particularly in Lake, Napa, Santa Clara and San Benito Counties, with the last two the most important.

Cinnabar is formed by solfataric (sulfur) waters depositing along the line of contact between veins of serpentine and the surrounding rock. Cinnabar is almost always associated with a white silica carbonate rock, which is formed by the hot solutions altering (changing) the serpentine just before depositing the cinnabar. The white, green and red colors are often beautiful.

Cinnabar was first mined by the Indians of California to use in the making of red paint. Many of them sickened from this use because of the mercury fumes they inhaled. At New Almaden in Santa Clara County a young Spanish officer, Andres Castillero, discovered in the 1830's that the region was rich in mercury ore. The mercury mined at New Almaden became vital to the progress of California when it was later found that mercury could be used with success in the great gold mines and placer dredges of the Sierra Nevada to separate gold from gravel or crushed rock.

Minerals of Weathered or Secondary Ore Veins

As the original primary ore veins become exposed by erosion, the part of each vein near the surface is exposed to weathering. Surface waters seep down through cracks in the rock and begin to change the nature of the minerals found in the veins. The original chemicals are replaced by new ones and so totally different minerals are formed. (See illustration on page 29.)

Since the weathered or secondary ore veins are always near the surface, these veins are those first mined out by the miners. So in California today we find only the remains of what were once magnificent secondary ore bodies.

Malachite and **azurite,** like Damon and Pythias, are almost always found together. Both are basic, cupric, hydrous carbonates, which means they were formed by the action of water and oxygen and carbon-dioxide gas in solution on the primary copper sulphide ores, such as chalcopyrite and bornite.

Prospectors on the lookout for copper ore bodies keep their eyes peeled for veins of the beautiful green malachite and blue azurite. Masses of either mineral are an almost sure sign of substantial primary copper ores deeper under the earth. For example, large masses of malachite discovered in the Genesee district of Plumas County led to the operation of the famous Bluebell Copper Mine.

The green crusts and coatings of malachite show the action of the ground water on the surface of the primary ore bodies, but the blue crystals of azurite seem to be precipitated inside the more extensive malachite or limonite as exquisite clusters of small crystals lining cavities and fissures.

Pegmatite dike exposed by erosion

Minerals of Pegmatite Dikes And Miarolitic Cavities

As a great body of semi-liquid hot rock lifts under the surface of the earth, it gradually cools and crystalized into the plutonic rock, granite. In the final stages of cooling a last pool of liquid gathers near the top in which are concentrated a

33

number of the minerals that did not find a place in the main rock.This liquid, largely water, is often forced up a crack or dike in the rock where the minerals in it begin to solidify and precipitate slowly in the form of unusually large crystals. These form a pegmatite or pegmatite dike. Of similar nature, but deeper in the granite, are cavities, caused by shrinkage of the rock, in which many other crystals are formed. These are called miarolitic cavities and should be looked for where granite has been cut.

The most interesting pegmatite dikes and miarolitic cavities of California are found in San Diego County where many rare and beautiful minerals are formed into crystals in such rocks. Such beauty and such largeness of size of mineral crystals makes one think of a pegmatite as a granite that has gone crazy! To the rock hound the pegmatite often proves a veritable treasure trove.

Translucent pink or green **tourmaline** is one of the mineral delights found in pegmatites and is particularly prevalent in San Diego County where some of the finest crystals in the world are found. The lovely color of these radiating, prismatic crystals, so beautiful in jewelry, is caused by the presence in the mineral of a tiny bit of the element lithium. (see pp. 68, 70.)

Pegmatite dikes are usually uncovered by thousands of years of erosion or by mining activities. They are immediately recognized by the immense crystals of quartz, feldspar and muscovite mica, which show the close connection with granite (see p. 64).

Minerals of Zeolitic Cavities in Lava

As the hot and liquid lava boils and tumbles up out of the crater of a volcano or from a volcanic fissure it carries with it large quantities of both water and air. When the lava hardens the air tends to form bubbles, which appear as cavities in the hardened lava rock. But the water in the lava often enters these cavities and deposits upon their walls the crystals of several different minerals (see chart on page 39).

Analcite is one of the commonest minerals formed on the walls of these zeolitic cavities. It forms as small, even, isometric (all sides equal) crystals that may fill such a cavity like a spray of tiny diamonds (see p. 21). Other interesting and rarer minerals leave their crystals in such cavities, showing the mysterious action of hot water, carrying many chemicals in solution.

34

Minerals Found In Lava

Besides the minerals of zeolitic cavities several other minerals are carried along in the main part of the lava flow and sometimes solidify as small crystals or masses in hard lava rocks. The mineral collector exploring over the many old lava beds and flows in California should keep an eye open for any unusual color or appearance that would lead him to the discovery of these minerals in the rock. (see p. 39)

VOLCANO AND LAVA FLOWS

Olivine is one of the commonest and most beautiful minerals found in lavas. Large crystals of olivine are rare, but if found are valuable gem stones because of their rich green color and hardness. In San Bernardino County in the Morongo District the olivine was apparently concentrated in large volcanic bombs where it is found in granular form.

Minerals Found in Plutonic Igneous Rocks

Plutonic igneous rocks are those rocks which formed from a semi-liquid magma beneath the surface of the earth (see illustration on page 41), but solidified slowly under the surface, usually forming crystals. The common minerals of such rocks are quartz, feldspar and various dark minerals such as augite, hornblende and biotite mica. However, a number of rarer and more unusual minerals may also crystallize in the rock.

Black tourmaline in long, prismatic, six-sided crystals is one of the interesting minerals found in many granites in the Sierra. In the slowly cooling granitic magma deep under the earth the aluminum boro-silicate that forms the tourmaline apparently concentrates in certain parts of the mass, often forming radiating crystals. While they do not have the gem quality of the beautiful green and red tourmalines of pegmatite dikes, they are worthy of the interest of any collector.

Minerals Found in Metamorphic Rocks

Metamorphic rocks (see p. 47), because of the stresses and strains to which they have been subjected and the action of hot and cold water solutions, are remarkable for the many interesting minerals that form within them. Besides the usual minerals derived from the igneous and sedimentary rocks from which they originated, many of these typical rock-forming minerals are here and there replaced by the unusual and beautiful.

Throughout many of the Coast Ranges of California **serpentine** is a mineral that has replaced by alteration (changing) of the chemical content many rocks rich in magnesium silicates such as olivine, peridotite, pyroxenite and gabbro. Instead of these dark minerals in the rock, hot water from deep under the earth has now replaced them with the beautiful greenish and white streaked serpentine. Sometimes the masses of serpentine are lined with veins of the fibrous and silky form called **chrysotile,** a good asbestos, used in fireproofing buildings.

Four rather remarkable minerals are found in many metamorphic schists and gneisses, **andalusite, sillimanite, kyanite,** and **staurolite.** The needle-like or fiber-like crystals of the second and third named are delightful finds for the mineral collection, while andalusite in the form called chiastolite is noted for its curious black, cross-like inclusions. Staurolite is often found in twin crystal form, each looking like a tiny cross 🔆 . All are the result of tremendous pressures altering rock.

Minerals in Sedimentary Rock

Most of the sedimentary rocks of California were laid down in ancient seas as layers of sediment carried by streams (see p. 44). In this sediment, however, water in solution carried many minerals other than the ordinary rock-forming ones such as calcite and quartz. These odd minerals were often deposited in cavities and crevices in the ordinary sedimentary rocks and one of the most interesting results of their action was their replacement of the bodies of animals and the leaves and stems of plants that had been trapped in the ancient mud. Thus were fossils formed.

Chalcedony, calcite, agate and **collophane** are minerals well-noted for their ability to make fossils by this replacement process. Sometimes extraordinarily beautiful fossilized wood or bone is found embedded in ordinary sedimentary rock with every part of cell and fiber shown in remarkable detail. Collophane is noted for its copying of the cellular structure of an ancient bone, while agate may exactly reproduce a tree trunk.

Minerals Found in Limestone and Marble Quarries

Properly speaking limestone is a part of the sedimentary rocks mentioned in the previous page, since limestone is laid down as sediment in the sea or in a lake (see p. 45). But limestone quarries are such good hunting places for certain definite minerals (see p. 40), that they are worth mentioning separately. The original limestone, for the most part, came from the calcareous or limey shells of ancient sea animals, but when the layers of lime gradually turned into rock and were later lifted above the sea by earth-pressures the new rock was infiltrated by ground water, which often replaced the original calcite with other minerals. Also when the rock near to limestone is metamorphosed (changed) by heat or pressure into marble, metamorphic minerals may be formed along the line of contact. Such a mineral is the beautifully fibrous **wollastonite** (see page 17).

Gypsum is often formed by the action of sulphate waters on limestone, and is very common. It takes on many beautiful and interesting forms such as selenite, satin spar, alabaster and gypsite, which can be carved or shaped into ornamental designs.

Minerals Found in Alluvium and Beach Sand

As erosion wears away the rock masses of the land small fragments of rocks and minerals are washed into streams. Some of these drop to stream beds where they form part of alluvial gravels, while others may be washed down to the ocean, there to form part of the beach sand. The ocean itself is also wearing away at the cliffs and rocks of the land, breaking the rock into fragments and forming more sand.

Quartz, feldspar and **chalcedony** are the commonest minerals in this alluvium and sand, but sometimes some quite rare and beautiful minerals are found there, especially those too hard to be dissolved by water. **Beryl,** in yellow, green and blue crystals; ruby-red **spinel,** and greenish **jade** are some semi-precious stones found in such places. But the real find is **gold,** which gathers because of its weight in the lowest part of a stream bed. The famous auriferous gold gravels of the Sierra are the result of the ages long erosion of the quartz veins of the Mother Lode. Sometimes such gold-rich gravel was trapped by rivers of lava, and many such trapped fortunes still wait finding.

Mineral Deposits of Old Lake Beds, Geysers And Hot Springs

In the deserts of southeastern California are many old and dry lake beds that are evidence of a time in our history when the climate was much wetter than it is today. As these ancient lake beds dried up, quantities of interesting minerals were deposited on their bottoms, including **borax** of twenty mule team fame.

The geysers of Sonoma County and the many hot springs of other parts of California carry several minerals in solution and these minerals are precipitated around the geyser and spring edges. **Travertine,** a form of calcite, leaves concentric rings of beautiful color about such hot water outlets.

Chart of Mineral Habitats

As you collect a mineral be sure to note the habitat where it is found and the other minerals found with it. Such facts help you identify the mineral and may lead to an important discovery. Check your mineral against minerals and habitats shown below.

The brackets in the chart show close mineral associates.

* Marks rare minerals not otherwise described in the book.

Primary ore veins of high & med. temps.	pyroxenes	Primary ore veins of low temperature.
tourmaline	amphiboles	silver
galena	olivine	*proustite (red)
pyrite	magnetite	*pyrargyrite (dark red)
chalcopyrite	garnet	barite
arsenopyrite	*ilmenite (black to red)	quartz
molybdenite	spinel	fluorite
pyrrhotite	scheelite	sphalerite
*enargite (black)	cassiterite	pyrite
tetrahedrite	topaz	realgar (see p. 69)
mariposite	wolframite	stibnite
gold	*sylvanite (silver-yellow striated crystals)	*marcasite (yellow)
quartz	*petzite (silver-yellow)	calcite
barite	bornite	opal
*siderite (brown)	covellite (blue)	cinnabar
silver	rhodochrosite	*stromeyerite (dk. grey)
fluorite	rhodonite	*metacinnabar (black)
apatite	*orpiment (yel.-orange)	*native mercury
dolomite	*argentite (dark-gray)	sylvanite
		gold

Weathered veins.

*native copper
chalcocite
malachite
azurite
chrysocolla
bornite
cuprite
limonite
*melanterite (green)
psilomelane
pyrolusite
hemimorphite (white)
smithsonite
cerussite
*pyromorphite (green
  to brown, resinous)
anglesite
epsomite
bauxite
*wulfenite (glitters)
*vanadinite (sp.gr. 7)
*orpiment (yel.-orange)
kaolinite
turquoise
autunite
gummite
hematite
gypsum
*tenorite (black)
*linarite (deep blue)
*chalcanthite (sky blue)
chrysocolla
*cerargyrite (gr.5.5)
*embolite (gray-green)
*boothite (blue)
*mirabilite (bitter)
*copiapite (yellow)
talc
benitoite
*inesite (rose red)
*bismutite (gray)
*alunite (basal clvg.)
alunogen (sol. in H₂O)
magnesite
*hydromagnesite
  (fizzes in HCl)

Pegmatites and miarolitic cavities

molybdenite
apatite
wolframite
topaz
cassiterite
quartz
corundum
muscovite
*amblygonite
  (fuzes easily)
lepidolite
tourmaline
spodumene
chlorite
beryl
feldspars
garnet
biotite
chalcedony
opal
uraninite
*allanite (fuses easily)
benitoite
analcite
*columbite (gr. 5–8)
sphene
epidote
pyroxenes
rutile
pyrrhotite
magnetite

Zeolitic cavities

analcite
calcite
*prehnite (fuses easily)
anhydrite
*heulandite (yel. flame)
*stilbite (✳ form)
*chabazite (◇ crystal)
natrolite
*mesolite (silky)
*laumontite (red flame)
*apophyllite (pearly)
topaz (in rhyolite)
quartz
opal
chalcedony
*tridymite

Minerals in lava.

*hypersthene (cl. ∟)
augite
*pectolite (silky)
olivine
zircon
feldspar

Min. in plutonic rock

biotite
corundum
magnetite
hematite
quartz
apatite
*ilmenite (magnetic)
chromite
molybdenite
hornblende
augite
feldspar
tremolite
actinolite
*hypersthene (cl. ∟)
olivine
*allanite (fuses easily)
zircon
*axinite (violet-brown)
dumortierite
pyrrhotite

Contact metamorphic zones & metamorphic rocks

*idocrase (⬡)
epidote
wollastonite
tremolite
graphite
quartz
garnet
calcite
feldspar
hornblende
actinolite
magnetite
*scapolite (⬡◇)
spinel
diopside
chlorite

galena
arsenopyrite
tetrahedrite
pyrite
sphalerite
chalcopyrite
pyrrhotite
bornite
biotite
corundum
muscovite
andalusite
tourmaline
kyanite
* sillimanite (satiny)
hematite
rutile
sphene
*ilmenite (black)
mt. leather
chrysotile
    (asbestos)
dolomite
talc
molybdenite
scheelite
nephrite (jade)
*ankerite (yel.-brown)
*lazulite (blue)
*pyrophyllite (soft,
    pearly)
mariposite
glaucophane
*pectolite (silky)
*lawsonite (pale blue;
    in schist)
*zoisite ( )
dumortierite

minerals of sedimen-
tary rocks
quartz
feldspar
dolomite
calcite
kaolinite
apatite
chalcedony

*alunite (purple
    flame)
carnotite
*collophane (like bone)
*vivianite (soft)
*halloysite (clay)
*montmorillonite (soft)
*piedmontite (red streak)
aragonite
*siderite (brown)
*strontianite (sol. in acid)
barite
anhydrite
*coquimbite (astringent)
magnetite

Limestone and
marble quarries
calcite
galena
sphalerite
chalcopyrite
dolomite
gypsum
aragonite
wollastonite
*idocrase (hard 6—6.5)
celestite
garnet
anhydrite
fluorite
*strontianite
    (clv. ∟)

Alluvium and beaches
quartz
feldspar
chalcedony
biotite
olivine
hematite
magnetite
zircon
*glauconite
    (greenish)
topaz
*axinite (violet-brown)

spinel
*ilmenite
    (magnetic)
gold
*diamond
*platinum
chromite
rutile

Old lake beds
halite
gypsum
anhydrite
kaolinite
*borax (sweet)
*ulexite (silky)
celestite
*trona (fizzes)
*howlite (green flame)
colemanite
*inyoite (breaks in heat)
*meyerhofferite (fibrous)
kernite
*thenardite
    (basal cleavage)
*gay-lussite
    (fizzes; cl. ∟)
*niter (explodes)
*hanksite (fuses easily)

Geysers & hot springs
sulphur
sal ammoniac (bitter)
chalcedony
gypsum
jasper
opal (geyserite)
aragonite
travertine
barite
celestite
*ankerite ( )
*siderite (brown)
fluorite

40

THE NATURE OF CALIFORNIA ROCKS

To give the reader an adequate picture of the rocks of California and something of their history in a small book of this kind is a very difficult task because of the tremendous complexity of California geology. If the information that follows can be thought of as a simplified and very brief introduction to a very complex subject, then the reader will not make the mistake of thinking the knowledge given is anywhere near complete or perfect, but perhaps will be encouraged to further study (see bibliography).

In this book we think of a rock as being a mixture of two or more minerals, though sometimes only one mineral plus some impurities. Thus in the rock section we speak of the rock serpentine, but it is very little different from the mineral serpentine in the mineral section of the book except for not being as pure a serpentine. Since rocks are made up of rock-forming minerals, it is wise to know something about these minerals before studying the rocks of which they are made. Study the chapter The Minerals of California starting on page 4 before reading this section. All the major rock-forming minerals are in bold capitals, as is **QUARTZ**.

The earth on which we live may be defined as a mass of igneous rocks covered with a thin skin of sedimentary rocks. Between these two main kinds of rock are found smaller quantities of metamorphic rocks (rocks that were changed by heat or pressure). We will start our study with the first rocks, the igneous.

Igneous Rocks

The word "igneous", as applied to rocks, comes from the old Greek word for fire. Igneous rocks are those that were made as a result of intense heat, heat so great that for a long time the rocks were in liquid form before they became solid.

Under the earth hot, semi-liquid rock, called magma, may form a vast mass in which minerals are mixed together. As

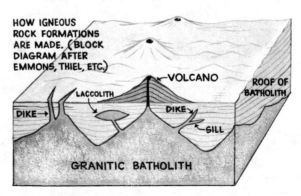

HOW IGNEOUS ROCK FORMATIONS ARE MADE. (BLOCK DIAGRAM AFTER EMMONS, THIEL, ETC.)

VOLCANO
ROOF OF BATHOLITH
LACCOLITH
DIKE→
DIKE
SILL
GRANITIC BATHOLITH

this magma begins to cool, it forms a granitic batholith, and connected with this batholith may be various intrusions (inside the earth's crust) and extrusions (outside the earth's crust) of igneous rock.

A laccolith and a dike, for example, are intrusions of magma, forced up through cracks in the rocks above, while the volcano and lava flows that come from it are extrusions. We then speak of the rocks formed under the earth as plutonic rocks and those formed on the earth's surface as volcanic rocks. Because the plutonic rocks are protected from contact with the cool atmosphere they cool very much more slowly than the volcanic rocks and so the minerals inside the rock have a chance to form crystals that are visible to the naked eye. On this basis we can divide igneous rocks into the following categories.

Igneous Rock Table

Type	Texture	Composition: Mineral and Chemical		
Plutonic	**Granular** with visible crystals that cooled slowly.	**Acid,** with mainly light minerals. **Granite**	**Intermediate** with ½ light and ½ dark minerals. **Diorite**	**Basic** with mainly dark minerals. **Gabbro**
Volcanic	**Fine-grained** or with invisible crystals. Cooled fast.	**Rhyolite**	**Andesite**	**Basalt**
Volcanic	**Prophyritic** with a few large crystals.	**Felsite Porphyry**	**Andesite Prophyry**	**Basalt Prophyry**
Volcanic	**Glassy** no crystals, cooled too rapidly.	**Obsidian Pitchstone Pumice**		**Basaltic Glass**

Fragmental: **Tuff   Breccia   Agglomerate**

Silicon dioxide (quartz) is acid-forming, so rocks high in silicon dioxide (and usually light-colored) are classified as "acid" rocks. The minerals of the acid rocks are mainly quartz, feldspar (pink kind) and either biotite mica or hornblende. Intermediate rocks are largely feldspar (white kind), and usually both biotite mica and hornblende. Basic rocks are mostly olivine, augite and a dark form of feldspar.

Interesting California Igneous Rocks

Granite. (See illus. p. 71.) This rock forms the backbone of the Sierra Nevada, as the great granitic batholith that was formed over a hundred million years ago (see p. 53) is now being exposed by erosion. Because it is a very hard rock, granite wears well and this accounts for the great cliffs of the Yosemite Valley and elsewhere in the Sierra retaining their essential form tens of thousands of years after they were first made by glacial action. The Sierra's gigantic granite domes show how the ancient batholith pushed huge knobs of molten rock up under the surface rock. As granite weathers it exfoliates, meaning the surface rock peels off in shells, gradually rounding off all sharp edges and explaining why we see today the well-rounded granite domes.

Rhyolite. (see illus. p. 60) This explosive lava rock is not as fluid as basalt and is full of explosive gasses which may cause it to be flung out of a volcano with great force. The flow lines in the rock often form very beautiful designs in various shades, making it an ornamental stone. Rhyolite of this type is common in southeastern California. Rhyolite breccias and volcanic necks form the weird-looking pinnacles of Pinnacles National Monument.

Basalt (see illus. p. 70) is the main rock in the vast lava fields of the northern Sierra and the Modoc Plateau. Most of it was spewed forth from the earth a million or more years ago in great volcanic and fissure eruptions brought about by the twisting of the earth's crust when the mountains were formed. Some of this dark rock flowed over ancient rivers burying fortunes in gold that had been caught in the auriferous gravels of the river beds. Some of these fortunes have been found, others will be.

Obsidian (see illus. p. 56) was much used by the California Indians for tools and weapons, as it is a very hard glassy rock that is easy to chip into the form desired. When lava cools almost instantly so there is no chance to form minerals, then it makes obsidian. Beautiful obsidian is found in Lake and Modoc counties.

Peridotite (see p. 72) is a most interesting basic rock that is rather rare in California except in Del Norte County. It is the darkest of all igneous rocks, being often made of only one or two dark minerals, such as olivine or pyroxene. As it weathers, it may make a blue clay similar to the famous blue clay of South Africa where the vast diamond fields were discovered.

Sedimentary Rocks

These are the rocks that cover over three-fourths of the earth's crust with a thick skin or accumulation of sediments that have been made into rock by pressure and cementing. They are of two main kinds: (1) those, such as conglomerate, sandstone and shale, that are made of rock fragments transported by wind or water and deposited in the sea, a plain or a valley, and (2) rocks formed by simple precipitation from solution, as is rock salt and some limestone, or secretions from organisms, as other limestone.

These rocks are tremendously important in helping us learn the geologic history of the earth. Seashells in a rock, for example, tell the story of an ancient sea that was once where now is solid land. Plant life of past ages, as shown in fossils, tells us much about the nature of ancient climates. When the plants were of luxuriant growth then the climate was damp and moist; when fossils of arid plants are found (such as cactus) then we know there were deserts. Thus fossil palms and similar plants found in Eocene sandstones of the foothills of the Sierra show that California had a moist and tropical climate about 50 million years ago. Tremendous accumulations of sedimentary rock, such as the 30,000 feet or more of Franciscan sandstones and shales in the Coast Ranges tell of the millions upon millions of years of relative calm in California during most of the Jurassic and Cretaceous Periods when sediments were washed down to the ancient California sea (see p. 53). The illustration on this page will give some idea of how such rocks were formed. The illustration first shows the rock layers as they appear today, second it shows the original granite bed rock, while the 3rd, 4th and 5th sections show sedimentary layers being formed.

How sedimentary rock beds are formed - Example: a series of beds is exposed (A) by a river's cutting of its canyon. How may beds have been formed?

Analysis: Suppose a great plain of granitic rock of the earth's crust (B)--

Prevailing wind brings sand from nearby desert. Crust slowly sinks under weight

until a rapid settling brings in sea, which deposits silt carried down by rivers.

More settling again sends sea inland. Now instead of silt there is deposition of lime skeletons, in billions, of tiny marine animals. Pressure and cementing action of sea-salts binds sandgrains to make sandstone and silt particles to make shale.

Sedimentary rocks may be classified as follows:

1. Mechanical—those caused by the depositing of particles formed through weathering and erosion.

Conglomerate—cemented pebbles—usually a sign of steep, nearby mountains, as only swift streams carry pebbles.

Sandstone—cemented sand grains—may be deposited from a stream of medium speed and so indicate rolling hill country, or it may be made by waves eroding the cliffs of a shore.

Shale—cemented silt or mud—is usually deposited from a large, slow-moving river, as this water carries only silt.

Limestone—cemented lime particles—may come from deposition of lime particles carried by water.

SEA LEVEL

SHOWING DEPOSITION
OF SEDIMENTS IN A SEA AS SEA RISES.

2. Chemical—rocks resulting from chemical reactions and precipitation from solution.

Limestone—cemented lime—usually caused by lime in solution being deposited on the ocean floor.

Dolomite—lime and magnesia—is usually caused by the sea water acting chemically on limestone.

Iron ores are often deposited from iron-oxide solutions.

Gypsum and anhydrite are salts deposited in dry lakes.

Magnesite and rock salt are also salt deposits in lakes, etc.

Chert was originally a silica gel deposited on a sea bottom.

3. Organic—rocks resulting from action of plant or animal life.

Limestone—(including chalk, coral limestone, coquina, etc.) may come from animal shells deposited on the sea bottom.

Coal and peat come from ancient plants that have turned into a form of rock by deep pressure and chemical change underground.

Chert is sometimes formed from the silica shells of certain sea animals, as is also diatomite (from the shells of diatoms).

Sediments—washed by water or blown by wind from their original rock source in the mountains or hills—usually end up in lowland valleys or shallow seas as vast accumulations that century after century press on the earlier sediments below. This weight bows down the earth's crust and eventually forms layers of rock thousands of feet deep. As the crust is bent downward, the tension of the crust keeps mounting until finally the accumulated pressures of the shrinking crust cause mountains to be upfolded.

It is exactly this process that caused the early folding of the ancestral Sierra Nevada way back in the Jurassic Period (see page 53), and the uplifting and folding of the Coast Ranges in the Pliocene and Pleistocene Epochs (see page 51). When these lifted and folded, rocks also slide up and down along faults, such as the famous San Andreas Fault of the California coast, then a real mixup of the ancient rock layers may appear. The geologist, who is a kind of super historical detective, uses these signs and others of past events to help unravel the great story of the ages.

Some Interesting California Sedimentary Rocks

Chert, which is found most often in California as a hard and often beautiful red rock with white veins running through it, was originally formed (in most cases) by the mixture of silica with very hot water into a silica gel. The silica spewed up through volcanic vents under the ancient California sea and spread out over the sea bottom to form a layer on which were later deposited layers of sediment brought down by rivers. The gel gradually hardened into chert rock beds, such as are common about the San Francisco Bay (see illustration page 70).

Limestone and **dolomite** (see illustration, p. 71) form some of the most ancient rocks in California, as most of them were laid down in very ancient seas, probably even before the lifting of the ancestral Sierra in the Jurassic Period 150 million years ago. The California Sea was deep then and the skeletons and shells of sea animals accumulated in great number. Since limestone is easily soluble in water, beautiful limestone caves have been hollowed out of limestone deposits in Calaveras and San Bernardino Counties. Sometimes crystallized limestone or dolomite form very handsome rocks with intricate patterns.

Diatomite, or diatomaceous earth, is the name of a peculiar, soft and porous rock of which California has the largest known deposits in the world. It is composed of the fossilized silica skeletons of extremely tiny plants that are found to this day in both fresh and salt water. 75 million of these plants fill only a cubic inch! Near Lompoc, in Santa Barbara County, diatomite is found in beds a thousand feet thick. It is used in various chemical processes, including the filtration of lime.

Sandstone concretions (see page 72) are found in sandstone beds where a foreign substance in the sandstone causes a changing in the surrounding minerals through oxidation and the action of acids. In the round reddish centers sometimes fossils are found.

46

Metamorphic Rocks

Metamorphic rocks are rocks that have been changed in their constitution and structure through pressure, heat or the action of water and the chemicals in it, resulting in the creation of a more compact and highly crystalline condition. They are almost always found in California where the crust of the earth has been heavily folded and twisted by pressure and where hot, semi-liquid rock magmas from under the earth have come in contact with the rock above. Since these two actions go together and are associated with the formation of mountains, metamorphic rocks are usually a sign of mountain building.

Types of metamorphism.

A. Contact metamorphism occurs on contact of a magma of molten igneous rock with the rock surrounding it. Minerals in solution in hot gas and water are deposited in nearby rock as crystals or veins, sometimes of considerable value.

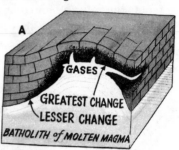

A. CONTACT. Intrusion of molten magma into a limestone, chemically changing it. New rocks formed are combinations of elements present in both magma and invaded rock. Of great effect are gases given off by molten rock.

B. DYNAMIC. Pressure and heat caused by great movements of the earth's crust crystallize and make denser the minerals of sedimentary rocks, changing shales to slates, etc.

B. Dynamic or regional metamorphism happens when tremendous pressure, due to the folding of rock

C. REPLACEMENT. water dissolves substance (e. g. wood), replaces it, molecule by molecule, with minerals in solution, keeping the exact form of the original.

Adapted from Am. Nat. Hdbk. (Little,Brown) with publ. permission.

layers, crystallizes sedimentary rocks, such as shales, and changes them to slates or schists.

C. Replacement metamorphism occurs when water, carrying minerals in solution, trades one mineral in a rock for another it has in solution. Petrified wood is often formed by the depositing of silica in the form of opal or agate to replace the wood fibers. Serpentine replaces other minerals to produce serpentine rock.

Results of Metamorphic Processes in Rocks

Development of new textures. The texture of a rock is often completely changed by the power of pressure and heat. When a shale is turned into a mica schist (see p. 62), the mica in the original shale

47

is concentrated and then crystallized into the innumerable thin flakes that form the schistose layers. The layered texture of a gneiss, on the other hand, is much coarser (see illustrations on p. 62), with large, partly flattened crystals. The granulated structure of a quartzite (p. 64) is like myriads of tiny beads jammed tightly together. Packed so tight are the quartz grains that they break through the middle instead of around the grains as in a sandstone, the rock from which quartzite comes.

Development of new minerals. The action of heat and hot water and gas on rocks is often to completely replace minerals that were previously in the rocks or force minerals that are there to change their chemical nature so that they become new minerals. Thus the kaolin (aluminum silicate) of common mud shale is changed by terrific heat and pressure into mica (a potassium aluminum silicate), the added potassium coming from the surrounding rock. Quartz, feldspars, hornblende, garnet, serpentine, wollastonite and glaucophane are other completely new minerals produced in rocks by metamorphism.

Chart of Metamorphic Rock Changes

Original rock	Changed by	Metamorphic rock
sedimentary conglomerate	pressure	conglomerate gneiss or schistose conglomerate
sandstone	heat	quartzite, quartz-feldspar rock
shale limestone	and	slate, phyllite, mica schist marble
igneous granitic rocks	chemical	granite gneiss, etc.
fine-grained acid or felsitic rocks	action	mica schist, feldspar schist, quartzite
fine-grained basic rocks, peridotite, etc.	to:	hornblende schist, serpentine

Sometimes metamorphism produces several stages. As shale becomes slate, small mica flakes form along new cleavage surfaces to give a shiny luster. The slate is metamorphosed into phyllite where the crystals are larger and more micaceous. When the phyllite turns into mica schist, the rock becomes almost completely micaceous.

Interesting California Metamorphic Rocks

Chlorite schist is a common and beautiful green rock of Death Valley and other parts of southeastern California and the Coast Ranges. The flakes of chlorite do not have the elasticity of the mica flakes in mica schist so that the rock is more brittle. This has a soft, soapy feeling.

Glaucophane schist. This beautiful blue schist is distinctive of the Coast Ranges of California. It is one of the Jurassic Franciscan group of rocks, telling of a time of rugged mountain building over a hundred million years ago. Recent erosion exposed it.

Schistose conglomerate is an interesting rock because it shows the result of extreme pressure. The original round pebbles of the conglomerate have been flattened out in the same way a piece of clay would be flattened by a steam roller, flattened so much that they become thin flakes.

Granite gneiss is a common metamorphic rock of the Sierra where it is found in the contact zone along the edges of the Sierra batholith. It looks very much like granite but is easily told by the wavy dark line of the mica crystals.

Marble, of the quality needed for building, is not common in California, but there are stretches of marble where limestone masses have been contacted by hot magmas and where the pressure from folding of the rock strata has also altered the limestone. Where such marble has been infiltrated by other minerals from the magma, such as psilomelane, dendrites (feathery lines) and other beautiful designs on the rock are occasionally found. Often near such places are pockets of valuable minerals.

Serpentine in California has largely come through the movement of hot water up cracks and faults in the rock from deep underground magmas. The beautiful green masses of serpentine with their white mottling and veins are found mainly in the Coast Ranges and the foothills of the Sierra. Often associated with them are such valuable minerals as chromite, magnesite and chrysotile asbestos. Some of the better looking and harder mottled serpentines may be cut or carved into decorative stone.

Slate of a quality good enough to be used for blackboards in school classrooms is found in the Sierra Nevada. It is interesting that the metamorphism of shale to slate seems to destroy all traces of fossils in the rock, and yet the apparent difference between the two rocks is very slight. The new cleavage surfaces produced by small mica flakes give the slate a shiny appearance.

BRIEF HISTORY OF CALIFORNIA ROCKS

Most of the rocks of California are of comparatively recent age, not nearly so old, for example, as the rocks of the Grand Canyon. To give an outline picture of the great events of California geology that led to the formation of our present rocks we are showing first a simplified and composite cross-section of the rocks of a part of central California to show how the layers of rock each tell a story of a great epoch or period of the past. Second is a Chart of the Geologic History of California with cross-sections of the state in different stages of that history, and third a geologic map of California (see page 54) which shows the major geologic units of the state.

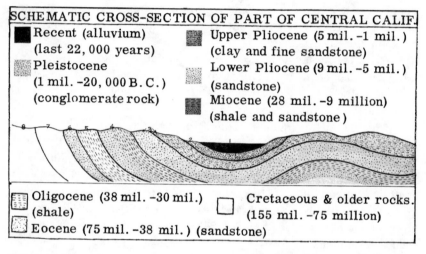

SCHEMATIC CROSS-SECTION OF PART OF CENTRAL CALIF.

■ Recent (alluvium) (last 22,000 years)

▨ Pleistocene (1 mil. –20,000 B.C.) (conglomerate rock)

▨ Upper Pliocene (5 mil. –1 mil.) (clay and fine sandstone)

▨ Lower Pliocene (9 mil. –5 mil.) (sandstone)

▨ Miocene (28 mil. –9 million) (shale and sandstone)

▨ Oligocene (38 mil. –30 mil.) (shale)

▨ Eocene (75 mil. –38 mil.) (sandstone)

□ Cretaceous & older rocks. (155 mil. –75 million)

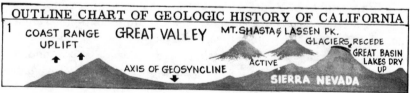

OUTLINE CHART OF GEOLOGIC HISTORY OF CALIFORNIA

1 COAST RANGE UPLIFT   GREAT VALLEY   MT. SHASTA & LASSEN PK.

AXIS OF GEOSYNCLINE   ACTIVE   GLACIERS RECEDE   GREAT BASIN LAKES DRY UP

SIERRA NEVADA

Recent epoch—Started about 22,000 years ago.

Major Changes: Coast Ranges still lifting; large lakes in east dry up, leaving salt deposits. Glaciers vanished, then came back slightly. San Francisco Bay formed. Volcanic eruptions in N.E.

Rocks formed. Gravel and clay sediments laid down in valleys; deep canyons eroded in Sierra exposing old schists and gneisses of Paleozoic time; also old crystalline metamorphic coast rocks exposed by erosion; basalt and rhyolite lavas in northeast.

Pleistocene epoch—Began about 1 million years ago.

Major changes: Great glaciers cover the higher mountains, receding and coming back about 4 times; climate moist, so many lakes formed in E. Calif.; active mountain building throughout Calif.

Rocks formed: Many lava eruptions, forming basalt, obsidian and andesite in N.E. and rhyolite and basalt in center and south. Pleistocene sediments, mostly gravel, sand and clay, formed in valleys. Erosion and glacial action carve new valleys and canyons, exposing much of granite batholith in the Sierra Nevada.

Pliocene epoch—Began about 9 million years ago.

Major changes: Mts. elevated in both Coast Range and Sierra as climate cools, in Sierra by uptilting of Sierra block toward west. Great Basin block begins to shear away and down from Sierra block after first rising with it. Low temp. ore veins, such as cinnabar (mercury ore) formed in Coast Ranges. Volcanic action in N. Sierra covers much of range under lava and mud flows.

Rocks formed. Sheets of basalt formed in N. Sierra, often trapping gold-bearing gravels; rhyolite lava in S.E. Erosion of gold-bearing quartz veins forms auriferous gravels. Erosion of block mountains in south begins to form alluvial plains.

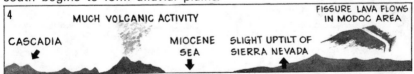

Miocene epoch—Began about 28 million years ago.

Major changes. Mts. rise high enough to cut off moisture, making E. Calif. more arid; first tilting of Sierra block lifts mts. to about 3000 ft. altitude. Great Valley mostly under sea; Coast Ranges as islands at first, then begin to rise above sea. Fissure eruptions of lava in Modoc Plateau. Volcanoes active in center, particularly in region of present Pinnacles National Monument.

Rocks formed. Basalt lava in northeast; rhyolite lava and breccia formed in Pinnacles region by explosive eruptions; Miocene sandstone and shales laid down in sea, some from land area off present West Coast (called Cascadia); some oil shales formed.

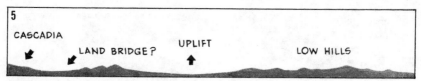

Oligocene epoch—Began about 38 million years ago.

Major changes. California seas shrink, so that most of present state is above water and possibly joined to land area of Cascadia off present West Coast. Some uplift, but land not high, mostly low hills and plains. Mountains of previous epoch eroded away.

Rocks formed. Land-laid sediments in wide flat valleys form about only record of Oligocene. Shale formed from this shows country was largely flat with few mountains.

Paleocene & eocene epochs—Began about 75 million yrs. ago.

Major changes. Most of record from Eocene. Ancestral Cascades and Sierra bowed upward into ridge mts. during this period. Moist climate with luxuriant tropical vegetation. Sea covers most of Great Valley and coast (with few islands), but land sometimes rises above sea. Land off present West Coast (Cascadia) rises steeply and much erosion brings down sediment.

Rocks formed. Lava eruptions in Klamath Mt. region; beginning of oil and gas formations in heavy vegetation of swampy areas. Eocene conglomerates, sandstones and shales formed in sea.

Cretaceous period—Started about 130 million years ago.

Major changes. Records scanty because this was a period when most of land was under a shallow sea, but ancestral Sierra continued high and erosion began to expose gold ore. Land of Cascadia off coast eroded and uplifted two or three times during this period. Santa Lucia Mts. and some other mountains uplifted at end of this period by folding and faulting.

Rocks formed. Cretaceous sandstones and shales laid down in shallow sea, with the shales deposited when Cascadia was a low-lying land mass, and the sandstones and conglomerates deposited when it was a rugged land of high mountains. Some of these sediments thousands of feet thick show long period of quiet.

Jurassic period—Started about 155 million years ago.

Major changes. Great debris-filled trough of early California geosyncline is crumbled into mountain ridges of ancestral Sierra Nevada at close of period; deep batholith underneath forms granite rock of Sierra backbone and sends out quartz veins bearing gold of the Mother Lode. Similar batholith under upfolding of Klamath and desert ranges. Mountains of Cascadia send down much sediment.

Rocks formed. Chert formed by gelatinized silica; lava eruptions on bottom of shallow sea; granite in inner mountans; volcanic eruptions of basalt, andesite, rhyolite and breccia in Sierra and elsewhere; sandstones and shales laid down to depths of 30,000 ft.

Pre-Jurassic time

During the Triassic period (first period of the Mesozoic era), and the Paleozoic era, which preceded it, the so-called "basement rocks" of California were laid down in ancient and wide-spread seas that covered most of what is now California. In the foothills of the Sierra, parts of the Santa Cruz Mts. and elsewhere these very ancient rocks are exposed today by erosion. Most of them are metamorphic rocks, such as schists, gneisses and crystalline limestones that show the result of much twisting and heating of the earth's crust.

Explanation of California Geologic Map on Page 54.

The map on the next page shows the major rock units of the State of California. The lines between these units should not be thought of as sharp as they are shown on the map, since the units, for the most part, grade into each other gradually. Also many non-typical rock masses are found scattered here and there.

Cenozoic volcanics. The Cenozoic Era, which extends from the beginning of the Paleocene Epoch to the present, saw tremendous volcanic activity in N.E. California. In the late Cenozoic great sheets of basalt lava from fissure eruptions covered most of the Modoc Plateau. Later the Cascades rose as volcanos.

Cenozoic sediments. The Great Valley of California and much of the present coast country were under the sea during large parts of the last 75 million years, and into this sea from land masses to the east and west great quantities of sediment were washed by erosion. Sediment was also deposited on valley floors by floods.

Cretaceous sediments. The sediments laid down in the ancient Cretaceous sea of 75 to 130 million years ago are mostly sandstone, and show a long quiet period of geologic history.

Jurassic-Franciscan group. These are cherts, shales and sandstones laid down in the Jurassic sea between 130 and 155 million years ago. Many of them are full of ancient sea fossils. Tens of thousands of feet of these sediments show the great influence of the once mountainous land of Cascadia off the West Coast.

Mesozoic-Paleozoic metamorphic-granitic rocks. The great granite batholiths that pushed up under the Sierra and Klamath Ranges 135 million or so years ago are now being exposed by erosion. Still earlier metamorphic rocks are exposed also.

Basin Ranges and Mohave Desert rock complex. Block mountains and valleys rising and lowering along fault lines have been formed above small granite batholiths and with masses of volcanic rocks.

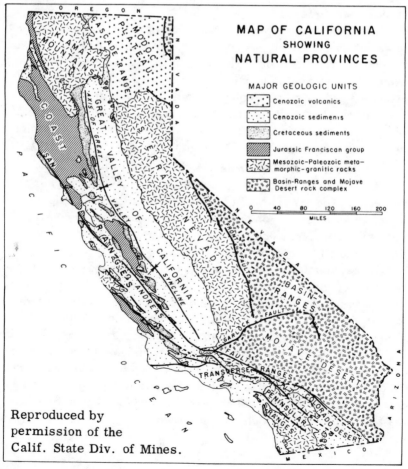

MAP OF CALIFORNIA
SHOWING
NATURAL PROVINCES

MAJOR GEOLOGIC UNITS

Cenozoic volcanics
Cenozoic sediments
Cretaceous sediments
Jurassic Franciscan group
Mesozoic-Paleozoic meta-morphic-granitic rocks
Basin-Ranges and Mojave Desert rock complex

0   40   80   120   160   200
MILES

Key to Common California Rocks

Rocks in particular are often very difficult to classify because, unlike minerals, they are mixtures of different things and grade into each other gradually. In using the following key try to come as close as you can, but remember it is very easy to be mistaken. You can check on your efforts with the key by showing the rock to an expert, who will tell you the right name, or by taking the rock to a museum and comparing it with specimens that are shown there on display. Since minerals form rocks, it is wise to study the rock-forming minerals first. (Indicated by bold capitals in the mineral key starting on page 4.)

When you drive through a city to reach the house of a friend, you are always making choices, usually between two alternate streets each time the choice is made. By making the right turn each time, you come eventually to your friend's house.

This key works the same way. Each time you are given two (a and b) or sometimes three (a, b and c) choices under each number of the key. The number on the right, opposite the letter, then tells you where to turn to find the next choice in the key. Finally you come down to the description and name of the rock you are trying to identify. If you find a rock that seems to fit half way between two choices, the only thing to do is to follow down each line of attack until you finally come to a do is to follow down each line of attack until you finally come to a description that seems to fit the rock you have. Take your time, study carefully each step in the key, and don't be afraid to start over.

(Key adapted from "A Key to Common Rocks" by Dr. Matthew Vessel of San Jose State College, and from "An Artificial Key to the Classification of Rocks" by W.F. Hoover of Univ. of Illinois.)

1a. Rock with visible grains on surface. The rock is made up of either clearly visible and tightly packed crystals (igneous rocks), or of grains of gravel, sand or other rock pieces cemented together. The appearance may be either fine or coarse grained, or it may be lumpy with pebbles of many sizes, but no magnifying glass is needed to see the grains **3**

1b. Rock without visible grains on surface (or only a few scattered ones). The appearance of the surface may be glass-like or soap-like or so very fine-grained that the individual grains can be seen only under a magnifying glass. The rock may be very solid (compact) or it may be full of small holes (porous or cellular), or it may be turned into powder by rubbing between the fingers (chalk-like) **2**

2a. Rock usually glasslike or pitchlike. It may be full of holes or be frothy like spun glass. When the rock is solid, it cannot be scratched with a knife. (Glassy igneous rocks.) **5**

2b. Rock generally dull (not like glass). The rock may be shiny if worn smooth by water or both slick and shiny if green or greenish-black (such a rock can usually be scratched easily with a knife). It may also be full of holes or easily crumbled in the fingers. Sometimes has a few scattered crystals.. **7**

3a. All of rock made up of visible mineral grains. These are usually one or several kinds of crystals which give some sparkle in bright light . . . **4**
3b. Rock made up of rock fragments (including pebbles), or sand or gravel cemented together. Fossils of shells, other animals, plants, etc. may be found in the rock; occasional crystals............ **28**

4a. Rock appears banded (with darker and lighter lines) or with irregular layers. The layers may be mixed with numerous, shiny mica flakes, with the flakes usually lined up parallel with each other. Magnified crystals look flattened **31**
4b. Rock appears neither banded nor layered and crystals are rarely flattened. (Large grained igneous rocks.)..................... **34**

5. Glasslike Igneous Rocks

These rocks appear like glass because the red-hot liquid lava from which they came cooled too rapidly to form any crystals.

5a. A solid, medium-weight rock, not scratched by knife....... **6**
5b. A very light-weight rock, full of holes or frothy like spun glass, usually scratched by a knife. Light gray to whitish color, either dull or with a sheen like silk. If holes are small with thin walls, a **pumice;** if holes large and thick-walled, a **scoria** (see illus. p. 57).

6a. Rock without any visible crystals; very glassy; breaks into shell-like or curved (conchoidal) pieces; color black, dark gray, brown, or reddish (rarely green)..................... **obsidian**
Note: obsidian may be mistaken for chert (see 22a), but chert is duller (like "petrified chewing gum") and does not usually break into very good curved chips.

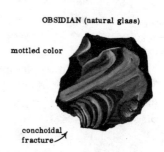

OBSIDIAN (natural glass)

mottled color

conchoidal fracture

6b. Rock with a few visible crystals embedded in the glass. (see note 32a.) .... **vitrophyre** (or **obsidian porphyry**)

7. Small-Grained Rocks

These rocks appear grained, but the grains can usually be seen clearly only under a magnifying glass, though there may be a few scattered large crystals (porphyrytic rocks).

7a. Rock bubbles or froths when touched with acid (acetic or dilute hydrochloric) especially along a scratch. Touch the rock in several places with the acid and make sure the frothing is not caused by just a thin surface layer or a vein in the rock. This rock often holds bits of shells or scattered crystals **26**
7b. Rock does not bubble or froth when touched with acid. Veins or thin surface layer of calcite may froth, so be sure to test the rock in many places **8**

8a. The rock does not powder easily between the fingers. Sometimes full of tiny holes, but usually solid (compact) **10**
8b. The rock is usually easily powdered between the fingers. Color whitish to white, sometimes with parallel lines............... **9**

9a. Rock when powdered is usually very fine (like talcum powder). The rock absorbs water very quickly..................... **diatomite**
9b. Rock when powdered feels gritty. Water absorbed slowly. (see also note under 18a.)................................... **tuff**

10a. A very hard rock, not easily scratched with a knife, but if full of small cells or holes, it may seem to scratch due to walls of the holes breaking down. Try to find wide surface..................... **19**
10b. Rock easily scratched by a knife **11**

11a. Rock full of holes, often tiny. . . . **12**
11b. Rock solid, not full of holes **13**

12a. Rock light in color (grayish to whitish), and usually light in weight. If holes are large and with thick walls, it is **scoria;** if holes are tiny and thin-walled (floats in water), it is......... **pumice**
12b. Rock black, purplish, dark gray or reddish, and usually of medium weight; holes usually few in number. (see 24a) .... **basalt**

PUMICE (glossy appearance; light-colored -- sometimes brown on red)

porous

silky fibers

will float

13a. Rock does not show layers or can't be split into layers. **14**
13b. Rock appears in layers which can be split apart. **17**

14a. Surface of rock feels waxy or slick (at least partly) **15**
14b. Surface of rock not waxy or slick; usually gritty, but may be smooth and with clay odor when wet. **16**

15a. Can't be scratched by fingernail; color dark greenish gray or greenish with the weathered surfaces sometimes rusty, often mottled whitish or with greenish-white veins. . . . . **serpentine**
15b. Can be scratched by fingernail; color usually white or gray; easily carved; valued by Indians. . . . . **steatite** or **soapstone**

16a. Rock of many colors, but usually gray or brownish; usually with a clayey odor and taste when wet . . . . **shale** or **siltstone**
Note: shale is made of a mixture of so many substances that there is wide variation in color, compostion and appearance. Shales which do not split are generally **mudstone.** Shales with much sand are called **sandy shale.** If shale fizzes or foams when touched with hydrochloric or acetic acid, it has some calcite in it from seashells and is called **limy shale.** White, hard and gritty shales are usually made partly of volcanic ash (so related to tuff). (see illustrations on page 59)
16b. Rock white or whitish; may have clayey odor, but more gritty than above, and with angular particles visible under a magnifying glass. (see also 18a) . . . . **tuff**

17a. Rock breaks into slabs with flat or curving and shell-like surfaces or into sharp chips. It may hold shells or other fossils. It usually has a clayey odor when wet **18**
17b. The rock splits into thin slates (like the slate on a blackboard) or into thicker slabs with very flat surfaces which are not easily scratched with a knife, and which have a shiny surface. Color usually gray or black, but also brown, yellowish-brown, greenish, reddish or purplish. Surface sometimes banded different colors. No fossils present. (see p. 72) . . . . **slate**

SLATE (dark gray to black, some red, green, purple and brown variations)
conchoidal fracture
sharp edges
often fine mica flakes

17c. Rock breaks into thickly irregular slabs; usually the blue color of glaucophane. Found mainly in the Coast Ranges . . . . **glaucophane** or **amphibole schist**

18a. Rock usually breaks up into sharp chips with smooth fracture, and these, when ground up, have a gritty feel. When moistened, may give sight odor of clay. Color whitish, light gray, pinkish, yellowish or other light color. Tiny glass shards usually are visible under magnifying glass . . . . **tuff**

Note: Tuff comes from volcanic ash, but when this ash is mixed with mud or other sediment, then tuffs grade gradually into shales and it is hard to draw the line between them.

18b. Rock usually breaks into shell-like or curved chips (conchoidal fracture); when ground into dust is usually smooth and not gritty. If moistened, the rock usually smells strongly of clay. (see 16a.) . . . . **shale**

SHALE (black, white, dark greens and reds)

thin layers, clay particles & little sand

conchoidal (shell-like) fracture

19a. Rock with large, scattered crystals embedded in its surface. (see also no. 34a) . . . . **porphyry**
19b. Rock without such crystals   **20**

20a. Rock plainly banded in different colors or with layers **21**
20b. Rock not in bands or layers **23**

21a. Rock obviously banded. **22**
21b. Rock in parallel layers (no obvious bands) that can be broken apart into approximately rectangular pieces. Looks like shale, but has greater hardness due to silica . . . . **cherty shale**

22a. Rock with white, soft, chalky layers between dark, hard layers. Absorbs water easily . . . . **cherty diatomite**
22b. Rock shows flow bands; light colored. (see 25a) . . . **rhyolite**
22c. Rock with darker or lighter strips, but all of same hardness.
. . . . see **quartzite** (39b), **slate** (17b), **felsite** (24b).
23a. Rock under magnifying glass shows no tiny holes or pores; usually brittle with somewhat curved or shell-like fracture; commonly reddish or yellow-brown in color, but often greenish and sometimes black or white; often criss-crossed with white quartz veins; often in hard water-worn pebbles. . . . . **chert**
(see also notes under 6a and 23b, and page 70)
23b. Rock under magnifying glass may appear with tiny holes. If not present, not brittle nor with curved chips when broken **24**

59

24a. Rock dark-colored, & usually black, purplish, dark rusty or dark greenish-gray; always heavy & often with round gas holes in it. The commonest lava rock.................................. **basalt**
Note: Basalt varies from the aphanitic type in which the grains are just barely visible to scoria type where there are numerous round gas holes and to amygdaloidal basalt where the round holes are filled with mineral. Basalt porphyry has angular spots.

24b. Rock light-colored, usually gray, white, yellowish-brown, cream, pink, greenish or purplish; sometimes a few white or dark red light bands or lines are visible, which were caused by the flow of the lava. Freshly-broken chips show white or semi-transparent edges.... **25**

BASALT (mostly dark)

usually porous

often has green inclusions of olivine

RHYOLITE (a felsite)

veins of color

often porous

generally banded
May be several colors, but all light of tone

25a. Often has visible quartz crystals or grains, and may appear almost glassy or at least very fine-grained in texture..... **rhyolite**
25b. No quartz, otherwise very similar to rhyolite....... **andesite**
Note: Felsitic rocks such as rhyolite and andesite show so many different colors and textures they may be mistaken for basalt (24a) when very dark, or chert (23a) when very fine-grained, or compact tuff (18a), or very fine-grained quartzite (40b).

LIMESTONE (white and many colors)
Often found in caves, quarries. Fizzing under acid is best test.

26a. Rock firm, does not easily crumble, though it sometimes is easily scratched with a knife; color whitish, gray, brownish, yellowish or black; may hold parts of shells or crystals.......... **limestone**
Note: Limestone in pure form is fairly hard, but it may be mixed with impurities such as clay (clayey limestone) or sand (sandy limestone). If formed in patterns or

banded deposits by hot water, called travertine.
26b. Rock easily powdered and scratched by fingernail....... **27**

27a. Gray color and clayey odor (when wetted) . . . . **marl**
27b. White color and without clayey odor . . . . **chalk**

28. Cemented Rocks with Visible Grains

Sedimentary rocks made up of either gravel or sand or other rock particles cemented together; often contain fossils; rarely a few scattered crystals. Cement of calcite, clay, iron oxide, etc.

28a. Rock made up mainly of pebbles or angular pieces of rock which are generally as large as or larger than peas. **30**

28b. Pieces smaller than peas. **29**

29a. Course or fine sand cemented more or less firmly together; color varies greatly from yellowish-brown to brown, red, yellow, gray or whitish; rock may hold shells or other fossils and scattered crystals. Magnifying glass shows rounded & angular grains of quartz and other minerals . . . . **sandstone**

Note: sandstones vary greatly in texture. If dark gray, called gray-wacke; if it fizzes with acid, limy sandstone (see 26a); if very fine-grained, clayey sandstone, which is close to shale.

29b. Fine gritty rock fragments (volcanic ash or cinders) cemented together. Magnifying glass shows sharp pieces. Color varies from white to light yellowish-brown or gray (18a) . . . . **tuff**

SANDSTONE (white to brown)

quartz

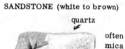

often
mica
flakes

grains of feldspar

Split slabs = flagstone

Slabs containing much reddish feldspar = brownstone.

CONGLOMERATE ("Puddingstone",
variable color)

Rounded pebbles
often quartz

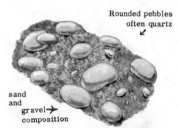

sand
and
gravel→
composition

30a. Rounded pebbles cemented in sand and clay . . . **conglomerate**
30b. Angular pieces of rock cemented together by calcite, etc., or the pieces are mixed with fine sand, clay or volcanic ash, which acts as a cement . . . . **breccia**

31. Banded, Crystallized or Schistose Rocks With Visible Crystals or Grains.

These are crystalline, metamorphic rocks, which have been changed from other rocks by heat or pressure. They are usually easily flaked or split into layers because of the parallel design of the flattened crystals.

31a. Rock fizzes or foams when touched with acetic or hydrochloric acid, especially along scratch. Has one color or with crudely-colored bands. (37a)......................................**marble**

31b. Rock does not fizz or foam when touched with acid..... **32**

MARBLE (white, gray)

often
banded
with
impurities

calcite or dolomite
crystals sparkle

SCHIST (variable in color)

mica flakes
common

fine
layered

32a. Rock not banded, but thickly layered with numerous, shiny, silvery flakes of mica, most of the flakes lying in parallel planes. Layers can usually be split into irregular slabs, or can be crumbled **mica schist**
Note: There are many other kinds of schists, depending on the mineral content, such as chlorite schist (light green), garnet schist (reddish), talc schist (whitish), glaucophane schist (blue), etc.

32b. Rock generally banded with dark streaks or lines........ **33**

33a. Rock made mainly of quartz sand grains so fused together they break directly through grains when rock is broken (with some mica visible but not in bands); cannot be scratched with knife. Color reddish, brownish, or greenish, rarely black. (see also 40b)...... **quartzite**

33b. Rock made up of many kinds of minerals including rough layers or bands of mica between layers of quartz and feldspar, rock often looks like granite (see 40a), but the mica appears in continuous, streaky, wavy or straight bands .... **gneiss**

GNEISS (variable color, coarse banding)

layered
bands of
feldspar and quartz usually present

34. Unbanded Rocks With Visible Crystals or Grains

These rocks have easily visible crystals, tightly packed together, but not flattened as in the rocks in the section above. These crystals or grains sparkle in bright light.

34a. Rocks not made of even grains or crystals, but with scattered large crystals (usually of one kind of mineral) placed among much smaller crystals of other kinds of minerals (the smaller crystals

62

sometimes being too small to see without a magnifying glass). The rock looks as if covered with angular flecks, usually darker than rest of rock, but may be lighter .... **prophyry**
Note: Prophyrys are named according to the kind of rock in which the large crystals (called phenocrysts) grow: basalt porphyry (24a); felsite porphyry (25a and b); granite prophyry (40a); obsidian porphyry (6a).

PORPHYRY (many colors)
Large crystals found in rock called phenocrysts

34b. Rock made up of grains or crystals of about the same size (either all small or all large) though not always of the same shape. Some minerals may be shapeless when molded around other mineral crystals **35**

35a. Rock does not fizz or foam with hydrochloric or acetic acid, even 'when scratched or turned to powder........................**37**
35b. Rock fizzes or foams when touched with acid, especially along a scratch or when powdered. Color white, gray, red, yellow or almost black, frequently veined or blotched **36**

36a. Rock fizzes easily on surface without scratching. (See 31a for fuller description and illustration.) .... **marble**
36b. Rock fizzes only along a scratch or when powdered. (See page 16 for illus. plus mineral description)................. **dolomite**

37a. Rock made up of large crystals, larger than a pea....... **42**
37b. Rock made up of small crystals, smaller than a pea **38**

38a. Rock made up of both light and dark colored minerals... **39**
38b. Rock of almost all the same color, either light or dark... **41**

39a. Rock having approximately 75% light minerals and 25% dark minerals... **40**
39b. Rock having approximately 75% dark minerals and 25% light minerals; with square, chunky, dark green grains of augite; the quartz is generally absent and the feldspar is often a dark variety, though showing typical feldspar cleavage when looked at with magnifying glass (see page 42) .... **gabbro**
39c. Rock having approximately 50% light minerals and 50% dark minerals; quartz always absent; plagioclase feldspar is always whitish, never reddish as in granite (see p. 42).................. **diorite**

40a. Rock made up mainly of orthoclase feldspar (pinkish or milky and showing good cleavage), quartz (glassy white), and slender, dark crystals of hornblende or flaky dark crystals of biotite mica (or sometimes both present). ...... **granite**

GRANITE (mottled appearance) composition of feldspar, quartz, mica, hornblende, etc.

mica flakes often present

light weight

40b. Similar to granite, but lighter colored and with no quartz present; less mottling. ...... **syenite**

40c. A rock midway between diorite and syenite that contains half plagioclase and half orthoclase feldspar, no quartz. . . . . **monzonite**

41a. Rock usually colored dark greenish-gray or almost black because of the dark-colored minerals (most often olivine). The surface often has smooth, shiny (even greasy) spots where the rock has changed to serpentine (see 15a) . . . . **peridotite**
Note: a fine-grained rock of this type will probably be basalt (24a). The rock should be carefully studied under a magnifying glass, as the presence of a dark feldspar with the typical feldspar cleavage (see p. 42) will show it to be a diorite (39c), while the dark green or black of augite indicates of gabbro (39b). Varieties are pyroxenite, with dark crystals of augite only; dunite, with very hard crystals of olivine; hornblendite, with black or dark green hornblende crystals.

41b. Rock almost white. (see 40b) . . . . **syenite**

41c. Rock whitish, reddish, brownish or greenish (but not dark); under magnifying glass shows tiny quartz crystals embedded in quartz. Can't be scratched with knife. The grains break straight through instead of around, and the pieces are very splintery. . . . . **quartzite**

42a. Very large crystals of quartz, orthoclase feldspar and mica or hornblende. It is found in dikes or large veins, often with beautiful gem minerals and other rarities. (see p. 33) . . . . **pegmatite**

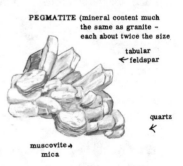

PEGMATITE (mineral content much the same as granite – each about twice the size

tabular ←feldspar

quartz ←

muscovite→ mica

42b. A rock composed of very large crystals such as garnet, epidote, pyroxenes, calcite, magnetite, pyrite and wollastonite. It is a contact metamorphic rock formed by the intruding of a limestone rock mass by a hot igneous mass. . . . . **tactite**

California Minerals and Rocks in Color

The following pages show illustrations of 32 minerals and 16 rocks in full color. The minerals are arranged in alphabetical order first, followed by the rocks, beginning with basalt. All of these beautiful pictures are reproduced by courtesy of Mr. W. Scott Lewis of Palm Springs, California, and selected from his extensive collection of kodachromes.

ACTINOLITE (an amphibole) — Cajon Pass, California. Nephrite jade when compact and tough.

BARITE — A mass of crystals from Palos Verdes, California. Also called "heavy spar" because of heavy weight.

BENITOITE — San Benito Co., California. Six-sided crystals in narrow veins of natrolite in serpentine.

AGATE — "Thunder Egg" from Mohave Desert, California. Agate formed inside geode.

BAUXITE — Death Valley, California. Also called pisolite because of fish-egg shape.

CALCITE — Iceland spar from Sierra Nevada, California. Shows rhombic cleavage and optical doubling.

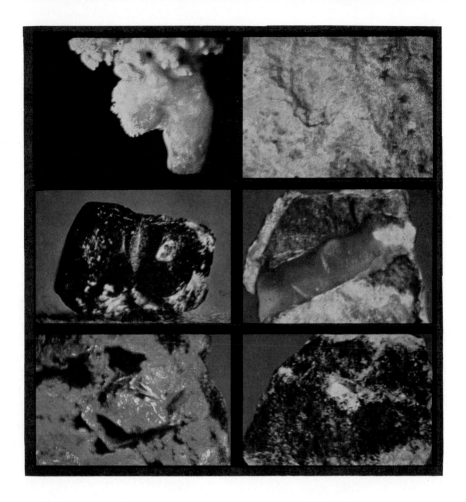

CALCITE — A stalactite from a cave in the Mohave Desert, California. Calcite precipitates as water drips from ceiling.

CARNOTITE — Disseminated in tuff, Kern County, California. A key uranium mineral.

CASSITERITE — This twin crystal from Oak Grove, California, shows adamantine luster.

CHRYSOPRASE — This green form of chalcedony is from Tulare County, California. Often used as a gem.

CINNABAR — New Almaden, California. Massive form, showing sparkling, adamantine luster.

CORUNDUM — Blue-green corundum in massive form, Mono County, California.

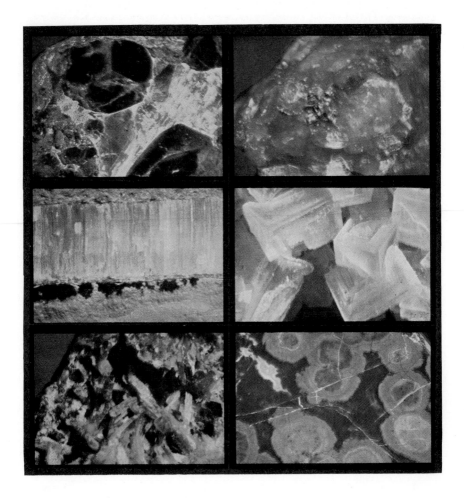

GARNET (Grossularite) — Crest-more, California. Typical garnet crystals shown, but garnet has many varieties.

GOLD in QUARTZ — Mother Lode Country, California. Typical quartz vein showing gold caught in matrix.

GYPSUM — Satin spar fibrous var-iety in rock of Calico Mountains, California. Formed by evaporation in drying lake beds.

HALITE — Death Valley, California. Notice cubic, hopper-shaped crystals.

JADEITE — Rare crystals in vug, northern California. Jade is some-times found on California beaches.

JASPER — Orbicular jasper from Morgan Hill, California. In large orbs.

JASPER — Brecciated jasper from Monterey County, California. Polished to emphasize colors.

LEPIDOLITE with RUBELLITE — Pala, California. Crystals of red tourmaline (rubellite) in granular lepidolite (a mica).

MAGNETITE or LODESTONE — San Bernardino County, California. When magnetite acts like a magnet it is called a lodestone.

MOLYBDENITE — Inyo County, California. Crystallized rosette in rock. The chief ore of molybdenum.

PSILOMELANE — Dendrites (fernlike growths) of psilomelane on rock in the Mohave Desert, California.

PSILOMELANE — Botryoidal form from the Cady Mountains, California. The chief ore of manganese.

QUARTZ — Quartz crystals formed in hollow in rock (geode) in Mohave Desert, California.

QUARTZ — Rose quartz of Kern County, California. Sometimes valuable as a gem stone.

OPAL — Precious opal in basalt rock, from Kern County, California. The fiery luster adds value.

REALGAR — Prismatic crystals on rock at Skaggs Springs, California. An ore of arsenic.

RHODONITE — A polished slab from Tulare County, California, with black inclusions. A manganese ore.

SERPENTINE in MARBLE — Notice the white streaks in the serpentine. The veins were deposited by warm water.

TOURMALINE — Mesa Grande, California. Sometimes of gem quality; notice striations in crystals.

TURQUOISE — Mohave Desert, California. Blue, massive incrustations. Used in gems.

Rocks

BASALT — Lava columns at Devil's Post Pile, Madera County, California.

CHERT — Ornamental chert, Buellton, California. Gelatinized silica rock, colored by iron oxide.

BRECCIA — Opalite breccia, Mohave Desert, California. Bits of opal in angular rock fragments.

CONGLOMERATE — Santa Monica, California. Cemented rock pebbles.

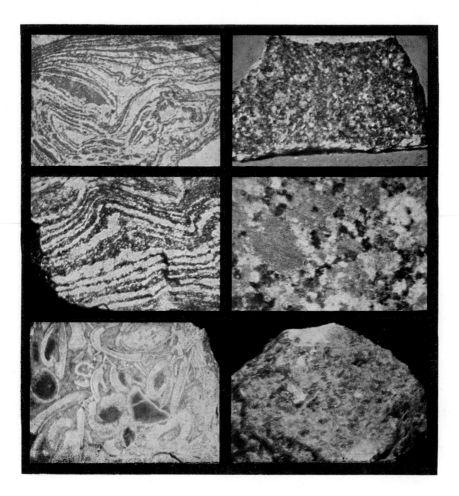

DACITE LAVA FLOW — Rosamond, California. A light-colored felsitic lava.

GNEISS — Sunland, California. Rock twisted and pressed into rough layers by pressure.

LIMESTONE — Fossiliferous limestone from Kern County, California. Shells of ancient sea animals are cemented in the rock.

GABBRO — San Diego County, California. A very dark plutonic rock with large grains like granite.

GRANITE — Quartz monzonite variety. Mt. Whitney, California. Crystals of quartz, feldspar and mica are visible.

MARBLE — Blue calcite marble from Crestmore, California. A metamorphic rock.

PEGMATITE — Mesa Grande, California. A very coarse-grained granite in which quartz and feldspar crystals have grown very large.

QUARTZITE — Mohave Desert, California. Sand grains of sandstone have been fused together.

SLATE — Mohave Desert, California. Ancient ripple marks show on this metamorphic rock.

PERIDOTITE — Del Norte, California. Made of dark minerals, olivine or augite.

SANDSTONE SPIKE — Colorado Desert, California. Sand cemented together in a strangely-shaped concretion.

TUFF — Tuff beds of Rosamond, California. Volcanic ash cemented into sedimentary rock beds.

LOCALITY MAPS

HOW TO USE THE MAPS

The maps on the following pages show those parts of California which have the most interesting and extensive deposits of minerals and unusual rocks. The key map of the state of California on page 74 shows where the different map sections are located in relation to the counties. Find those map sections that cover areas in your neighborhood and study them carefully.

We have purposely eliminated from these two color maps all lines, names, and so forth that would interfere with locating the deposits of minerals and rocks noted. For example, all county lines are cut out of the maps, as these lines cannot be seen in the countryside anyway, and you have the county lines on the key map. The most important things for locating the deposits are roads, rivers, creeks, hills and mountains. These are emphasized on our maps. You will note that in the high mountains we have indicated peaks as if they were hills. The steepest parts of each peak are indicated by rows of parallel lines. On a hike watch for these steep places in relation to the map and use them to help you locate the specimens for which you are looking.

The main map in each case is in black while the symbols used for rocks and minerals are in red. The minerals are always shown as numbers on the maps, with the names given opposite the numbers at the bottom of the page. But the rocks have different markings, as shown below.

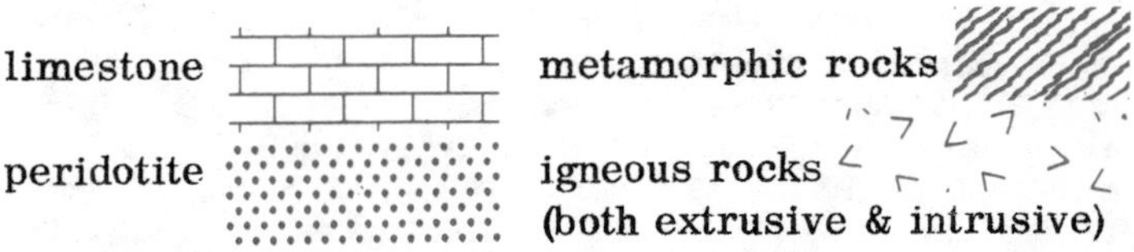

limestone   metamorphic rocks

peridotite   igneous rocks
(both extrusive & intrusive)

Areas on the map that are not marked with rock symbols are where there are alluvium or sedimentary rocks such as chert, shale or sandstone, or where there is not sufficient information to be found on the area. The rocks shown are those that will most likely have interesting mineral deposits in them.

Do not be too disappointed if you do not immediately find the mineral you are looking for at the place shown on the map. A good collector knows specimens must be carefully searched for.

73

KEY TO ROCK AND MINERAL LOCALITY MAPS

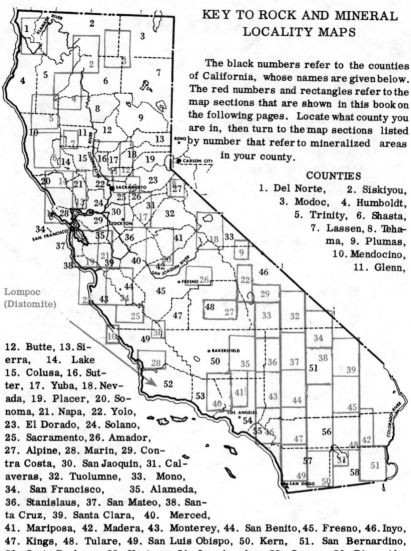

The black numbers refer to the counties of California, whose names are given below. The red numbers and rectangles refer to the map sections that are shown in this book on the following pages. Locate what county you are in, then turn to the map sections listed by number that refer to mineralized areas in your county.

COUNTIES

1. Del Norte, 2. Siskiyou, 3. Modoc, 4. Humboldt, 5. Trinity, 6. Shasta, 7. Lassen, 8. Tehama, 9. Plumas, 10. Mendocino, 11. Glenn,

Lompoc (Diatomite)

12. Butte, 13. Sierra, 14. Lake 15. Colusa, 16. Sutter, 17. Yuba, 18. Nevada, 19. Placer, 20. Sonoma, 21. Napa, 22. Yolo, 23. El Dorado, 24. Solano, 25. Sacramento, 26. Amador, 27. Alpine, 28. Marin, 29. Contra Costa, 30. San Jaoquin, 31. Calaveras, 32. Tuolumne, 33. Mono, 34. San Francisco, 35. Alameda, 36. Stanislaus, 37. San Mateo, 38. Santa Cruz, 39. Santa Clara, 40. Merced, 41. Mariposa, 42. Madera, 43. Monterey, 44. San Benito, 45. Fresno, 46. Inyo, 47. Kings, 48. Tulare, 49. San Luis Obispo, 50. Kern, 51. San Bernardino, 52. Santa Barbara, 53. Ventura, 54. Los Angeles, 55. Orange, 56. Riverside, 57. San Diego, 58. Imperial.

CONVENTIONAL MAP SYMBOLS USED

Railroads	+---+---+	Intermittent str.	Open water
Dismantled R. R.	+---+---+	Towns ○	Swamp
Roads	———	Cities ◎	Dry lake
Streams		Well, spring · ⌒	
Disappearing str.	⌁→ →→	Mine ⚒	SCALE OF MILES: 9 miles = 1 in

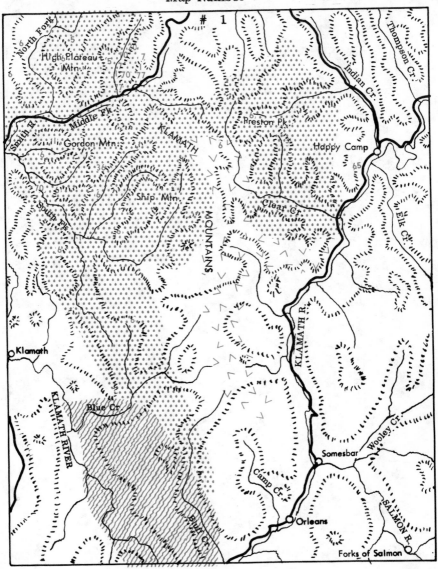

1	gold	7	quartz	65	rhodonite
3	bornite	10	chalcopyrite	70	garnet
5	cinnabar	20	pyrrhotite	77	arsenopyrite
6	chromite	36	magnesite		

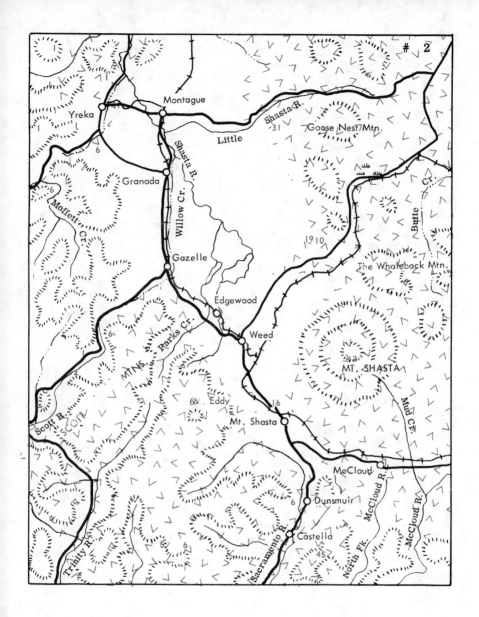

1 gold

4 galena

5 cinnabar

6 chromite

10 chalcopyrite

16 graphite

17 sulfur

19 molybdenite

31 opal

45 barite

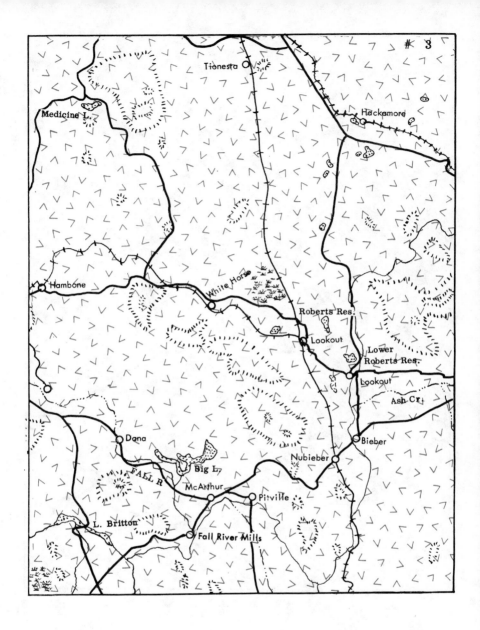

The above area is one of great interest in volcanic rocks and volcanic features. In exploring this region be sure to use those sections of the Habitat Chart on pages 38–40 that deal with the minerals of volcanic rocks and zeolitic cavities. It is these minerals that you can hope to find as you explore here.

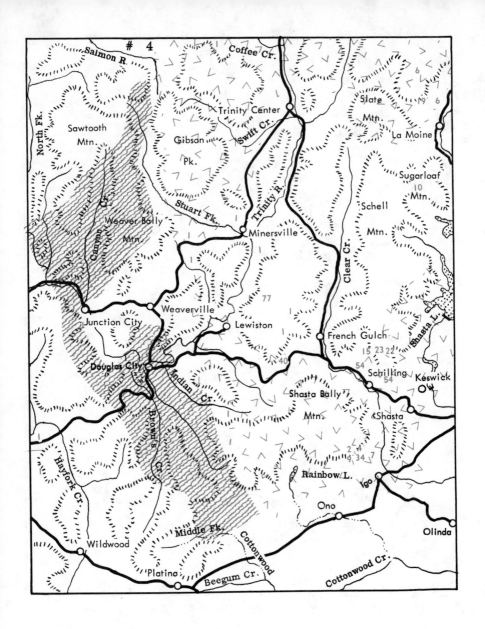

1	gold	9	sphalerite	23	magnetite
2	silver	10	chalcopyrite	34	calcite
4	galena	15	pyrite	40	azurite
6	chromite	19	molybdenite	54	talc
7	quartz	22	hematite	77	arsenopyrite

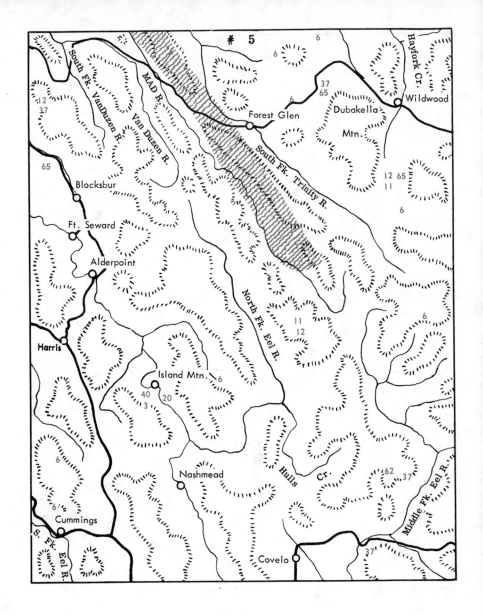

3	bornite	12	psilomelane	40	azurite
6	chromite	20	pyrrhotite	62	nephrite
11	pyrolusite	37	rhodochrosite	65	rhodonite

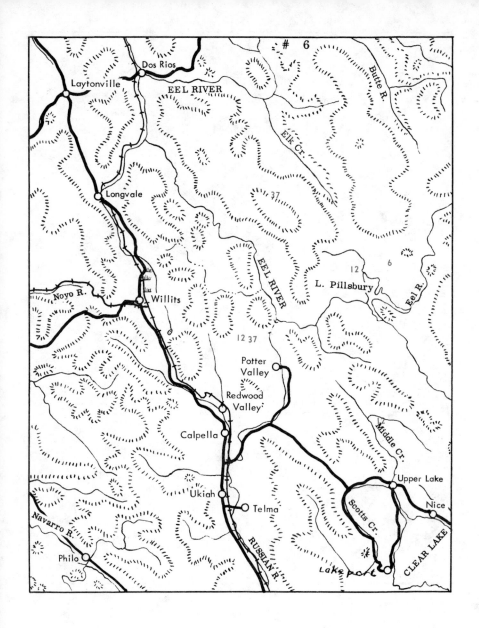

6 chromite   12 psilomelane   37 rhodochrosite

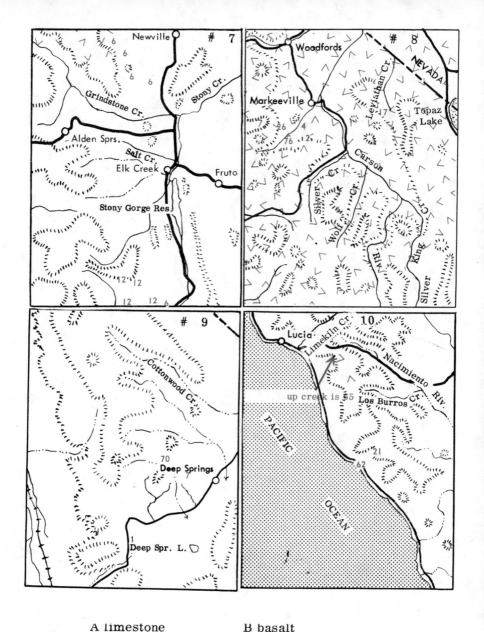

A limestone		B basalt
2 silver	17 sulfur	62 nephrite
4 galena	21 stibnite	65 rhodonite
6 chromite	26 rutile	70 garnet
7 quartz	34 calcite	71 epidote
12 psilomelane		76 andalusite

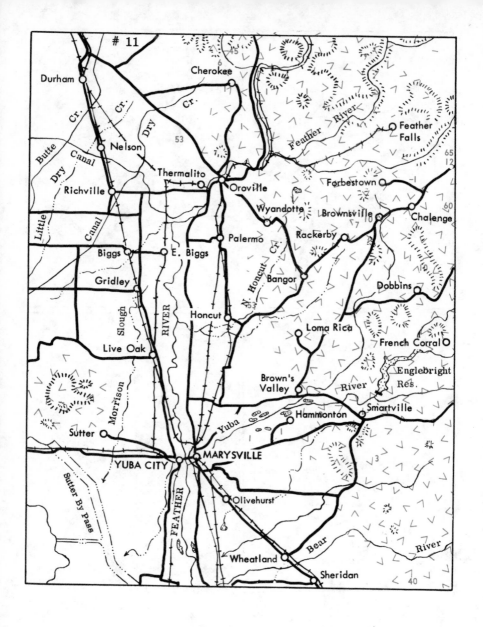

11

1	gold	10	chalcopyrite	45	barite
3	bornite	11	pyrolusite	53	kaolinite
6	chromite	12	psilomelane	60	tremolite
7	quartz	40	azurite	65	rhodonite

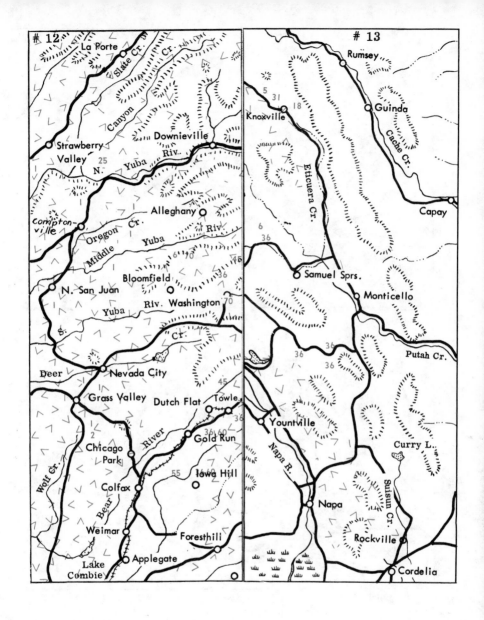

1	gold	18	marcasite	45	barite
2	silver	25	corundum	55	serpentine
5	cinnabar	31	opal	60	tremolite
6	chromite	36	magnesite	70	garnet

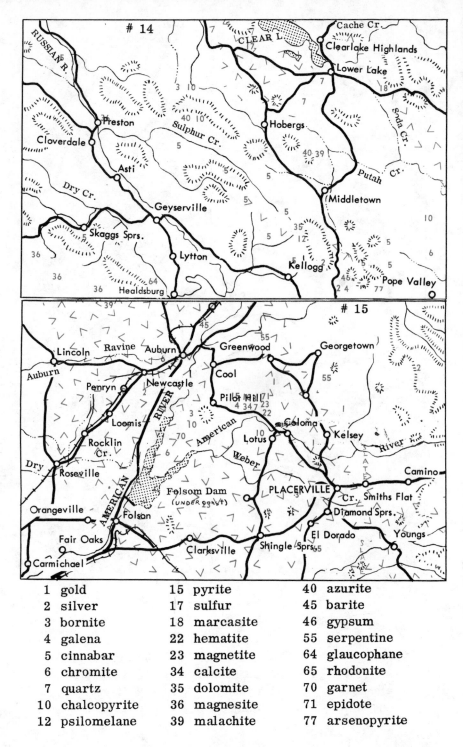

14

15

1	gold	15	pyrite	40	azurite
2	silver	17	sulfur	45	barite
3	bornite	18	marcasite	46	gypsum
4	galena	22	hematite	55	serpentine
5	cinnabar	23	magnetite	64	glaucophane
6	chromite	34	calcite	65	rhodonite
7	quartz	35	dolomite	70	garnet
10	chalcopyrite	36	magnesite	71	epidote
12	psilomelane	39	malachite	77	arsenopyrite

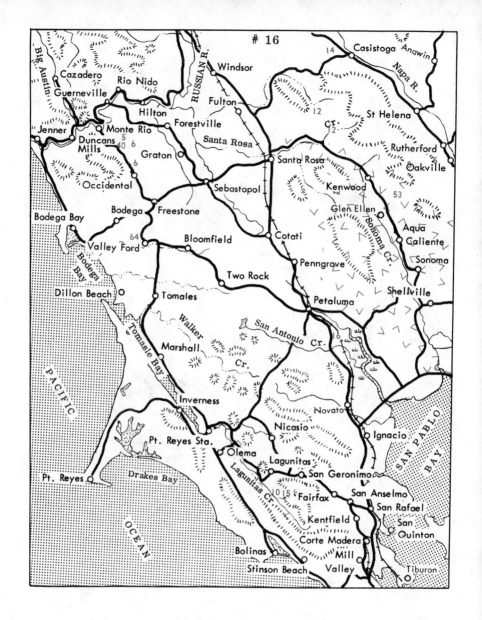

16

5 cinnabar	15 pyrite
6 chromite	16 graphite
10 chalcopyrite	40 azurite
12 psilomelane	53 kaolinite
14 chalcedony	64 glaucophane

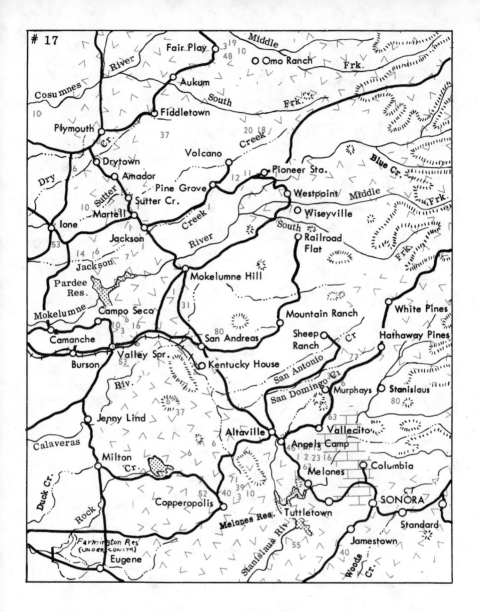

1 gold	12 psilomelane	23 magnetite	52 orthoclase
2 silver	14 chalcedony	31 opal	53 kaolinite
3 bornite	15 pyrite	34 calcite	55 serpentine
6 chromite	16 graphite	37 rhodochrosite	63 hornblende
7 quartz	18 marcasite	39 malachite	71 epidote
10 chalcopyrite	19 molybdenite	40 azurite	77 arsenopyrite
11 pyrolusite	20 pyrrhotite	46 gypsum	80 uranium

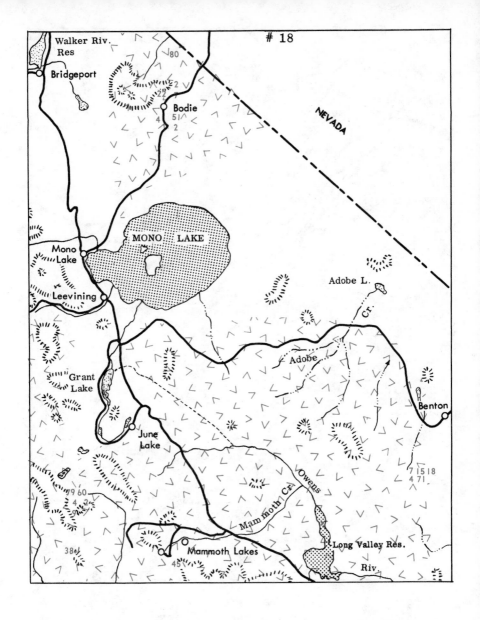

2 silver	18 marcasite	60 tremolite
4 galena	22 hematite	71 epidote
7 quartz	38 aragonite	79 cerrusite
9 sphalerite	45 barite	80 uranium
15 pyrite	51 plagioclase	

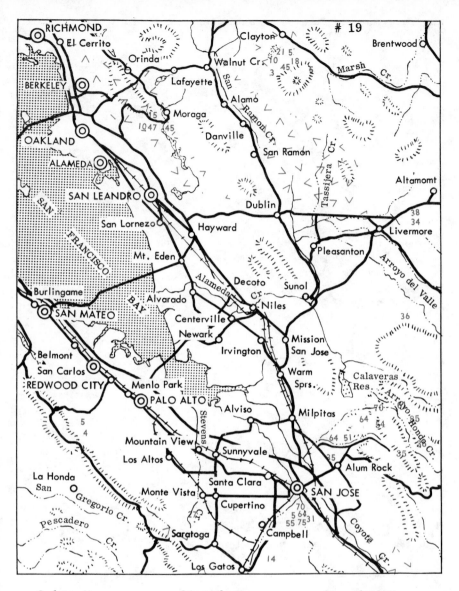

19

3 bornite	21 stibnite	47 anhydrite
4 galena	27 jasper	51 plagioclase
5 cinnabar	31 opal (hyaline)	54 talc
6 chromite	34 calcite	55 serpentine
10 chalcopyrite	35 dolomite	61 actinolite
14 chalcedony	36 magnesite	64 glaucophane
15 pyrite	38 aragonite	70 garnet
18 marcasite	45 barite	75 pyroxene
		85 chlorite

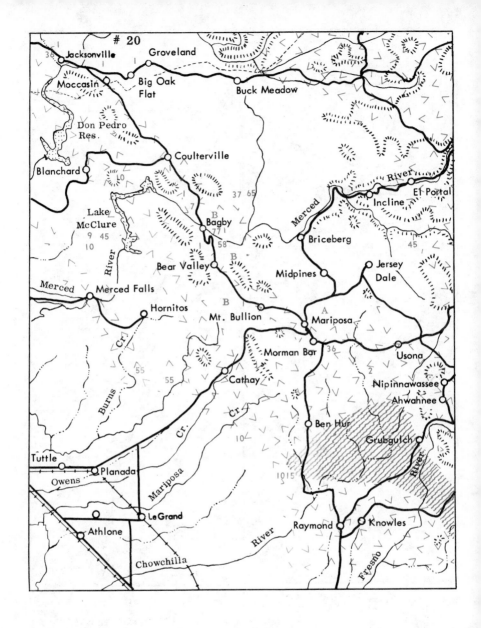

1	gold	15	pyrite	57	mariposite
2	silver	36	magnesite	65	rhodonite
7	quartz	37	rhodochrosite	77	arsenopyrite
9	sphalerite	45	barite	A	soapstone
10	chalcopyrite	55	serpentine	B	schist

89

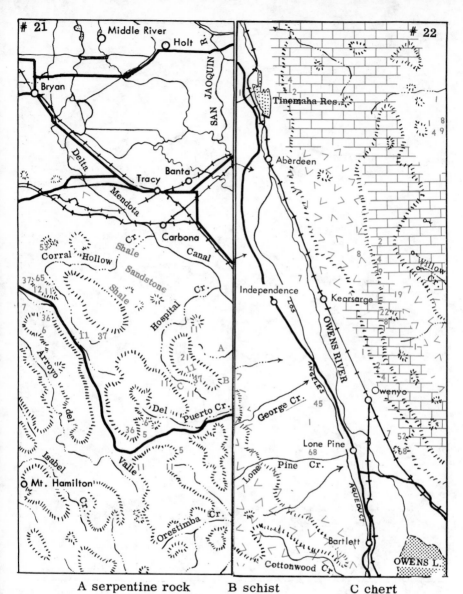

A serpentine rock   B schist   C chert

1 gold	9 sphalerite	37 rhodochrosite
2 silver	11 pyrolusite	45 barite
4 galena	12 psilomelane	52 orthoclase
5 cinnabar	19 molybdenite	53 kaolinite
6 chromite	21 stibnite	65 rhodonite
7 quartz	22 hematite	68 beryl
8 scheelite	36 magnesite	

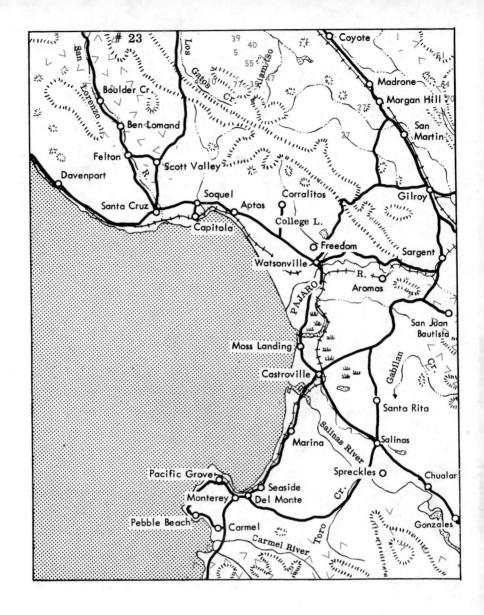

5 cinnabar	39 malachite	55 serpentine
10 chalcopyrite	40 azurite	64 glaucophane
27 jasper	47 epsomite	70 garnet
35 magnesite	51 plagioclase	77 arsenopyrite

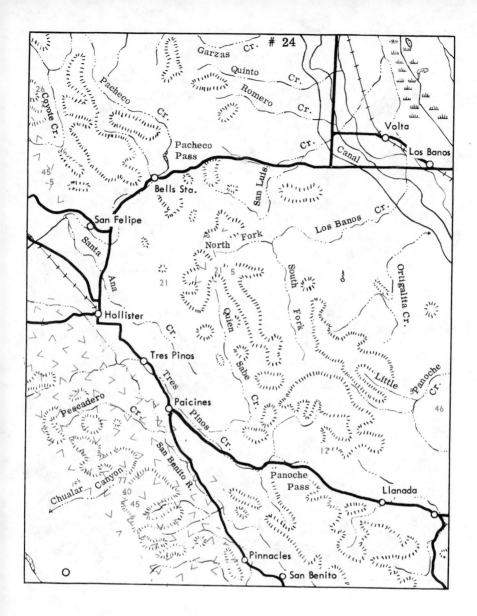

24

5 cinnabar	26 **rutile**
7 quartz	**40 azurite**
12 psilomelane	45 barite
21 stibnite	46 gypsum
	77 arsenopyrite

92

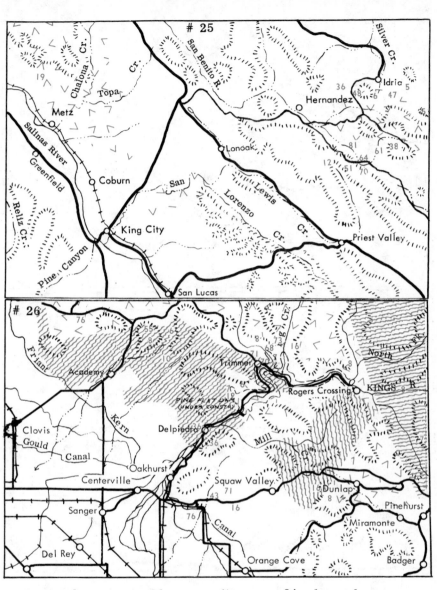

5 cinnabar	36 magnesite	64 glaucophane
6 chromite	38 aragonite	68 beryl
7 quartz	43 apatite	70 garnet
8 scheelite	47 epsomite	71 epidote
10 chalcopyrite	48 anhydrite	73 topaz
12 psilomelane	51 plagioclase	76 andalusite
16 graphite	55 serpentine	77 arsenopyrite
19 molybdenite	61 actinolite	81 benitoite

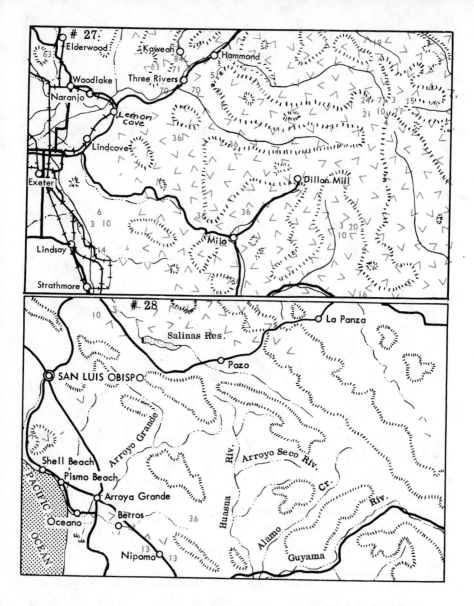

3	bornite	15	pyrite	36	magnesite
4	galena	16	graphite	51	plagioclase
6	chromite	19	molybdenite	63	hornblende
7	quartz	20	pyrrhotite	70	garnet
10	chalcopyrite	21	stibnite	71	epidote
13	agate	24	limonite	77	arsenopyrite
14	chalcedony			84	wollastonite

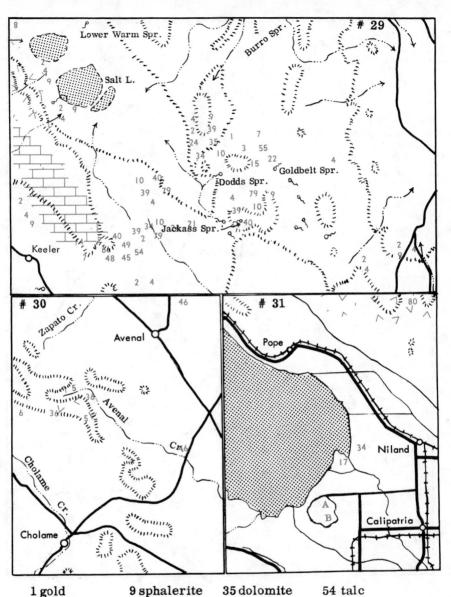

1 gold	9 sphalerite	35 dolomite	54 talc
2 silver	10 chalcopyrite	36 magnesite	55 serpentine
3 bornite	15 pyrite	39 malachite	66 chrysocolla
4 galena	17 sulfur	40 azurite	79 cerussite
5 cinnabar	21 stibnite	45 barite	80 uranium
6 chromite	22 hematite	46 gypsum	A obsidian
7 quartz	24 limonite	48 anhydrite	B pumice
8 scheelite	34 calcite	49 anglesite	

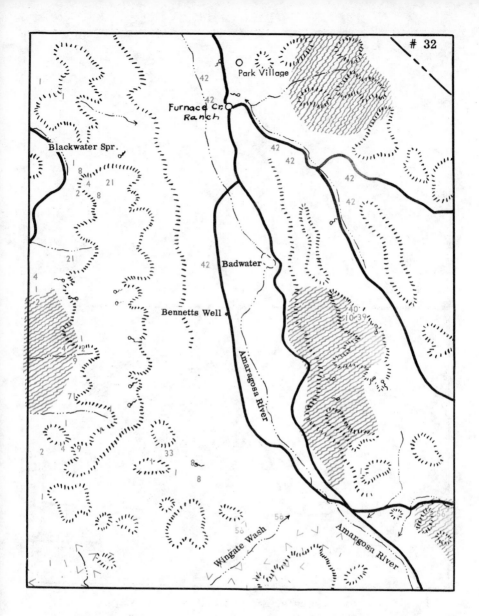

1	gold	33	fluorite
2	silver	39	malachite
4	galena	40	azurite
8	scheelite	42	colemanite
9	sphalerite	56	muscovite
10	chalcopyrite	71	epidote
21	stibnite		

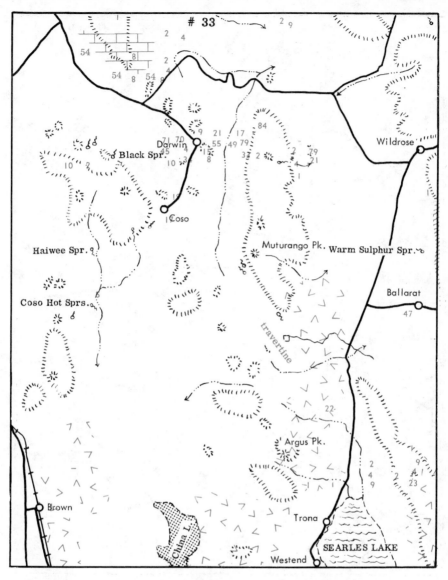

33

1 gold	17 sulfur	47 anhydrite
2 silver	19 molybdenite	49 anglesite
4 galena	21 stibnite	54 talc
5 cinnabar	22 hematite	55 serpentine
8 scheelite	23 magnetite	70 garnet
9 sphalerite	33 fluorite	71 epidote
10 chalcopyrite	34 calcite	79 cerussite
15 pyrite	45 barite	84 wollastonite

97

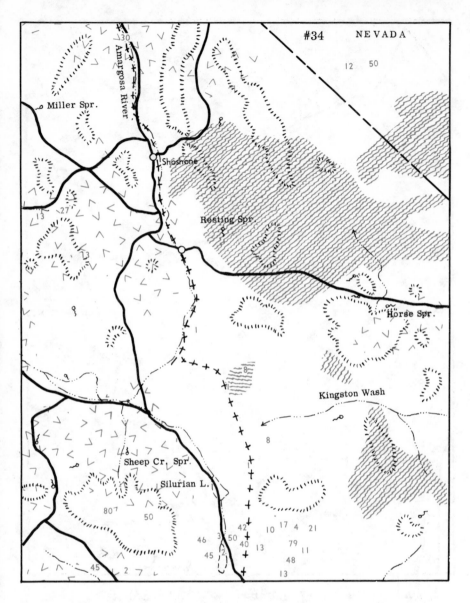

1 gold	12 psilomelane	42 colemanite
2 silver	13 agate	45 barite
3 bornite	17 sulfur	46 gypsum
4 galena	21 stibnite	48 anhydrite
8 scheelite	27 jasper	50 celestite
10 chalcopyrite	30 bloodstone	79 cerrusite
11 pyrolusite	40 azurite	80 uranium

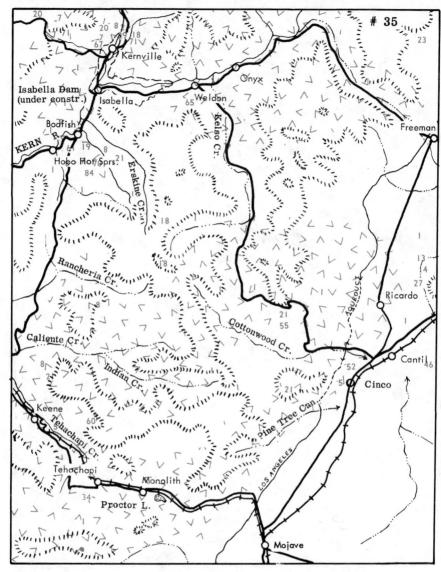

1 gold	20 pyrrhotite	55 serpentine
5 cinnabar	21 stibnite	60 tremolite
7 quartz	23 magnetite	61 actinolite
8 scheelite	27 jasper	65 rhodonite
13 agate	29 rose quartz	67 tourmaline
14 chalcedony	34 calcite	70 garnet
18 marcasite	46 gypsum	71 epidote
19 molybdenite	52 orthoclase	84 wollastonite

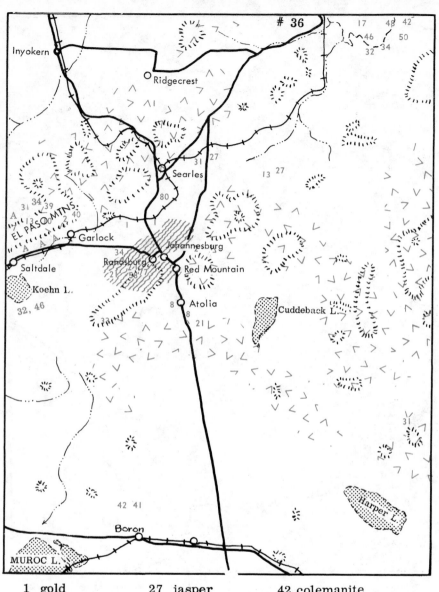

36

1	gold	27	jasper	42	colemanite
2	silver	31	opal	46	gypsum
7	quartz	32	halite	48	anhydrite
8	scheelite	33	fluorite	50	celestite
10	chalcopyrite	34	calcite	58	mariposite
13	agate	39	malachite	77	arsenopyrite
17	sulfur	40	azurite	80	uranium
21	stibnite	41	kernite	A	igneous area of great interest

100

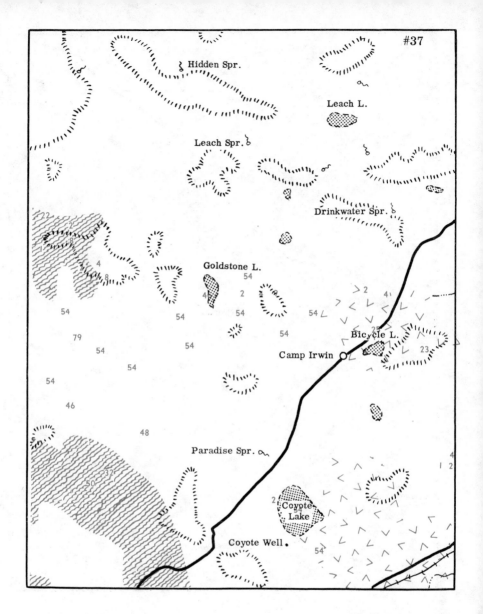

1	gold	25	corundum
2	silver	32	halite
4	galena	46	gypsum
8	scheelite	48	anhydrite
9	sphalerite	50	celestite
22	hematite	54	talc
23	magnetite	79	cerrusite

101

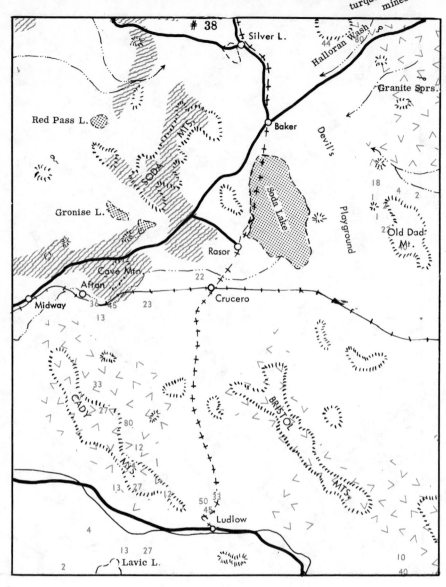

38

Silver L.

turquoise mines

Halloran Wash

Granite Sprs.

Red Pass L.

Baker

Devil's

SODA MTS.

Gronise L.

Soda Lake

18
4   2

Playground

23   Old Dad Mt.
40

Rasor

22

Cave Mtn.

Afton

Crucero

Midway
36   45
23
13

CADY

33

27

80

12

MTS

BRISTOL

MTS.

13   27

12

50   33
45

Ludlow

4

13   27

Lavic L.

10

2

40

1 gold	14 chalcedony	36 magnesite
2 silver	18 marcasite	40 azurite
4 galena	22 hematite	44 turquoise
10 chalcopyrite	23 magnetite	45 barite
12 psilomelane	27 jasper	50 celestite
13 agate	33 fluorite	80 uranium

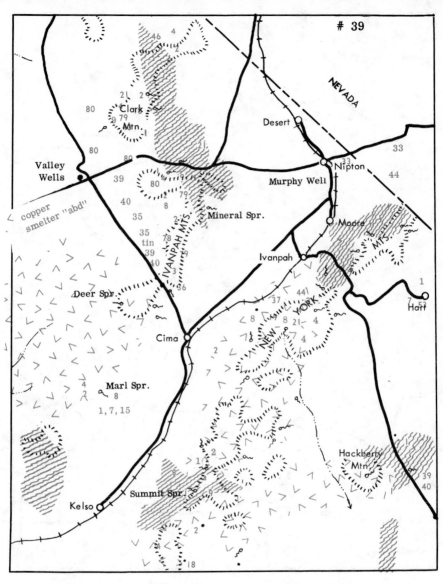

1 gold	15 pyrite	40 azurite
2 silver	18 marcasite	44 turquoise
3 bornite	19 molybdenite	46 gypsum
4 galena	21 stibnite	53 kaolinite
7 quartz	33 fluorite	78 cassiterite
8 scheelite	35 dolomite	79 cerrusite
9 sphalerite	36 magnesite	80 uranium
	37 rhodochrosite	

103

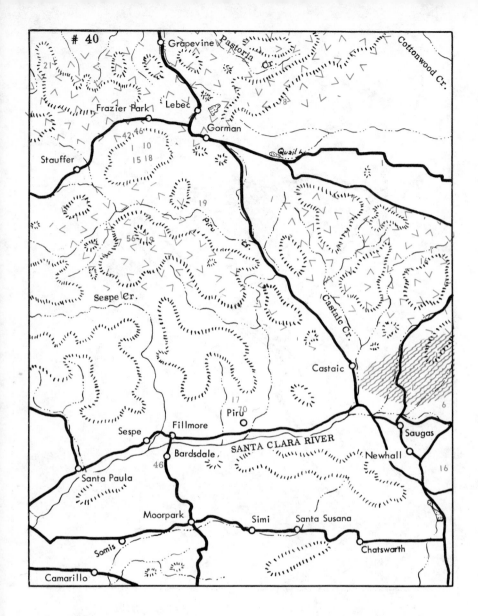

1	gold	19	molybdenite
6	chromite	21	stibnite
10	chalcopyrite	42	colemanite
15	pyrite	46	gypsum
16	graphite	56	muscovite
17	sulfur	70	garnet
18	marcasite	78	cassiterite

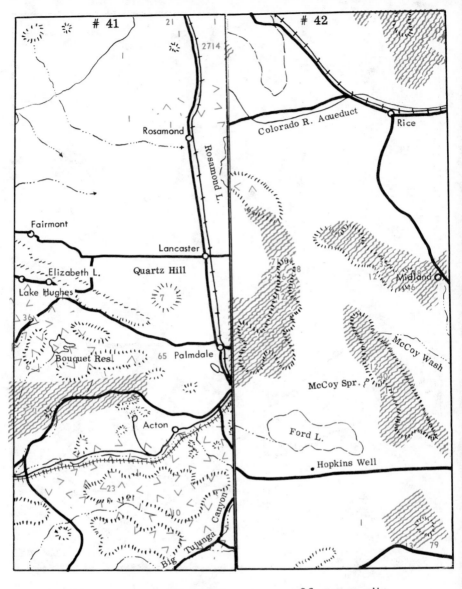

1 gold	13 agate	36 magnesite
2 silver	14 chalcedony	40 azurite
6 chromite	21 stibnite	46 gypsum
7 quartz	23 magnetite	48 anhydrite
9 sphalerite	27 jasper	65 rhodonite
10 chalcopyrite	33 fluorite	71 epidote
11 pyrolusite	34 calcite	79 cerussite
12 psilomelane		

105

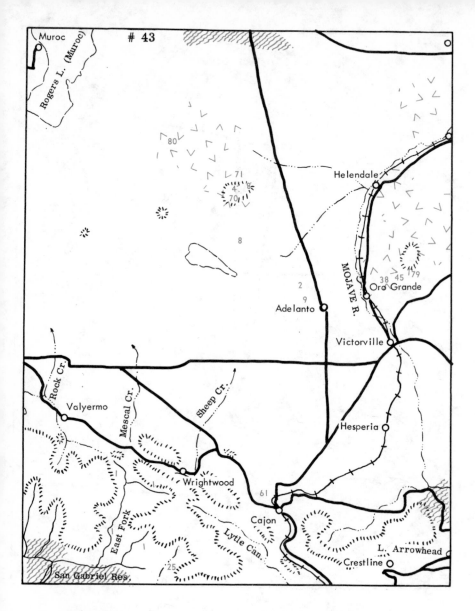

43

1 gold	45 barite
2 silver	61 actinolite
8 scheelite	70 garnet
9 sphalerite	71 epidote
25 corundum	79 cerussite
38 aragonite	80 uranium

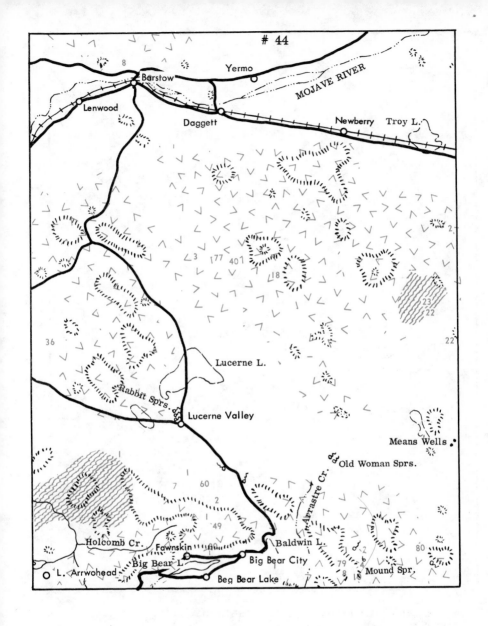

1 gold	18 marcasite	60 tremolite
2 silver	22 hematite	77 arsenopyrite
3 bornite	23 magnetite	79 cerussite
4 galena	36 magnesite	80 uranium
8 scheelite	40 azurite	
10 chalcopyrite	49 anglesite	

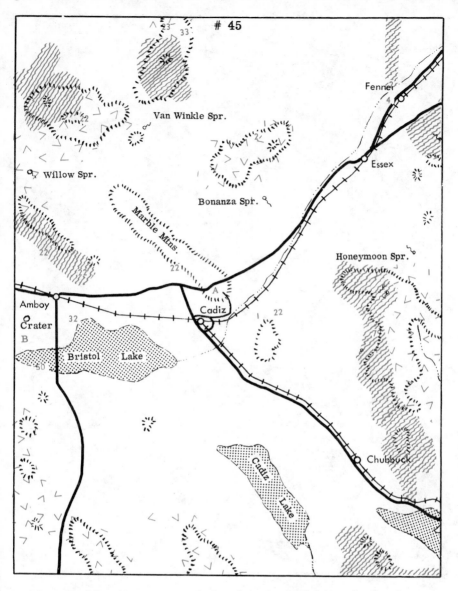

A - marble, limestone, shale, fossils (trilobites & algae)
B - basalt

1	gold	22	hematite	33	fluorite
2	silver	23	magnetite	50	celestite
4	galena	32	halite	79	cerussite

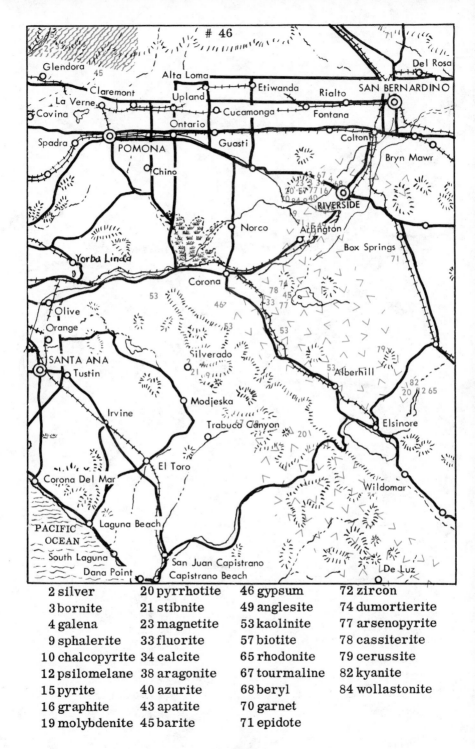

46

2 silver	20 pyrrhotite	46 gypsum	72 zircon
3 bornite	21 stibnite	49 anglesite	74 dumortierite
4 galena	23 magnetite	53 kaolinite	77 arsenopyrite
9 sphalerite	33 fluorite	57 biotite	78 cassiterite
10 chalcopyrite	34 calcite	65 rhodonite	79 cerussite
12 psilomelane	38 aragonite	67 tourmaline	82 kyanite
15 pyrite	40 azurite	68 beryl	84 wollastonite
16 graphite	43 apatite	70 garnet	
19 molybdenite	45 barite	71 epidote	

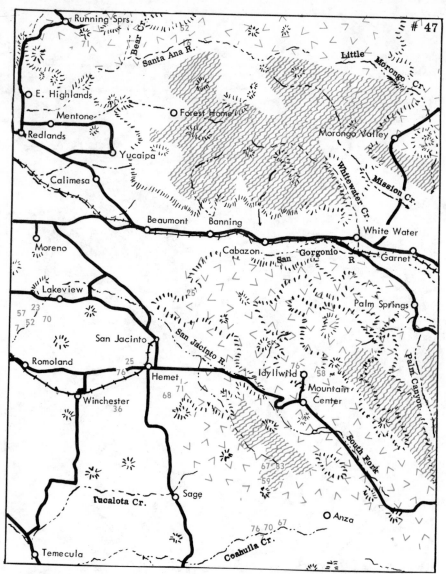

47

7 quartz
16 graphite
23 magnetite
25 corundum
36 magnesite
52 orthoclase feldspar
57 biotite
58 mariposite

59 lepidolite
67 tourmaline
68 beryl
70 garnet
71 epidote
76 andalusite
83 spodumene

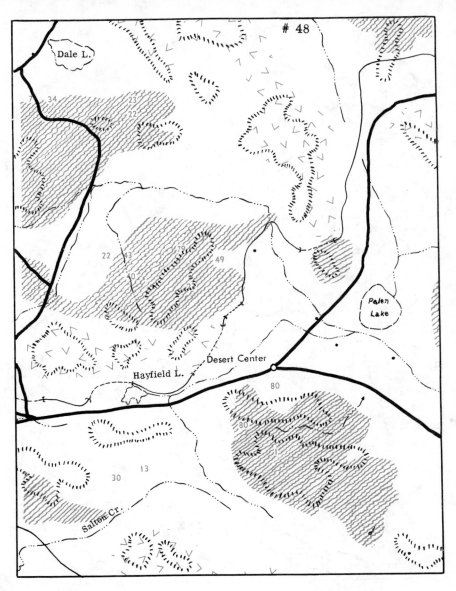

48

Dale L.

Palen Lake

Desert Center

Hayfield L.

Salton Cr.

1	gold	40	azurite
4	galena	43	apatite
13	agate	49	anglesite
22	hematite	71	epidote
23	magnetite	79	cerussite
30	bloodstone	80	uranium
34	calcite		

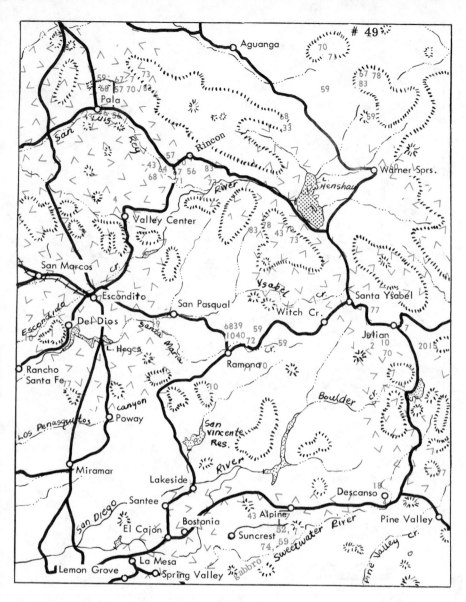

2 silver	20 pyrrhotite	59 lepidolite	72 zircon
4 galena	33 fluorite	60 tremolite	73 topaz
7 quartz	39 malachite	64 glaucophane	74 dumortierite
10 chalcopyrite	40 azurite	67 tourmaline	76 andalusite
15 pyrite	43 apatite	68 beryl	77 arsenopyrite
18 marcasite	56 muscovite	70 garnet	78 cassiterite
19 molybdenite	57 biotite	71 epidote	83 spodumene

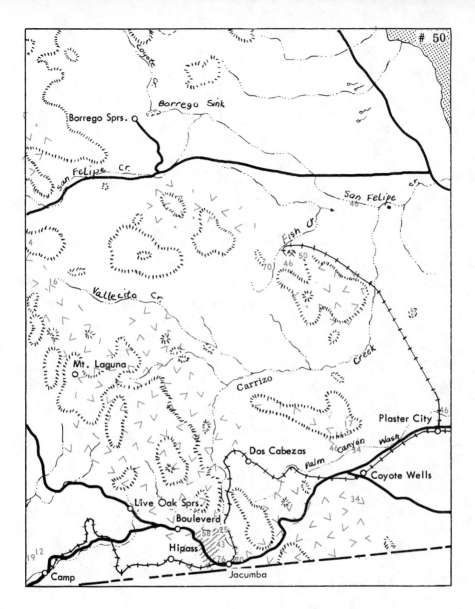

4 galena	43 apatite
12 psilomelane	46 gypsum
16 graphite	50 celestite
17 sulfur	68 beryl
19 molybdenite	70 garnet
25 corundum	76 andalusite
34 calcite	

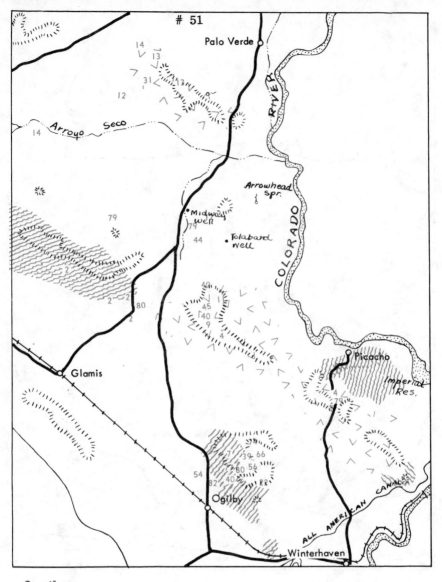

2	silver				
4	galena	22	hematite	56	muscovite
7	quartz	31	opal	66	chrysocolla
9	sphalerite	39	malachite	74	dumortierite
11	pyrolusite	40	azurite	77	arsenopyrite
12	psilomelane	44	turquoise	79	cerussite
13	agate	45	barite	80	uranium
14	chalcedony	54	talc	82	kyanite

A supplementary list and brief descriptions of some rocks and minerals that were not previously mentioned in the text and can be located with the use of the Quadrangle Map information.

MINERALS

Acmite *(Aegirine)*—A pyroxene, a silicate of sodium and iron
Albite—A plagioclase feldspar, a silicate of sodium and aluminum
Allanite—A complex silicate of cerium, thorium, aluminum, iron, etc.
Alunite—A hydrous sulfate of aluminum and potassium
Analcime—A hydrous sodium aluminum silicate
Andalusite—An aluminum silicate
Andradite—One of the commonest kinds of garnet
Anglesite—Lead sulfate, an alteration of galena
Annabergite—A hydrous arsenate of cobalt and nickel
Antigorite—A member of the serpentine group
Aragotite—A hydrocarbon, reported from several cinnabar mines in Calif.
Argentian—An alloy of gold and silver
Atacamite—A basic chloride of copper
Aurichalcite—A carbonate-hydroxide of zinc and copper
Axinite—A basic borosilicate with aluminum, calcium, iron, and manganese

Barkevikite—An amphibole rich in alkalies and ferrous iron
Bementite—A basic manganese silicate
Betafite—A rare earth oxide
Bindheimite—A pyroantimonate of lead
Bismuthinite—A rare mineral containing bismuth
Botryogen—A sulfate of magnesium and iron
Braunite—A manganese silicate
Brochantite—A basic sulfate of copper
Bromyrite—A bromide of silver

Calaverite—A gold telluride mineral
Caledonite—A carbonate-sulfate of lead and copper
Calomel—A chloride of mercury
Cervantite—An oxide of antimony
Chloropal *(Nontronite)*—A basic hydrous silicate of iron and aluminum
Cleavelandite—A lamellar variety of albite
Clinochlore—A variety of chlorite
Clinozoisite—A member of the epidote group of minerals
Cobaltite—Cobalt sulfarsenide
Connellite—A hydrated basic chloride-sulfate-nitrate of copper
Coronadite—An oxide of lead and manganese
Cryptomelane—A hydrous oxide of manganese with potassium
Cuprodescloizite—A vanadate (salt) of copper, lead and zinc
Cuprotungstite—A basic copper tungstate
Curtisite—A hydrocarbon
Cyrtolite—A silicate of zirconium with some uranium and other rare earth metals

115

Deweylite—A mineral near serpentine in composition
Duftite—A basic arsenate of copper and lead

Electrum—Gold containing 20-30% silver
Erythrite—A hydrous arsenate of cobalt and nickel

Ferberite—A tungstate of iron
Fibroferrite—A basic sulfate of ferric iron
Freibergite—Silver bearing variety of tetrahedrite

Garnierite—A green hydrous silicate of nickel and magnesium
Glauberite—A sulfate of sodium and calcium
Goslarite—A hydrous zinc sulfate

Hausmannite—An oxide of manganese
Hectorite—A clay mineral of the montmorillonite group
Hedenbergite—A silicate of calcium and iron, a pyroxene mineral
Hohmannite—A hydrated basic sulfate of ferric iron
Hubnerite—A tungstate of manganese
Hydrozincite—A carbonate-hydroxide of zinc

Jade—A valuable gemstone, there are two varieties, nephrite and jadeite
Jamesonite—A sulfide of antimony and lead
Jarosite—A basic sulfate of potassium and iron

Kammererite *(Penninite)*—Is a peach-blossom red variety of penninite associated with chromite
Kermesite—A red oxide of antimony
Knoxvillite—A basic sulfate of magnesium and iron
Kunzite—A lilac colored variety of spodumene

Lazurite—A beautiful rich blue gemstone
Leadhillite—A basic sulfate-carbonate of lead
Loellingite—An arsenide of iron
Ludwigite—A borate of iron and magnesium

Massicot—A monoxide of lead
Metatorbernite—A hydrated phosphate of copper and uranium
Millerite—A nickel sulfide
Mimetite—A chloride-phosphate-arsenate of lead
Minium—An oxide of lead, scarlet or brownish-red mineral
Monazite—A phosphate of the rare earth metals
Montroydite—An oxide of mercury
Myrickite *(Chalcedony)*—A local name applied to chalcedony containing cinnabar

Neotocite—A manganiferous opal
Niccolite—An arsenide of nickel

116

Northupite—A chloride-carbonate of sodium and magnesium

Phlogopite—"Amber mica", similar in composition to Biotite
Picrolite—A variety of serpentine
Pirssonite—A hydrated carbonate of sodium and calcium
Pisolite—A concretionary form of calcite (rounded rock 1" or more in size)
Pitchblende—A massive variety of uraninite that has a pitchy luster
Plumojarosite—A basic sulfate of lead and iron
Polybasite—A silver antimony sulfide with some copper
Posepnyte—An oxygenated hydrocarbon
Powellite—A calcium molybdate with tungsten
Probertite—A hydrated borate of sodium and calcium

Redingtonite—A complex sulfate of iron, magnesium, nickel, chrome, etc.
Riebeckite—An alkali amphibole
Roscoelite—A vanadium mica
Rubellite—Red or pink variety of tourmaline (lithium-bearing)

Schroeckingerite—A hydrated fluo-carbonate-sulfate of sodium, calcium, and uranium
Sericite—A fine-grained variety of muscovite
Smaltite—An arsenide of cobalt and nickel
Specularite—A variety of hematite with a metallic splendent luster
Spessartine—Reddish-brown garnet, a silicate of manganese and aluminum
Stephanite—A sulfide of silver and antimony

Teepleite—A hydrated borate-chloride of sodium
Tephroite—A manganese silicate
Thermonatrite—Hydrous sodium carbonate
Tiemannite—Mercury selenide
Torbernite—A hydrated phosphate of copper and uranium

Uraconite—A sulfate of uranium
Uranophane—A hydrous calcium uranyl silicate
Uvarovite—Emerald green variety of garnet

Veatchite—A hydrated strontium borate
Vermiculite—A mica, related to the chlorites
Voltaite—A hydrated sulfate of iron and potassium

Willemite—A zinc silicate, noted for its green fluorescence

Zincite—An oxide of zinc

ROCKS

Alaskite—A granite, composed chiefly of quartz and alkali-feldspar
Anorthosite—Chiefly plagioclase-feldspar with little pyroxene

117

Aplite—Light colored, fine-grained rocks with a granitic composition

Barkevikite syenite—A rock-like granite but containing little or no quartz

Calc-silicate hornfels—A dense, fine-grained metamorphic rock containing lime and silica

Calcareous tufa—Porous or spongy limestone

Claystone—Indurated or lithified clay

Dacite porphyry—Like andesite but contains quartz

Diabase—Crystalline igneous rock containing plagioclase-feldspar and pyroxene

Diabase porphyry—Characterized by porphyritic texture

Diorite porphyry—Characterized by phenocrysts of feldspar and hornblende, pyroxene or biotite in a ground mass of the same minerals

Eclogite—Metamorphic rocks with dense green garnets (Franciscan formation)

Felsite—Dense, fine-grained volcanic rocks, light colored

Graphic granite—Feldspar cleavage faces show irregular crystals of quartz that resemble the character of Arabic writing

Granodiorite—A variety of monzonite containing more plagioclase feldspar than orthoclase feldspar

Graphite slate—A slate which contain graphite

Graphite schist—A schist containing graphite

Greenstone—A metamorphic rock generally colored green by chlorite

Hornblende diorite—A diorite that has hornblende as the dominant mineral

Hornblende gabbro—A gabbro that contains abundant hornblende

Hornblende granodiorite—A granodiorite with hornblende as a prominent mineral

Hornblende schist—A schist containing hornblende

Hornfels—A dense, fine-grained, metamorphic rock

Kaolinised—Feldspar mineral altered to clay (Kaolin)

Lignite—An impure variety of coal

Monzonite—A rock resembling granite but distinguished by having orthoclase and plagioclase-feldspar in almost equal amounts

Norite—A rock composed of lime-soda feldspar and rhombic pyroxene

Obsidian—A glassy volcanic rock with a conchoidal fracture

Onyx marble—Banded or mottled marble, generally translucent

Perlite—A glassy rock composed of small ball-shaped masses produced by shrinkage during cooling

Perthite—Intergrowth of feldspar albite and microcline

Pumicite—Is volcanic ash

Quartz latite—Is the extrusive equivalent of quartz monzonite

Quartz diorite—A coarse-grained igneous rock containing plagioclase feldspar, quartz, a little orthoclase, and one or more iron-magnesium minerals

Quartz porphyry—A siliceous igneous rock containing quartz as phenocrysts

Quartz monzonite—A coarse-grained igneous rock having orthoclase and plagioclase in nearly equal amounts and containing quartz

Saxonite—A rock containing olivene and enstatite

Siltstone—Indurated or lithified silt

Silica-carbonate rock—A hard, dense, fine-grained rock formed by the hydrothermal alteration of serpentine

Talc schist—A schistose rock having a pearly luster and a greasy feel due to the presence of talc

Volcanic cinders—Solid or porous fragments that are larger than ash, reaching the size of walnuts

HOW TO USE THE QUADRANGLE MAP INFORMATION

(See Foreword for more map information)

Address for ordering maps on page 195.

Notice on the quadrangle maps that Township (T) numbers are printed on the left and right hand margins of the map. Townships are listed North (N) or South (S). Range (R) numbers are printed at the top and bottom margin of the map. Ranges are either listed East (E) or West (W).

DIAGRAM OF A TOWNSHIP

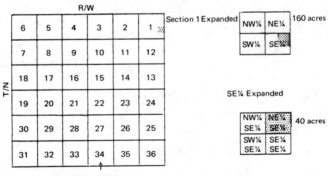

1 square mile or 640 acres

Notice that each T. and R. line encloses 36 sections or 36 square miles. The section numbers read from right to left and top to bottom. After you obtain your quadrangle maps first locate the township and range numbers, and reading from right to left locate your section number and your area. For example NE¼SE¼1, T. 11N, R. 10W: In township 11, north and range 10 west find section 1. Then find the southeast quarter of section 1. Your mineral area is in the northeast quarter of the southeast quarter of section 1.

AMADOR COUNTY

Amador City Quadrangle 7½'

	SECTION	T.	R.
Gold, Pyrite, Arsenopyrite, Quartz, Greenstone, Slate.	25,36	7N	10E
Gold, Quartz, Pyrite, Arsenopyrite, Pyrophyllite, Slate, Greenstone.	SW¼8	6N	11E
Gold, Quartz, Slate, Greenstone.	SW¼24	7N	10E
Gold, Quartz.	NW¼6	6N	11E
Gold, Quartz.	SW¼3	7N	10E
Gold (placer).	6,7	7N	11E
Rhodochrosite, Chert.	NW¼10	7N	11E

Aukum Quadrangle 7½'

Quartz crystals in gravels between Dry and Big Indian Creeks, northeast of Fiddletown.

Fiddletown Quadrangle 7½'

Gold, Pyrite, Quartz, Slate.	E½W½14	8N	10E
Gold (placer).	SW¼28	8N	11E

Goose Creek Quadrangle 7½'

Pumice.	SE¼19	6N	9E

Ione Quadrangle 7½'

Calcite, Pyrite, Chalcopyrite, Chalcocite, Amphibole and Chlorite schist, Sericite, Quartz.	SW¼28	6N	10E
Gold, Chalcopyrite, Pyrrhotite, Graphite, Molybdenite, Tetrahedrite.	20	6N	10E
Limonite.	NW¼SW¼16	5N	10E

Irish Hill Quadrangle 7½'

Stibnite, Chalcopyrite, Greenstone.	2	6N	9E

Jackson Quadrangle 7½'

Chromite.	W½SE¼34	6N	10E
Chromite.	NE¼SW¼34	6N	10E
Chromite.	NW¼SW¼2	5N	10E
Gold, Pyrophyllite, Pyrite, Galena, Quartz, Greenstone, Slate.	SW¼SW¼16	6N	11E
Gold, Chalcopyrite, Molybdenite.	20	6N	11E
Tremolite.	NE¼20	6N	10E
Rhodonite, Chert, Greenstone.	SW¼27	6N	10E
Sandstone (dimension stone), fine-grained, bright red.	27	5N	10E
Limestone, bluish-gray, fossiliferous.	SW¼13	6N	10E
Chrysoprase (apple-green Chalcedony) in Serpentine.	34	6N	10E

Latrobe Quadrangle 7½'

	SECTION	T.	R.
Pyrite, Malachite, Azurite, Chalcopyrite, Sphalerite, Chalcocite, Bornite, Limonite, Volcanics, Amphibole schist.	SE¼34	8N	9E

Pine Grove Quadrangle 7½'

	SECTION	T.	R.
Marble.	N½19	7N	12E
Diamonds (small) have been found in Jackass Gulch.			
Rhyolite tuff.	17,18	7N	12E
Rhodochrosite.	NW¼10	7N	11E
Pyrolusite, Psilomelane, Rhodochrosite, Chert.	SE¼10	7N	11E
Pyrolusite, Psilomelane, Rhodonite, Chert.	NW¼35	7N	12E
Rhodonite.	SW¼35	7N	12E
Psilomelane, Pyrolusite, Schist.	SW¼15	7N	12E
Placer Gold.	S½18	7N	12E
Gold, Quartz, Pyrite, Galena, Slate.	NE¼32	7N	12E
Gold, Pyrite, Chalcopyrite, Bornite, Slate, Schist.	NE¼32	7N	12E
Gold, Quartz, Bornite, Sphalerite, Slate.	SE¼32	7N	12E
Gold, Quartz, Pyrite, Arsenopyrite, Greenstone, Granite.	NE¼5	6N	12E
Gold, Quartz, Pyrite, Chalcopyrite, Galena, blue and brown Opal, Greenstone.	W½9	6N	12E
Gold, Pyrite, Chalcopyrite, Galena, Quartz, Granodiorite.	SW¼23	7N	13E
Gold, Pyrite, Chalcopyrite, Galena, Greenstone.	SE¼5	6N	12E

West Point Quadrangle 7½'

	SECTION	T.	R.
Gold, Silver, Quartz, Pyrite, Galena, Sphalerite, Pyrrhotite, Granodiorite.	NW¼26	7N	13E
Gold, Pyrite, Galena, Chalcopyrite, Granodiorite, Quartz.	SE¼27	7N	13E
Gold, Quartz, Pyrite, Galena, Sphalerite, Marcasite, Pyrrhotite, Chalcopyrite, Granodiorite.	SE¼SW¼29	7N	13E
Gold, Bornite, Arsenopyrite, Pyrite, Chalcopyrite, Granodiorite.	SW¼SE¼29	7N	13E
Gold, Quartz, Pyrite, Schist, Slate.	E½2	7N	12E
Gold, Quartz, Pyrite, Galena.	NE¼33	7N	13E
Gold, Quartz, Malachite, Chalcopyrite, Granodiorite.	SW¼26	7N	13E
Gold, Quartz, Pyrite, Galena.	NE¼33	7N	13E
Gold, Quartz, Pyrite, Galena, Chalcopyrite, Granodiorite.	SW¼23	7N	13E
Gold, Quartz, Pyrite, Granodiorite.	SE¼20	7N	13E
Psilomelane, Chert.	SE¼24	7N	12E

CALAVERAS COUNTY

Angels Camp Quadrangle 7½'

	SECTION	T.	R.
Gold, Quartz; Schist, Phyllite.	center NE¼31	3N	13E
Gold, Quartz.	SE¼SE¼3	2N	13E
Gold, Quartz; (vein 10-50' wide), Greenstone.	NE¼SW¼3	2N	13E
Gold, Quartz.	SW¼SE¼30	3N	13E
Gold, Quartz, Slate, Schist.	SE¼NW¼4	2N	13E
Pyrite, Ankerite, Gold, Amphibolite.	NW¼NW¼3	2N	13E
Gold, Quartz.	NE¼SW¼29	3N	13E
Gold, Slate, Phyllite, Quartz.	NE¼SW¼30	3N	13E
Rhodonite, Chert, Schist, Phyllite.	SW¼35	3N	13E
Psilomelane, Phyllite.	NE¼NE¼3	2N	13E

	SECTION	T.	R.
Gold, Quartz vein (massive vein in mother lode).	E½14	2N	13E
Talc (soapstone).	S½11,N½14	2N	13E
Gold, Quartz, Diorite, Schist, Slate.	NW¼NE¼33	3N	13E
Gold, Quartz, Pyrite, Arsenopyrite, Amphibolite, Chlorite, Schist.	NW¼33	3N	13E
Gold, Quartz, Schist, Slate, Phyllite.	center S½30	3N	13E
Gold, Quartz, Pyrite, Chlorite and Amphibolite Schist.	SW¼SE¼14	2N	13E
Gold, Quartz, Slate, Phyllite.	NW¼NW¼33	3N	13E
Gold, Quartz, Amphibolite and Chlorite Schist.	center SE¼33	3N	13E
Gold, Quartz, Greenstone, Schist.	NW¼32	3N	13E
Gold, Quartz, Talc, Slate, Amphibolite Schist.	NE¼33	3N	13E
Gold, Quartz, Pyrite, Amphibolite Schist.	SE¼SE¼33	3N	13E
Gold, Quartz, Schist.	SE¼3,NE¼10	2N	13E
Gold, Quartz, Greenstone, Amphibolite Schist.	S½33	3N	13E
Gold, Quartz, Calcite, Pyrite, Schist, Slate, Phyllite.	SW¼SE¼30	3N	13E
Gold, Quartz, Pyrite, Arsenopyrite, Amphibolite Schist.	NW¼SE¼32	3N	13E
Gold, Quartz, Chlorite Schist.	SW¼28	3N	13E
Gold, Quartz, Pyrite, Amphibolite Schist.	NE¼SW¼3	2N	13E
Gold, Quartz, Ankerite.	SW¼11	2N	13E

Bachelor Valley Quadrangle 7½'

	SECTION	T.	R.
Gold, Chalcopyrite, Sphalerite, Pyrite, Galena, Barite, Quartz, Calcite, Kaolinite.	S½3,N½10	1N	11E
Rhodonite, Psilomelane, Chert.	W½34	2N	11E
Quartz vein, 100' long and 35' wide in Greenstone.	S½16	1N	11E

Blue Mountain Quadrangle 15'

	SECTION	T.	R.
Bluish-black Quartz vein in Granodiorite.	1	6N	13E
Marcasite, Quartz (white and dark), Pyrite, Pyrrhotite, Galena, Sphalerite, Granodiorite.	NE¼SE¼1	6N	13E
Pyrite, Galena, Quartz, Granodiorite.	center 12	6N	13E
Scheelite, Chalcopyrite, Idocrase, Garnet, Epidote, Molybdenite.	6,7	7N	16E
Scheelite, Chalcopyrite, Molybdenite.	7	7N	16E

Calavaritas Quadrangle 7½'

	SECTION	T.	R.
Gold, Quartz, Graphitic Slate, Quartz-mica Schist.	SE¼NE¼34	4N	13E
Gold, Quartz.	center S½SE¼28	4N	13E
Gold, Quartz, Galena, Pyrite, Mica Schist.	NW¼SW¼22	4N	13E
Gold, Quartz, Slate, Schist.	NW¼33	4N	13E
Gold, Talc, Quartz, Graphitic Slate.	SE¼NW¼34	4N	13E
Gold, Quartz, Mica Schist.	NW¼27,NE¼28	4N	13E
Gold, Quartz, Mica Schist.	SE¼SW¼14	4N	13E
Gold, Quartz, Pyrite, Galena, Sphalerite, Slate, Mica Schist.	E½20,W½21	4N	13E
Gold, Quartz, abundant Galena, Slate, Mica Schist.	21	4N	13E
Gold, Quartz, Pyrite, brown Opal, Schist, Slate.	SW corner 10, SE corner 9	4N	13E
Tremolite.	SW¼1	3N	13E
Chrysotile, Serpentine.	S½NE¼2	4N	13E
Chromite, Serpentine.	SW¼SW¼2	3N	13E
Chromite, Serpentine.	center SW¼2	3N	13E
Magnetite, Antigorite.	SE¼NE¼2	3N	13E

Columbia Quadrangle 7½'

	SECTION	T.	R.
White Marble (in Skunk Gulch).	NE¼33	3N	14E
White Marble (near head of Skunk Gulch).	NW¼28	3N	14E
White Rhyolite Tuff.	SW¼17	3N	14E
Gray Rhyolite Tuff.	SW¼19	3N	14E
Gold, Mariposite, Graphite, Talc (15' wide zone).	SE¼24	2N	13E
Gold, Quartz, Pyrite, Chlorite and Talc Schist.	NW¼26	3N	14E
Blue Quartz vein in Slate.	12	3N	13E

Melones Dam Quadrangle 7½'

	SECTION	T.	R.
Chrysotile.	15,16,21,22	1N	13E
Chromite, Dunite, Saxonite.	NE¼16	1N	13E
Chromite, Uvarovite.	9,16	1N	13E
Chromite. and	NE¼NE¼8	1N	13E
	SW¼NW¼9	1N	13E
Chromite, Serpentine, Talc, Kammererite.	NW¼9	1N	13E
Uvarovite (Green Garnet).	SW¼9	1N	13E
Chalcopyrite, Limonite, Schist.	NW¼NW¼18	1N	13E
Pyrite, Chalcopyrite, Greenstone.	NE¼20	1N	13E

Mokelumne Hill Quadrangle 7½'

	SECTION	T.	R.
Placer Gold, Quartz crystals, opalized wood in gravel. and	S½NE¼24	5N	11E
	N½SE¼24	5N	11E
Fine grained compact Tuff resting on Eocene Quartz gravel, Tuff is pink and purplish-gray.	W½25	5N	11E
Talc and Soapstone, up to 50' wide and 1,000' long.	3	5N	12E

Murphys Quadrangle 7½'

	SECTION	T.	R.
Gold, Quartz, Pyrite, Galena, Mica Schist.	NE¼SW¼7	4N	14E
Gold, Quartz, Black Slate.	NE¼NE¼26	4N	13E
Gold, blue Quartz, Mica Schist.	SE¼SE¼30	4N	14E
Gold, pink and white Quartz, Schist, Slate.	NE¼NE¼1	3N	13E
Gold, Quartz, Slate, Mica Schist. and	NE¼NW¼36	4N	13E
	SW¼NE¼1	3N	13E
Gold, Quartz, Quartzite, Mica Schist. and	center S½SE¼1	3N	13E
	center S½NE¼25	4N	13E
Gold, Quartz, Slate, Mica Schist.	NE¼SE¼1	3N	13E
Gold, Quartz, Mica Schist.	NW¼NW¼18	4N	13E
Gold, Quartz, Quartzite, Pyrite, Galena,Smaltite, Slate.	center S½NW¼21	4N	14E
Gold, pink and white Quartz, Mica Schist.	NE¼NE¼36	4N	13E
Gold, Quartz, Galena, Stibnite, Tetrahedrite, Limestone, Diorite.	SE¼NE¼6	3N	14E
Gold, Pyrite, Galena, Quartz, Schist, Slate, Diorite.	NW¼SW¼20	4N	14E
Gold, Quartz (white, blue, dark), Pyrite, Chalcopyrite,	S½SE¼7	4N	14E
Galena, Sphalerite, Schist. and	NE¼NE¼23	4N	13E
Gold, blue and white Quartz, Mica Schist.	29	4N	14E
Silver, Galena, Limestone.	5	3N	14E
Hematite, Limonite, in Mica Schist.	center SW¼32	4N	14E

Railroad Flat Quadrangle 7½'

	SECTION	T.	R.
Galena, Pyrite, Quartz, Gold, Mica Schist.	SW¼SE¼35	6N	13E

123

	SECTION	T.	R.
Gold, Quartz, Granodiorite.	NE¼SE¼18	6N	13E
Chalcopyrite, Galena, Pyrite, dark Quartzite, Slate, Schist, Gold.	center SE¼30	6N	13E
Tetrahedrite, Stibnite, Galena, Chalcopyrite, Pyrite, Quartzite, Schist, Gold.	W½SE¼35	6N	12E
Gold, Quartz, Schist, Slate.	SW¼NE¼26	6N	13E
Gold, Quartz, Schist, Granodiorite.	NW¼35	6N	12E
Quartz (white, dark gray), Pyrite, Chalcopyrite, Slate, Quartzite, Gold.	SE¼SW¼35	6N	13E
Gold, Quartz, Schist.	NE¼NE¼21	6N	13E
Sulfides (abundant), Gold, Calcite, Quartz, Diorite, Schist.	NE¼15	6N	13E
Garnet (good quality Andradite crystals), Mica Schist, Quartzite, Gold. On Jesus Maria Creek.	N½24	5N	12E
Pyrite (abundant); Calcite, Quartz; Mica Schist, Gold.	20	6N	13E

Salt Spring Valley Quadrangle 7½'

Chrysotile in Serpentine.	center N½15	2N	12E
Chromite in Serpentine.	SW¼14,NE¼23	2N	12E
Gold, Silver, Chalcopyrite, Pyrite, Sphalerite, Slate, Diabase, Diorite.	NE¼9,NW¼10	2N	12E
Bementite, Rhodochrosite, Psilomelane, Chert.	SW¼11,NW¼14	3N	11E
Bementite, Rhodochrosite, Tephroite.	S½4	2N	12E

San Andreas Quadrangle 7½'

Dark-mottled Marble.	center 7	4N	12E
Gold, Uraconite, Uraninite.	NW¼34,NE¼33	4N	12E
Ankerite.	center 7	4N	12E

Valley Springs Quadrangle 7½'

Pyrite, Chalcopyrite, Sphalerite, Bornite, Galena, Tetrahedrite, Slate, Rhyolite, Basalt, Tuff, Quartz Porphyry.	and 3,4	4N	10E
	33	5N	10E
Limonite.	E½11	4N	10E
Sandstone, white, thick beds, shallow dip.	23	4N	10E

West Point Quadrangle 7½'

Galena, Pyrite, Chalcopyrite, Gold, Granodiorite.	W½8	6N	13E
Gold, Quartz, Pyrite, Granodiorite.	SE¼NW¼4	6N	13E
Gold, Quartz, Galena, Granodiorite.	NW¼SE¼4	6N	13E
Pyrrhotite, Quartz, Gold, Granodiorite.	SE¼SW¼32	7N	13E
Galena, Pyrite, Chalcopyrite, Quartz, Gold, Diorite.	center W½SW¼5	6N	13E

COLUSA COUNTY

Clearlake Oaks Quadrangle 15'

Native Copper, Chalcopyrite, Cuprite, Tenorite, Serpentine.	20	16N	6W

	SECTION	T.	R.
Chalcopyrite, Pyrite.	19,20	16N	6W

Stonyford Quadrangle 15'

	SECTION	T.	R.
Aragonite (white and transparent crystals), native Copper, Cuprite.	17	17N	6W

Wilbur Springs Quadrangle 15'

	SECTION	T.	R.
Cinnabar, Calcite, Chalcopyrite, Gold, Argentian (Gold and Silver alloy), Marcasite, Metacinnabar, Pyrite, Sulfur (good crystals), Sandstone; Shale, Conglomerate, Serpentine.	NE¼29	14N	5W
Rhodochrosite, Manganese Oxides, Chert.	12	15N	6W
Rhodochrosite, Manganese Oxides, Chert.	1,2	15N	6W
Cinnabar, abundant Sulfur, Calcite, Magnesite, Opal, Shale, Serpentine.	SE¼13 and 18	14N 14N	6W 5W
Cinnabar, silicified Serpentine, Shale, Sandstone.	28,29	14N	5W
Ammonite fossils (Lower Cretaceous), 100' W and 2,400' S of NE corner, found in Sandstone bed in Bear Creek near culvert across road, 1½ miles N of turnoff to Wilbur Springs.	16	14N	5W
Ammonites (Upper Jurassic), in larger section layers in gully, SW corner 50-100' E of Bear Creek Road; 1 mile N of Wilbur Springs bridge and 1 1/3 miles above mouth of Sulfur Creek.	15	14N	5W

DEL NORTE COUNTY

Crescent City Quadrangle 15'

	SECTION	T.	R.
Chromite, Serpentine; on Rowdy Creek.	SW¼26	18N	1E
Chromite, Serpentine.	NE¼12	18N	1E
Chromite, Serpentine.	E½33	18N	1E
Copper minerals, some 15% Ore was mined here.	35	18N	1E

Gasquet Quadrangle 15'

	SECTION	T.	R.
Chromite, Serpentine.	SW¼7	16N	3E
Chromite, Serpentine.	29	16N	2E
Chromite, Serpentine.	29	18N	2E
Chromite, Serpentine.	21	18N	2E
Chromite, Serpentine.	near center 19	16N	3E
Chromite, Serpentine.	29	18N	3E
Chromite, Serpentine.	28	18N	2E
Chromite, Serpentine, Uvarovite, Kammererite.	NE¼6	16N	2E
Chromite, Serpentine.	NW¼21	18N	3E
Chromite, Serpentine.	NE¼28	18N	2E
Chromite, Serpentine.	NW¼20	18N	3E
Chromite, Serpentine, Uvarovite, Kammererite.	19	16N	3E
Chalcocite (abundant), Magnetite, Serpentine.	34	18N	2E
Gold, Quartz, Specular Hematite, Copper ($15 Gold Ore).	1	18N	3E

	SECTION	T.	R.
Placer Gold, 8' gravels on Serpentine bedrock, Gold coarse, some nuggets recovered. Patrick Creek.	33	18N	3E
Cinnabar, native Mercury (was abundant), Andesite, Peridotite.	SE¼20	18N	3E
Native Mercury.	18	18N	3E
Cinnabar, fissure fillings in large mass of altered Diorite, 3-5 lb. Ore. On California-Oregon state line.	36	19N	2E
Cinnabar, Quartz, Serpentine.	NW¼11	18N	2E

EL DORADO COUNTY

Camino Quadrangle 15'

	SECTION	T.	R.
Bornite (massive), Garnet (large crystals of Grossular), Molybdenite (broad foliated plates), Axinite, Azurite, Epidote, Chalcopyrite, Diopside (fine crystals), Hornblende (large cleavage masses), Powellite, Limestone; Amphibolite Schists, Pegmatite.	24,25	9N	12E

Clarksville Quadrangle 7½'

	SECTION	T.	R.
Magnetite, two veins 4½' wide in coarse grained Gabbro.	center NE¼18	10N	9E
Chromite, Serpentine.	NE¼3	10N	8E
Chromite, Serpentine.	SW¼NW¼13	10N	8E
Chromite, Serpentine.	SW¼NW¼35	10N	8E
Chromite, Serpentine.	SE¼35	10N	8E

Coloma Quadrangle 7½'

	SECTION	T.	R.
Chromite, Serpentine.	NE¼SE¼5	11N	10E
Chromite, Serpentine.	SE¼NE¼5	11N	10E
Chromite, Dunite, Kammererite.	SW¼NE¼5	11N	10E
Chromite (lens to 20' wide), Serpentine.	SE¼SE¼6	11N	10E
Garnet (crystals), Epidote, Magnetite, Calcite, Idocrase, Pyrite, Galena, Bornite, Ilmenite, Specular Hematite, Scheelite, Euhedral Magnetite crystals, Hornfels, Marble, Granodiorite.	SW¼NW¼3	11N	9E
Malachite, Chalcopyrite, native Copper, Gold, in veins of Talcose Schist between walls of Granodiorite and Serpentine.	S½NW¼23	11N	9E
Roscoelite (very rare mineral) in green or clove-brown scales (micaceous), native gold, in a Quartz vein. Vein is in Greenstone and Slate between Serpentine and Granodiorite.	SE¼24	11N	9E
Roscoelite in Quartz.	7	11N	10E
Chromite, Talc, Serpentine.	NW¼8	11N	10E
Wollastonite, Garnet, Marble, Sericite, Copper minerals.	9	11N	9E

Fiddletown Quadrangle 7½'

	SECTION	T.	R.
Gold, Quartz, Meta-andesite, some small high grade pockets, recent output was specimen material.	center SW¼27	9N	10E
Bornite, Chalcopyrite, Pyrite, Gold, Silver, Quartz; Meta-diabase.	center 18	9N	11E
Bornite, Chalcopyrite, Pyrite; Schist, Quartz.	NW¼NW¼18	9N	11E

Garden Valley Quadrangle 7½'

	SECTION	T.	R.
Scheelite (some coarse crystals), Calcite, Chlorite Schist.	SE¼4	11N	11E
Gold, Quartz; Slate, produced ½ million up to 1878.	SE¼SE¼3	11N	10E
Chalcopyrite, Bornite, Pyrrhotite, Sphalerite, Tuffs, Slate.	NE¼3	11N	10E
Gold, Quartz, Slate.	NW¼3	11N	10E
Gold, Quartz; Slate, Porphyry.	NW corner 13	11N	10E
Gold, Quartz; Slate (to $26 a ton).	NW¼13	11N	10E
Gold, Quartz; (one pocket yielded $14,000).	SE¼13	11N	10E
Gold, Quartz; Slate, Greenstone.	NW¼14	11N	10E
Gold, Quartz.	NE¼14	11N	10E
Auriferous Pyrite, Quartz.	center W½15	11N	10E
Several fine specimens of crystallized Gold from this area in the 1930's. Specimen Ore from seams in a dike.	SW¼NW¼24	11N	10E
Gold, Quartz.	NE¼NE¼24	11N	10E
Gold, in pockets in 18" vein.	center E½24	11N	10E
Gold, Quartz; Talc, Calcite, Slate.	center S½24	11N	10E
Quartz; Gold, Pyrite, Galena, Ankerite, Slate, Schist, (Gold $1.80-$6.40 a ton).	SW¼24	11N	10E
Quartz; Diabase, Slate, Gold, ($7-$15 a ton).	NE¼SW¼26	11N	10E
Gold, Quartz; Slate.	SW¼NE¼36	11N	10E
Gold, Quartz; Pyrite, Schist, Slate.	SW¼SW¼21	12N	10E
Gold, Quartz; Slate, Greenstone, produced $1,000,000.	SW¼21	12N	10E
Chromite, Serpentine, Uvarovite, Kammererite.	SE¼NE¼23	12N	10E
Quartz (12' vein), Schist, native Copper, Copper Sulphides.	NW¼24	12N	10E

Georgetown Quadrangle 7½'

	SECTION	T.	R.
Gold, Quartz; vein in Slate, 6' wide.	NW¼2	12N	10E
Coarse Gold from Alluvium and seams in Slate, produced 2 million dollars prior to 1880.	SW¼NE¼3	12N	10E
Rich seam diggings, narrow Quartz seams and veins in Chlorite Schist and Slate, some beautiful specimens of crystallized Gold from here. Produced $6,550,000.	NE¼NW¼3	12N	10E
Pyrolusite, Psilomelane, Chert, Quartzite.	SE¼NE¼9	12N	10E
Gold, silicified mineralized Amphibolite Schist, Diorite and basic dikes, produced over $1,000,000.	NW corner 11	12N	10E
Copper, Slate, Serpentine, Limonite.	NW¼13	12N	10E
Gold, Quartz; Slate, 12' wide vein.	center S½15	12N	10E
Gold, Quartz; minor Sulfides, Amphibolite.	SE¼16	12N	10E
Gold, Quartz; Slate, 6' wide vein.	NE¼8	13N	11E
Gold, Quartz.	center E½18	13N	11E
Chromite, Serpentine.	NE¼NW¼19	13N	11E
Hydraulic and Gold drift mine, gravel $1.33 a ton.	SW¼12	13N	10E
Chromite, Serpentine.	NE¼25	13N	10E

Greenwood Quadrangle 7½'

	SECTION	T.	R.
Gold, Quartz; Slate (20' vein).	SE¼NE¼6	12N	10E
20' zone of Gold Quartz seams in Slate.	SW¼SW¼6	12N	10E
Gold Quartz vein in Slate (3-8' wide).	NW¼7	12N	10E
Gold, Meta-andesite, Gold finely disseminated in Greenstone with Pyrite.	SE¼NW¼7	12N	10E
Gold, Quartz; Slate, (4' vein).	center S½7	12N	10E
Mineralized Schist, Pyrite, ($15 Ore).	NE¼SW¼17	12N	10E
Seam Gold yielded $14,000.	NW¼12	12N	9E

127

	SECTION	T.	R.
Gold in seams.	SE corner 12	12N	9I
Chromite, Peridotite.	NE¼SE¼23	12N	9E
Limestone, blue-gray.	NW¼NW¼4	12N	9E
Gold, Quartz; Slate, Amphibolite Schist.	SW¼24	13N	9E
Gold, Quartz.	NW¼NE¼36	13N	9E
Gold, Pyrite, Arsenopyrite, Ankerite, siliceous Slate, Amphibolite, Ore zone 30' wide, 60% of the Gold is in the Sulfides. Produced over 2 million dollars.	NW¼36	13N	9E
Veins and veinlets in Slate yielded much specimen Gold	SW¼36	13N	9E
Limestone, blue-gray.	SW¼34	13N	9E
Gold, Quartz; Calcite veins in Slate and Amphibolite Schist, abundant coarse Pyrite, 3 veins to 20' thick, ($18 Ore).	NW¼30	13N	10E
Gold Quartz seams in zone 200-300' wide.	NW¼NW¼29	13N	10E
Placer Gold in gravel 8' thick over Slate bedrock.	center NW¼29	13N	10E

Latrobe Quadrangle 7½'

Gold, Quartz; Pyrite, Galena, Slate, Serpentine, Gold occurred here in pockets.	SW corner 1	8N	9E
Some 4% Copper Ore mined here in 1917.	SW¼SW¼2	8N	9E
Chalcopyrite, Pyrrhotite, Meta-volcanics, Copper to 10%.	E½NW¼3	8N	9E
Soapstone.	NE¼SE¼9	8N	9E
Chromite, Uvarovite, Kammererite, Serpentine.	NW¼9	8N	9E
Greenstone, Manganese Oxides, Limonite.	NW¼NE¼13	8N	9E
Magnetite, Hematite lens to 25' wide and 60' long.	NE¼SE¼14	8N	9E
Chromite, Serpentine.	SE¼SE¼14	8N	9E
Chromite, Uvarovite, Kammererite, Serpentine.	NE¼14	8N	9E
Chromite, Serpentine.	SW¼SE¼14	8N	9E
Cinnabar, Pyrite, Slate, Quartzite.	center N½4	8N	10E
Chromite, Dunite.	SW¼SW¼7	8N	10E
Chromite, Dunite.	NW¼NE¼7	8N	10E
Chromite, Serpentine.	NW¼NW¼30	8N	10E
Chromite, Serpentine.	SW¼NW¼30	8N	10E
Talc Schist, large outcrop.	SW¼23	9N	9E
Soapstone, greenish-blue in Greenstone and Meta-sedimentary rock.	NW¼SE¼35	9N	9E
Good Copper Ore produced here in 1870, Schist country rock.	center 22	9N	9E
Auriferous Pyrite, Quartz; Schist.	NE¼SE¼19	9N	10E
Gold, Pyrite, Pyrrhotite, Albite, Quartz; Ankerite, large producer.	NW¼NW¼29	9N	10E
Gold, Quartz; Slate, Serpentine.	NE¼SE¼30	9N	10E
Auriferous Pyrite, Metadiabase, Chalcopyrite,($20-$30 for Ore).	NW¼NW¼31	9N	10E

Omo Ranch Quadrangle 7½'

Limestone.			
Gold, Quartz; Granite, abundant Sulfides.	24,25,26	9N	12E
Gold, Quartz; Granite, abundant Sulfides.	SW¼32	9N	13E
Gold, Quartz; Granite.	E½32	9N	13E
	SW¼SW¼33	9N	13E

Pilot Hill Quadrangle 7½'

	SECTION	T.	R.
Chromite, Dunite.	center 12	11N	8E
Chalcopyrite, Pyrite, Bornite, Quartz.	NW¼11	11N	8E
Limestone, 4,000' long, 100' wide.	NW¼15	11N	8E
Chromite, Serpentine.	NE¼22	11N	8E
Chromite, Serpentine.	21	11N	8E
Chromite, Uvarovite, Kammererite, Garnierite, Penninite.	NW¼NW¼28	11N	8E
Galena, Sphalerite, Chalcopyrite, Pyrite, Amphibolite, Mica Schist, Granodiorite, (Gold, to $14 a ton).	SW¼29	11N	8E
Chromite, Serpentine.	S½33	11N	8E
Gold, Quartz; Amphibolite, some high grade Ore.	SW¼SW¼25	12N	8E
Stromeyerite.	SE¼17	11N	8E
Sphalerite, Chalcopyrite, Mica Schist, Amphibolite Schist.	SW¼NE¼28	11N	8E
Chromite, Serpentine.	SW¼NE¼28	11N	8E
Chromite, Serpentine.	NW¼SW¼28	11N	8E
Chromite, Dunite, Magnesite, Yellow Serpentine, common Opal.	SE¼SW¼21	11N	8E

Shingle Springs Quadrangle 7½'

	SECTION	T.	R.
Pyrite, Chalcopyrite, Magnetite, Bornite, Stibnite, specular Hematite, Sphalerite, Molybdenite, Galena, Arsenopyrite, Greenstone, Schist, Granodiorite, Quartz.	SE¼5	10N	10E
Chromite, Serpentine.	NW¼6	10N	10E
Chromite, Serpentine, Slickentite.	NW¼7	10N	10E
Auriferous Pyrite, Amphibolite Schist.	SW¼SE¼17	10N	10E
Gold, Quartz; Arsenopyrite, Tellurides, Serpentine, Metavolcanics.	NW¼NW¼33	10N	10E
Gold, Quartz; Granodiorite, ($10,000 from a pocket in 1860).	NW¼3	10N	9E
Gold, Quartz; Pyrite, Chalcopyrite, Galena, Greenstone, Meta-diorite.	SE¼NE¼10	10N	9E
Gold, Quartz; Gabbro, Pyrite, Galena (Gold $1-$5 a ton).	SE¼SE¼10	10N	9E
Gold, Quartz; Mariposite, Ankerite, Pyrite, Amphibolite Schist. Produced $1,000,000.	NW¼13	10N	9E
Soapstone, Greenstone.	SW¼7	9N	10E
Gold, Quartz; Hornblende Porphyry, some small rich shoots.	SW¼NE¼16	9N	10E
Gold, Quartz; Calcite, Pyrite, Amphibolite-chlorite Schist. Gold values to $11 a ton.	NE¼SE¼18	9N	10E

Slate Mountain Quadrangle 7½'

Calaverite, Petzite, Quartz; Slate, (Gold, $5-$6 ton).	NW¼SE¼33	12N	11E
Gold, Calcite, Quartz; Talc, Serpentine.	NE¼NW¼6	11N	11E
Gold, Quartz; Arsenopyrite, Pyrite, Schist, Graphite Schist, Slate, high grade pockets, one yielded $500,000.	SW¼SE¼6	11N	11E
Gold, Quartz.	NE¼7	11N	11E
Gold, Quartz; Granodiorite, Ore to $65 a ton.	SE¼23	11N	11E

Sly Park Quadrangle 7½'

Gold Galena, Pyrite, Chalcopyrite, Sphalerite, Epidote, Clinozoisite, Slate, Green Schist, Quartzite, Metachert, Quartz. Considerable high grade Ore at vein junctions.	SE¼3	10N	13E

	SECTION	T.	R.
Gold, Quartz; Slate, Chlorite Schist, Granodiorite, Ore zone 400' wide x 3,500' long, $12, Ore.	NE¼NE¼21	10N	13E
Gold, Quartz; Slate.	SE¼SE¼23	10N	13E
Gold, Quartz; Granodiorite.	SW¼NW¼34	10N	13E
Scheelite, Garnet, Epidote, Schist, Quartzite, Gneiss.	SE¼32	10N	13E
Gold, Galena, Sphalerite, Pyrite, Stibnite, Quartz; Chalcopyrite, Arsenopyrite, Granodiorite, Ore to $25, ton.	SW¼NW¼3	9N	13E
Gold, Pyrite, Galena, Sphalerite, Granodiorite, Schist.	SE¼SE¼4	9N	13E
Gold, Quartz; Granodiorite, Pyrite, Galena, Sphalerite.	NW¼10	9N	13E
Gold, Quartz; some high grade Ore.	NW¼16	9N	13E
Gold, Pyrite, Galena, Sphalerite, Chalcopyrite, Quartz; Granodiorite, Schist, produced $1,000,000.	center 16	9N	13E
Gold, Quartz; Granite.	NW¼SE¼16	9N	13E
Gold, Quartz; Mica Schist, $12, Ore.	SW¼16	9N	13E
Gold, Quartz; Ore $12, ton from a shoot several hundred feet long.	center 16	9N	13E

FRESNO COUNTY

Academy Quadrangle 7½'

	SECTION	T.	R.
Andalusite, dark reddish-violet, radiating and prismatic, crystals up to 10 x 15 cm. in a Pegmatite 1½ miles east of Sharpsville.	S½20	11S	22E
Hornblende Diorite (used for monuments).	13	12S	22E

Chounet Ranch Quadrangle 7½'

	SECTION	T.	R.
Apatite, Psuedomorphs after Fossil Wood in the Moreno formation at head of Escarpado Canyon.	NW¼7	15S	12E
Diatomite.	8	15S	12E
Gypsite.	W½30,19	14S	12E

Coalinga Quadrangle 15'

	SECTION	T.	R.
Satin Spar, San Joaquin Coal Mine.	26	20S	14E

Friant Quadrangle 7½'

	SECTION	T.	R.
Pyrrhotite, Chalcopyrite, Pyrite, Galena, long euhedral needles of Hornblende.	SW¼10	12S	21E

Humphreys Station Quadrangle 7½'

	SECTION	T.	R.
Vermiculite, in nodules with Talc.	22	11S	23E
Chalcanthite, Chalcopyrite, Chalcedony (large white masses).	34	11S	23E
Chalcopyrite (abundant), Pyrite, Galena, Sphalerite, Gold, Quartz; Amphibolite and Mica Schist.	SE¼3	12S	23E
Clinochlore, Penninite.	E½11	12S	23E
Chrysotile, Serpentine.	22	11S	23E
Chromite, produced several thousand tons, a Chromite belt extends northwest across Hog Mountain in a belt of Serpentine about 1 mile wide from 19, 12S, 25E to 13, 11S, 23E.	NW¼25	11S	23E
Marl, in soil.	11	11S	23E

130

Kaiser Peak Quadrangle 15'

	SECTION	T.	R.
Limestone, Marble, Calc-silicate Hornfels, large deposit.	29,30	7S	26E

Millerton Lake Quadrangle 15'

Feldspar, Orthoclase, Quartz; in Pegmatite dikes in Granite.	23	9S	22E

Monocline Ridge Quadrangle 7½'

Gypsite, sand and gravel.	SW¼1	16S	12E
Gypsite, Sandstone.	6	16S	13E

New Idria Quadrangle 15'

Acmite, Barkevikite, Analcime, Albite, in cavities of Soda Syenite.	SE¼4	19S	13E
Aragonite, clusters of acicular crystals in Serpentine, Chromite.	34	18S	13E
Chrysotile, Serpentine.	21	19S	13E
Magnesite, Serpentine.	3,4,5	19S	13E
Cinnabar, Pyrite, Serpentine.	NW¼2,NE¼3	19S	13E
Cinnabar, Sandstone; Serpentine.	SW¼17	18S	13E
Cinnabar, Sandstone; Serpentine.	SW¼22,NW¼27	18S	13E
Cinnabar.	34	18S	13E

Patterson Mountain Quadrangle 15'

Arsenopyrite, abundant.	NW¼16	13S	27E
Beryl, Topaz in a Pegmatite.	34	11S	25E
Scheelite.	NW¼32	13S	26E
Scheelite, Tactite, Granite.	22	12S	27E
Scheelite.	E½3	12S	26E
Scheelite.	NE¼22	12S	27E
Scheelite, Garnet, Epidote, Limestone; Granite.	29	13S	26E

Shaver Lake Quadrangle 15'

Marble, white, blue and black.	36	8S	24E

Tehipite Dome Quadrangle 15'

Limestone, large deposit on the north side of the Kings River.	26	12S	27E

Trimmer Quadrangle 7½'

Limestone.	15	11S	24E
Scheelite.	18	11S	25E
Scheelite.	7	11S	25E
Scheelite, Granite, Limestone.	E½15	11S	24E

131

Tucker Mountain Quadrangle 7½'

	SECTION	T.	R.
Mica, some Muscovite in books up to 4" square in Pegmatite.	near east line of 12	14S	25E

GLENN COUNTY

Elk Creek Quadrangle 15'

Ammonites, several varieties Upper Jurassic. From 400' of strata exposed on and near Watson Creek east of the bridge on the road from Elk Creek to Newville.	NE¼NE¼16	21N	6W
Ammonites and Buchia fossils. On Watson Creek SE of the bridge.	1,100' W. and 800' S. of NE corner 16	21N	6W
Ammonites, Lower Cretaceous. Just north of the junction of Watson Creek and Grindstone Creek.	900' E. and 1,400' S. of NW corner 15	21N	6W
Ammonites, Upper Jurrasic. On south bank of Grindstone Creek.	775' W. of east line of 16	21N	6W
Ammonites, Lower Cretaceous. On south bank of Grindstone Creek.	300' W. of east line of 16	21N	6W

GLENN AND TEHAMA COUNTIES

Paskenta Quadrangle 15'

Ammonite fossil localities, Lower Cretaceous and Upper Jurassic:

Ammonites, Upper Jurassic. From unnamed eastern tributary of Heifer Camp Creek ¼ mile above junction with the north fork of Stony Creek.	250' E. and 1,400' N of SW corner 3	22N	6W
Ammonites, Upper Jurassic. On Heifer Camp Creek.	850' E. and 1,150' N. of SW corner 9	22N	6W
Ammonites, 3 varieties, Upper Jurassic in beds of Sandstone and Mudstone containing Limestone concretions. Located 300' SW of Oakes Ranch house (abandoned).	2,500' W. of SE corner and just N. of S. line of 30	25N	6W
Ammonites, Lower Cretaceous. Located on the S. side of road from Paskenta to Red Bluff, 800' SE of BM (Bench Mark) 870 near South fork of Elder Creek.	400' E. and 2,000' S. of NW corner 28	25N	6W
Ammonites, Lower Cretaceous. On south side of road to Red Bluff.	1,100' E. and 1,750' N. of SW corner 28	25N	6W

HUMBOLDT COUNTY

Alderpoint Quadrangle 15'

Braunite, Chert.	15	3S	4E
Limestone.	20,29	4S	5E

Arcata South Quadrangle 7½'

	SECTION	T.	R.
Limestone, on Jacoby Creek.	13,14	5N	1E

Blocksburg Quadrangle 15'

Bementite, Psilomelane, Rhodochrosite, Rhodonite, Chert.	2	1S	4E

Hoopa Quadrangle 15'

Bornite, Cuprite, native Copper.	29	10N	6E
Chalcopyrite (abundant), Sphalerite, Pyrite, Quartz; Schist, Gold (some 1 oz. assays).	2	8N	4E
Chromite, Serpentine.	24	10N	5E
Chromite, float on Hostler Ridge.	20,21	11N	6E
Rhodonite, Chert.	15	8N	4E

Orick Quadrangle 15'

Beach Placer Gold.		33	13N	1E
	and	4	12N	1E

Scotia Quadrangle 15'

Limestone, outcrop on west fork of Howe Creek.	10,16	1N	1W
Limestone.	4,9	2S	1W
Limestone.	SE¼SE¼11	1N	1W
Calcareous tufa.	5	1N	1W

Willow Creek Quadrangle 15'

Bornite, Chalcocite, Chalcopyrite, Chromite, native Copper (masses to 400 lbs. were found), Malachite (good specimens), Diorite, Schist, Serpentine, Gabbro.	33,34	6N	4E
Limestone.	33	7N	4E
Limestone.	18,19	6N	5E
Limestone, along state highway on Willow Creek.		6N	4E

IMPERIAL COUNTY

Borrego Mountain SE Quadrangle 7½'

Gypsum.		19,20,29,30,32	13S	9E
Gypsum.		NW¼18	13S	9E
	and	W½NW¼18	13S	9E

Durmid Quadrangle 7½'

Thenardite, Mirabolite, Blodite, Clay, Shale, Sandstone.	N½19	9S	12E
Thenardite, Mirabolite, Blodite, Clay, Shale, Sandstone.	S½13	9S	11E

Little Picacho Peak Quadrangle 7½'

Cerussite, Galena, Silver.	11	14S	22E

133

	SECTION	T.	R.
Malachite, Chalcopyrite, Schist.	1	14S	22E

Ogilby Quadrangle 15'

Gold, Quartz; Pyrite, Chalcopyrite, Galena, Sphalerite, rare purple Fluorite, Chalcocite, Covellite (thick veins here can be traced for 2 miles).	17	15S	21E
Gold, Quartz; Quartz Diorite, Pyrite, Chalcopyrite.	19	15S	21E
Gold, Quartz; Schist, Sulfides.	17	15S	21E
Gold, Granite, Quartz; ($20 Ore).	20,29	15S	21E
Kyanite, Andalusite, Pyrophyllite, black Tourmaline, Gneiss, Schist.	19,30	15S	21E

Quartz Peak Quadrangle 15'

Malachite, Azurite, Schist, Quartzite, Monzonite.		26	12S	20E
Malachite, Azurite, Chalcopyrite, Monzonite.		23,26	12S	20E
Gold, Quartz; Schist, (one pocket wire gold worth $3,000).		21	13S	19E
Cerussite, Galena, Argentite, Diorite, Granite, Gold, Silver.	and	19,30	11S	20E
		24,25	11S	19E
Psilomelane, Pyrolusite, Andesite.		18,19	11S	21E
Silver, Barite, Manganese Oxides, Granite Gneiss, Porphyry, Argentite.		3	12S	20E
Torbernite (Uranium), plus other Uranium minerals in Metamorphics.		14	12S	19E

INYO COUNTY

Big Pine Quadrangle 15'

Scheelite.	SE¼36	8S	32E
Scheelite, Epidote (large crystals), Garnet, Limestone; Quartz, Monzonite.	SE¼31	8S	33E
Scheelite, Marble, Epidote.	SW¼20	8S	33E
Scheelite, Garnet, Epidote, Wollastonite.	SW¼31	8S	33E
Pumice.	8	8S	34E
Scheelite.	SW¼36	9S	32E
Scheelite.	NW¼6	9S	33E
Feldspar, Kaolin, Granite.	SW¼2,NW¼14	9S	33E
Talc, Marble, Amphibolite, Granite.	SE¼31	9S	33E
Marble.	27,34	9S	33E
Perlite.	24,25	10S	33E
Gold, Granodiorite.	2	10S	33E
Talc.	SW¼28	10S	34E
Gold, Quartz; Granite.	NW¼,SW¼17	10S	34E
Gold, Silver, Galena, Pyrite, Chalcopyrite.	7,17,18	10S	34E
Volcanic cinders.	SW¼17	10S	34E
Perlite.	19,24,25,30	10S	34E
Scheelite.	SE¼11	11S	33E

Bishop Quadrangle 15'

Gold.	SW¼34	5S	33E
Gold.	NW¼25	5S	33E

	SECTION	T.	R.
Pumice.	N½12	6S	33E
Tuff.	18	6S	33E
Stibnite, Quartz.	SE corner 23	7S	32E
Scheelite.	W½8	7S	32E
Scheelite, Marble, Schist.	NE corner 25	7S	32E
Scheelite, Ferberite, Jarosite.	SW corner 22	7S	32E
Scheelite, Garnet, Epidote, Marble, Wollastonite.	SW corner 28	7S	32E
Gold, Silver, Lead, Pyrite, Limonite, Limestone; Quartz.	NW¼8	7S	34E
Barite, float in canyon at north end of sections 5 and 6.		7S	34E
Scheelite.	NW¼17	8S	32E

Blanco Mountain Quadrangle 15'

	SECTION	T.	R.
Cerussite, Galena, Sphalerite, Chalcopyrite, Smithsonite, Limestone.	13,14,23,24	7S	34E
Silver, Galena, Cerussite, Limestone, Schist.	15	6S	35E
Cerussite, Silver, Galena, Sphalerite, Smithsonite, Limestone.	6	7S	35E
Silver, Galena, Cerussite, Copper minerals, Limestone, Quartz Diorite.	14	7S	35E
Scheelite, Copper Oxides, Limestone.	7	6S	36E
Scheelite.	4	7S	36E

Chloride Cliff Quadrangle 15'

	SECTION	T.	R.
Borax.	30,31	28N	1E
Gold.	2,3	29N	1E
Chalcopyrite, Galena, Pyrite, Silver, Quartz; Schist.	6	29N	1E
Gold.	5,6	29N	1E
Cinnabar, Copper (native), Marcasite, Galena, Cerussite, Gold, Pyrite, Limestone; Granite.	28	30N	1E
Silver, Galena, Copper minerals, Talc.	29	30N	1E
Gold, Galena, Pyrite, Quartz; Schist.	31,32	30N	1E

Darwin Quadrangle 15'

	SECTION	T.	R.
Talc.	20,29,30	18S	40E
Galena, Cerussite, Hemimorphite.	NW¼NW¼12	19S	40E
Talc.	29,32	18S	40E
Cerussite, Hemimorphite, Galena.	SE¼SE¼31	18S	41E
Cuprite, Chrysocolla, Malachite, Garnet, Scheelite.	SW¼NW¼18	19S	41E
Anglesite, Cerussite, Galena, Azurite, Malachite, Pyrite, Hemimorphite, Wollastonite, Limestone, Granite.	Midpoint of boundary between 1,12	19S	40E
Cerussite, Galena, Limonite, Scheelite, Jarosite, pink and green Fluorite, Malachite, Calcite (rhombs to 2').	NW¼NE¼19	19S	41E
Stibnite, Limonite, Calcite.	NE¼NE¼2	19S	40E
Hydrozincite, Calcite, crystals.	SW¼SW¼2	19S	41E
Chalcopyrite, Galena, Sphalerite, Cerussite, Anglesite, Smithsonite, Hemimorphite, Wulfenite, Azurite, Malachite, Garnet, Epidote, Wollastonite.	E½SW¼2	19S	41E
Bismutite, Bismuthinite, Cerussite, Scheelite, Diorite, Tactite, Limestone.	center of 24	19S	40E
Talc, Chlorite.	31	18S	39E

	SECTION	T.	R.
Calcite (iceland spar), rhombs to 4".	SW¼NE¼3	19S	40E
Galena, Malachite, Azurite, Cerussite, Pyrite, Calcite, Limonite, Tactite.	SE¼SW¼18	19S	40E
Marble.	27	17S	40E
Chrysocolla, Cuprite, Malachite.	NW¼SW¼19	19S	41E
Argentite, Anglesite, Aurichalcite, Azurite, Bindheimite, Chrysocolla, Cerussite, Cerargyrite (euhedral olive-green crystals), Galena, Hemimorphite (abundant radial and divergent aggregates, gray to colorless associated with Cerargyrite), Malachite, Silver (native), Smithsonite, Tremolite, Barite, Calcite, Limestone.	23	17S	40E
Scheelite, Garnet, Epidote, Calcite, Limonite.	NW¼SW¼26	19S	39E
Cerussite, Anglesite, Galena, Pyrite, Calcite, Jasper, Fluorite, Jarosite.	NE¼SW¼1	19S	40E
Cerussite, Wulfenite, Plumbojarosite, Hydrozincite.	S½NE¼30	19S	41E
Chryscolla, Malachite, Cuprite, Chalcopyrite, Garnet, Limonite Pseudomorphs after Pyrite (Pyritohedrons).	24	19S	40E
Cerussite, Hemimorphite, Calcite, Pyrite, Sphalerite, Galena, Arsenopyrite, Chalcopyrite, Quartzite; Argillite, Limestone.	26,35	17S	39E
Talc.	28,29	18S	40E
Galena, Cerussite, Pyrite, Chrysocolla, Anglesite, Fluorite, Jasper.	NE¼13	19S	40E
Talc, Hematite (specular).	28,29,32,33	18S	40E
Talc.	23,24,25,36	18S	39E
Calcite, Fluorite, Cerussite, Galena, Garnet, Scheelite, Pyrite, Limestone.	N½SW¼18	19S	41E
Galena, Sphalerite, Cerussite, Anglesite, Azurite, Malachite, Hemimorphite (abundant masses of colorless, white, cream colored crystals mixed with Limonite), Limestone.	SE¼NW¼2	19S	41E
Galena, Cerussite, Chrysocolla, Chalcopyrite, Cuprite, Azurite.	SE¼NW¼11	19S	41E

Funeral Peak Quadrangle 15'

Barite, Copper minerals, Quartz.	23	23N	3E
Borates.	11,12	24N	4E
Copper minerals.	2,16,17,18,19,20,21,24,26,27,35,36	24N	3E
Copper minerals.	1,2,10,15,36	23N	3E

Furnace Creek Quadrangle 15'

Borates, Colemanite.	8,9,16,17,20,29,32	27N	1E
Ginorite.	SW¼9	26N	2E

Haiwee Reservoir Quadrangle 15'

Obsidian, Coso Hot Springs		22S	39E

Independence Quadrangle 15'

Gold, Silver, Copper minerals.	15	13S	36E
Gold, Silver, Cerussite, Cerargyrite, Galena, Siderite, Limestone, Granite.	28,29	12S	36E

	SECTION	T.	R.
Azurite, Chrysocolla, Malachite, Quartz.	31,32	11S	35E
Copper minerals.	1	13S	35E
Scheelite.	15	13S	36E
Gold, Silver, Sphalerite, Galena.	5	13S	36E
Silver, Galena.	30	12S	36E
Silver, Galena, Cerargyrite.	15	11S	36E

Keeler Quadrangle 15'

Clay, Fullers earth.	13,14,23	18S	38E
Hematite, Limestone, Granite.	1	19S	38E
Autunite, Shale, Sandstone.	N½25	19S	37E

Maturango Peak Quadrangle 15'

Stibnite.	26	21S	42E
Gold, Cerussite, Limestone.	34	19S	42E
Argentite, Cerargyrite, Anglesite, Embolite, Cryptomelane, Hydrozincite, Mimetite (small green crystals), Galena, Sphalerite, Pyrolusite, Limonite, Limestone, Diabase.	33,34	19S	42E

Mount Goddard Quadrangle 15'

Scheelite (crystals to 2″), Garnet, Epidote, Pyrrhotite, Hornblende.	SE¼,NW¼23	8S	31E
Scheelite, Garnet, Pyrrhotite, Pyrite, Bornite, Chalcopyrite, Marble, Quartzite.	SW¼27	8S	31E
Scheelite.	NE¼SE¼20	8S	31E
Arsenopyrite, Lollingite, Pyrrhotite, Wollastonite, Molybdenite, Quartzite; Granite.	W½29	8S	31E
Scheelite, Galena, Marble, Granodiorite.	NE¼30	8S	32E
Annabergite, Argentite, Erythrite, Cobaltite, Smaltite, Barite, Wollastonite.	SE¼23	9S	31E

Mountain Tom Quadrangle 15'

Scheelite.	SW¼35	6S	31E
Scheelite, Marble.	SW¼34	6S	31E
Scheelite, Garnet, Epidote, yellow-green Nontronite, Marble.	SE¼34	6S	31E
Cerussite (large crystals).	14	6S	31E
Scheelite, abundant Garnet, Epidote, Sphalerite crystals; pink Garnet.	NW¼13	7S	31E
Scheelite, Garnet, Epidote, Magnetite, Hematite, Hornblende Gabbro.	NW¼12	7S	31E
Scheelite.	SE¼11	7S	31E
Scheelite, Marble, Quartz Diorite.	SW¼12	7S	31E
Scheelite, Hornblende Gabbro.	center W¼12	7S	31E
Scheelite.	center E½9	7S	31E
Scheelite.	center 13	7S	31E
Scheelite.	center S½10	7S	31E
Scheelite.	SW¼1	7S	31E
Scheelite (well developed crystals to 2″), Epidote, Garnet.	NW¼21	7S	30E

	SECTION	T.	R.
Scheelite, Garnet, Epidote, Limestone; Granodiorite.	NE¼11	7S	30E
Scheelite, Marble, Granite.	SE¼15	7S	30E

New York Butte Quadrangle 15'

	SECTION	T.	R.
Lead, Silver, Gold, Copper, Quartz; Granite.	35	14S	37E
Anglesite, Anhydrite, Argentite, Atacamite, Aurichalcite, Azurite, Barite, Bindheimite, Calcite, Caledonite, Cerargyrite, Cerussite, Chrysocolla, Duftite, Galena, Halloysite, Hemimorphite, Hydrozincite, Leadhillite, Limonite, Linarite, Malachite, Mimetite, Pyrite, Silver, Smithsonite, Sphalerite, Stibnite, Tetrahedrite, Willemite, Wulfenite.	12,13,23,24,28	16S	38E
Cerargyrite, Galena, Silver, Zinc, Copper, Gold.	13	16S	38E
Marble.	4,10,11,13,14,24,25	16S	37E
Talc, Quartzite; Diabase.	4	16S	37E
Lead, Zinc, Copper, Limestone.	24	16S	37E
Galena, Cerussite, Silver, Copper, Gold, Limestone.	16,21	15S	37E
Copper minerals.	35	15S	37E
Lead, Silver, Copper.	14	16S	38E
Tremolite, Limestone.	25	16S	37E
Galena, Caledonite, Linarite, Cerussite, Wulfenite.	8	14S	38E
Galena, Cerussite, Limestone.	13	16S	37E
Cerussite, Galena, Smithsonite, Copper minerals, Gold.	11,12,13,14	16S	38E
Galena, Cerussite, Sphalerite, Tetrahedrite, Limestone, Quartz Monzonite.	23	16S	38E

Panamint Butte Quandrangle 15'

	SECTION	T.	R.
Cerussite, Smithsonite, Limonite, Mimetite, Jasper, Pyrolusite, Wulfenite, Bindheimite, Hemimorphite, Linarite, Specularite, Sphalerite, Limestone, Basalt.	26	17S	42E
Native Silver.	34	19S	42E
Bindheimite, Cerussite, Coronadite, Cryptomelane, Galena, Mimetite (yellow-green masses on Cerussite), Jasper, Cerargyrite, Limonite, Pyrolusite, Limestone.	28,29	19S	42E
Azurite, Argentite, Anglesite, Cerargyrite, Bindheimite, Cerussite (fine crystals), Cryptomelane, Hydrozincite, Pyrolusite, Galena, Smithsonite, Limestone, Diabase.	27,28	19S	42E
Malachite, Cerussite, Granite.	18	19S	42E
Sphalerite, Chalcopyrite, Pyrite, Azurite, Malachite, Smithsonite, Anglesite, Cerussite, Chrysocolla, Mimetite, Pyromorphite, Galena, Limestone.	19	19S	42E

Ryan Quadrangle 15'

	SECTION	T.	R.
Colemanite, Ulexite, Probertite (translucent satiny needles).	5	25N	3E
Borax.	8	25N	3E
Gypsum.	6	25N	4E
Borax.	33	26N	3E
Borax.	9,16	25N	3E
Howlite (white micaceous masses) in Gower Gulch near Ryan.	1	27N	2E
Gold.	1	27N	2E

Shoshone Quadrangle 15'

	SECTION	T.	R.
Gold, Silver, Tetrahedrite, Chalcopyrite, Galena, Barite.	27	21N	5E
Gold, Quartz, Hornblende Schist.	4,5	20N	5E
Talc.	7,18	20N	6E
Talc.	35	21N	5E
Bentonite.	25	22N	6E
Pumicite.	31,32	22N	7E
Perlite.	26	22N	6E
Hematite (Specular variety), Granite Gneiss.	24	21N	4E

Tecopa Quadrangle 15'

	SECTION	T.	R.
Gypsum, in Shale.	26	20N	7E
Gold.	21,22	22N	7E
Gold, Silver, Galena, Cerussite, Anglesite, Aurichalcite, Dolomite.	9,10,14,15,16,22,23,27	20N	8E
Nitrates, Gypsum (transparent).	27,33,34,38	20N	7E

Telescope Peak Quadrangle 15'

	SECTION	T.	R.
Galena, Sphalerite, Chalcopyrite, Bornite, Pyrrhotite, Pyrite, Quartz; Schist, Granite.	14	20S	44E
Chalcopyrite, Galena, Pyrite, Cerussite, Gold, Quartz; Limestone, Schist.	16	20S	44E
Gold, Lead, Quartz; Schist.	9	20S	44E
Silver, Galena, Copper minerals.	5	20S	45E
Gold, Quartz; Limonite.	21	20S	45E
Tetrahedrite, Bromyrite, Azurite, Malachite, Quartz; Schist, Limestone.	10,11,15,21,22	21S	45E
Siderite, Marcasite, Pyrrhotite, Pyrite, Chalcopyrite, Gold, Silver, Quartz.	11	21S	45E
Gold, Silver.	13	22S	44E
Gold, Galena, Chalcopyrite, Pyrite, Pyrrhotite, Quartz, Schist.	8	22S	45E
Siderite, Gold, Galena, Quartz; Schist.	1	22S	45E
Gold.	9	22S	45E
Chalcopyrite, Galena, Gold, Pyrite, Cerussite, Quartz; Limestone, Schist.	7	22S	45E

Trona Quadrangle 15'

	SECTION	T.	R.
Hematite, Magnetite, Granite, Limestone.	28,29,30	22S	43E
Stibnite, Metacinnabar.	29	22S	43E
Vari-colored Onyx Marble in Limestone. (In Shepard Canyon, green, red, brown, cream).	6	22S	43E
Gold.	24	23S	42E
Gold, Siderite, Hematite, Quartz; Granite.	30	23S	43E
Gold, Quartz; Granite.	31	23S	43E
Manganese Oxides, Garnet.	14,15,20,21	23S	43E
Gold.	31	23S	43E
Gold, Quartz; Calcite, Granite.	6	24S	43E
Gold, Pyrite, Limonite, Quartz Monzonite.	35	23S	42E
Galena, Cerrusite, Smithsonite, Wulfenite, Vanadinite, Limestone.	24	24S	43E

Ubehebe Peak Quadrangle 15'

	SECTION	T.	R.
Wulfenite, Axinite, Hemimorphite, Cerussite, Hydrozincite (colloform linings), Vanadinite, Sphalerite, Galena, Limestone, Diorite.	1,2	14S	40E
Malachite, Azurite, Marble, Granite.	26	14S	40E
Gold (Megascopic), Jarosite crystals; Chalcopyrite, Pyrite, Limonite, Calcite, Jasper, Quartz.	16	14S	41E
Silver, Copper minerals, Galena, Idocrase, Garnet.	10	15S	40E
Chrysocolla, Azurite, Malachite.	15	15S	40E
Galena, Smithsonite, Wulfenite, Limonite, Cerussite, Talc, Aragonite, Hemimorphite, Limestone; Quartz Monzonite.	13	15S	40E
Gold, Scheelite.	7,8	15S	41E
Silver, Galena, Cerussite, Azurite, Malachite.	16	15S	41E
Hubnerite.	31	13S	41E
Chalcocite, Cuprite, Tetrahedrite.	19	15S	41E
Malachite, Chrysocolla, Azurite, Garnet, Epidote, abundant Magnetite, Limonite, Hematite, Phlogopite, Marble, Antigorite, Chrysotile.	5	15S	41E
Malachite, Azurite, Magnetite, Scapolite, Marble, Quartz Monzonite.	21	15S	41E
Scheelite (to 2''), Cuprotungstite (yellow-green), Malachite, Chrysocolla, Garnet, Calcite, Hematite, Magnetite, Cuprite, Chalcocite, Chalcopyrite, Marble.	30	15S	41E
Ferberite, Quartz.	35	15S	41E
Argentite, Galena, Copper Minerals, Quartz.	19	16S	39E
Galena, Cerussite, Bindheimite, Gold, Silver, Chalcocite, Limestone; Quartz.	19	16S	39E
Tetrahedrite.	18	16S	39E
Cerussite, Cerargyrite, Galena, Limestone.	7	16S	40E
Galena, abundant Cerussite, Calcite, Covellite, Chalcocite Malachite, Limonite, Hematite.	1	16S	40E
Copper minerals.	4	16S	40E
Allanite, Chrysocolla.	21	16S	41E

KERN COUNTY

Breckenridge Mountain Quadrangle 15'

Petrified Wood.	1,2	30S	30E
Scheelite, Quartz Diorite, Schist.	SE¼NW¼34	28S	32E
Scheelite, Tactite, Schist.	NW¼35	28S	32E
Scheelite (to 4''), Garnet, Epidote.	S½27	28S	32E
Scheelite (fine to coarse crystals).	NW¼SE¼26	28S	32E
Scheelite (to ½''), Garnet, Epidote, Schist.	SE¼27	28S	32E

California Hot Springs Quadrangle 15'

Scheelite, Tactite, Limestone, Quartz Diorite.	E½17	25S	32E
Scheelite, Epidote, Garnet, Calcite, Quartz, Tactite, Limestone, Quartz Diorite.	NW¼17	25S	32E
Scheelite, Tactite, Limestone,Granodiorite.	center 16	25S	32E
Stibnite, Quartz, Granodiorite.	NW¼16	25S	32E
Epidote (large crystals), Scheelite, Garnet, smoky Quartz crystals, Tactite, Limestone, Quartz Diorite.	SW¼SE¼9	25S	32E

	SECTION	T.	R.

Scheelite, Garnet, Epidote.   NE¼9 25S 32E
Scheelite, Garnet, Epidote.   S½7 25S 32E
Scheelite, Garnet, Epidote, Marble.   NE¼9 25S 32E

Cantil Quadrangle 7½'

Bentonite.   NE¼8 30S 38E
Ulexite (balls to 3" in diameter).   8 30S 38E
Gypsum.   south side Koehn Dry Lake 28 30S 38E
Gypsum.   E½29 30S 38E
Bornite, Azurite, Malachite, Limonite.   6 30S 38E

Castle Butte Quadrangle 15'

Bloodstone, Agate, Palm Root.   23,35,36 32S 38E
Petrified Wood in lake beds; Chalcedony in Basalt.   3,4,14 11N 9W
Bentonite, Tuff, Basalt.   S½SE¼,SE¼SW¼2 11N 9W

Cross Mountain Quadrangle 15'

Quartz and Orthoclase crystals (Carlsbad Twins) in Gran-
    ite Pegmatite.   31 30S 37E
Variegated Claystone.   NE¼SE¼29 30S 37E
Autunite, Schroeckingerite, Uranophane, Rhyolite.   SE¼1 30S 36E
Metatorbernite.   SE corner 10 30S 36E
Wolframite, Scheelite, Granite.   common corner sections 10,11,14,15 30S 36E
Scheelite, Granodiorite.   NE¼NW¼29 30S 36E
Bentonite, Varicolored Tuff beds.   SW¼NE¼14 30S 36E
Claystone in Rhyolite.   NE¼34 30S 36E
Cinnabar.   NE corner 10 31S 36E
Stibnite, Granodiorite.   5 31S 36E
Stibnite, Quartz, Granodiorite.   SW corner 5 31S 36E
Stibnite, Quartz, Granodiorite.   NW¼8 31S 36E
Galena, Chalcopyrite, Limonite, Gypsum, Calcite.   NE¼6 31S 37E

El Paso Peaks Quadrangle 7½'

Chalcopyrite, Copper Oxides, Granodiorite.   19,30 28S 40E
Lode Gold, Silver, Copper Oxides, Quartz Monzonite,
    Diorite.   common corner of sections 20,21,28,29 28S 40E
Chalcopyrite, Galena, Copper Oxides, Limestone, Quartz
    Monzonite.   SE¼30 28S 40E
Placer Gold.   SE¼35 28S 40E
Gold, Limonite, Gypsum, Diorite.   SE¼SE¼6 29S 40E
Placer Gold.   1,12 29S 40E
Placer Gold and Scheelite.   22,23,24 29S 40E

Emerald Mountain Quadrangle 15'

Lode Gold in Quartz veins in Granite.   4,5,6,8,9,14,16,21,22,26,28,36 29S 34E
Lode Gold in Quartz veins in Granite and Rhyolite.   19,25,29,30,31,32 28S 34E
Scheelite in Tactite (Epidote, Garnet).   NW¼20 28S 34E
Scheelite, Molybdenite, Garnet, Epidote, Diopside, Pyrite,
    Quartz.   36 28S 33E
Scheelite (crystals to 100 lbs.), Limestone,Schist.   NE¼1 31S 33E
Cerargyrite, Bromyrite, Gold, Pyrite, Pyrrhotite, Rhyolite.   SW¼28,NE¼28 30S 33E
Barite, Limestone.   SW¼4 31S 33E
Aurichalcite, Sphalerite, Cerussite, Galena, Chalcopyrite,
    Goslarite, Zincite, Malachite, Hemimorphite Calcite,
    Pyrite, Pyrrhotite.   SW¼5 31S 33E
Stibnite, blue-gray Quartz, Rhyolite.   NW¼4 31S 33E

Garlock Quadrangle 7½'

	SECTION	T.	R.
Fluorite (red, green, white), Rhyolite.	NE¼SW¼12	29S	38E
Lode Gold, Silver, Malachite, Chalcopyrite, Pyrite.	SW¼SE¼29	28S	39E
Pumice, Tuff.	center 16	28S	38E
Jasper-agate, Basalt.	SW¼22	28S	38E
Placer Gold.	SW¼NW¼34	28S	38E
Placer Gold.	SE¼NW¼34	29S	38E
Placer Gold.	NE¼11	29S	38E
Chalcopyrite, Limonite, Quartz, Schist.	SE corner NE¼1	29S	38E
Gold, Chalcopyrite, Pyrite, Quartz, Schist.	N½SE¼1	29S	38E
Bornite, Chalcopyrite, Limonite, Manganese Oxides, Quartz, Granite.	NE¼12	29S	38E
Azurite, Malachite, Chalcopyrite, Quartz Diorite.	NW¼13	29S	38E

Glenville Quadrangle 15'

	SECTION	T.	R.
Scheelite, Garnet, Epidote.	E½3	28S	32E
Scheelite (coarse crystals), Quartz, Quartz Diorite.	SW¼26	27S	32E
Scheelite, Granite.	NW¼SW¼26	27S	32E
Scheelite, Granite.	NW¼26	27S	32E
Scheelite, Pyrite, Quartz Diorite.	SW¼23	27S	32E
Scheelite, Pyrite, Quartz Diorite.	SW¼NE¼14	27S	32E
Smoky Quartz crystals (large), Pegmatite in Quartz Diorite.	S½22	25S	32E
Scheelite (good crystals), Garnet, Epidote, smoky Quartz crystals.	NW¼27	25S	32E
Scheelite, Garnet, Epidote, Calcite, Tactite, Quartz Diorite.	S½NW¼20	25S	32E
Scheelite, Pyrite, Garnet, Epidote, blue Sulfates of Copper and Iron, Tactite, Quartz Diorite.	N½19	25S	32E
Epidote (coarse grained), Garnet, Clinozoisite, Calcite, Actinolite, Diopside, Molybdenite, Marble.	SW¼17	25S	32E
Scheelite, Epidote, Garnet, Clinozoisite, Calcite, Diopside.	S½SW¼17	25S	32E
Scheelite, Garnet (coarse), Epidote.	SE¼16	25S	32E

Inyokern Quadrangle 15'

	SECTION	T.	R.
Pumicite, Basalt.	SW¼5	28S	39E
Radioactive bones in Sandstone.	NW¼33	26S	38E
Scheelite, Garnet, Epidote.	center 10	26S	38E
Scheelite, Garnet, Epidote.	NE¼11	26S	37E
Scheelite, Garnet, Epidote.	NW¼24	26S	37E
Scheelite, Garnet, Clinozoisite, Calcite, Albite, Gold, Limestone.	2	26S	37E
Scheelite (crystals to 1").	SE¼34,SW¼35	25S	37E

Isabella Quadrangle 15'

	SECTION	T.	R.
Gold, Quartz, Chalcopyrite, Pyrite, Stibnite, Limestone, Schist.	NW¼18	28S	34E
Pyrite, Quartz, Chalcopyrite, Sphalerite, Limestone.	SW¼NE¼26	27S	33E
Stibnite, Quartz, Slate, Quartzite.	SW¼SW¼24	27S	33E
Scheelite, (to ¼"), Limestone.	N½SW¼23	27S	33E
Pitchblende, Gummite, Fluorite, Gneiss, Schist.	S½24	27S	33E
Garnet, Epidote, Scheelite, Quartz Monzonite.	N½14	27S	33E
Malachite, Chalcopyrite, Pyrite.	center of north edge of 10	27S	33E
Scheelite, Tactite.	E½SW¼30	27S	33E

142

Johannesburg Quadrangle 7½'

	SECTION	T.	R.
Lode Gold, Quartz, Limonite.	35,36	29S	40E
Lode Gold, Placer Gold, Kaolinite, Limonite, Scheelite, Mariposite, Pyrite, Stibnite, Miargyrite, Arsenopyrite, Talc, Manganese minerals, Actinolite, Rhodonite, Tourmaline, Chert, Schist, Rhyolite, Quartz Monzonite.	1,2,3,4,9,10,11,12,15,16,22	30S	40E

Keene Quadrangle 7½'

Cinnabar, Granite.	SE¼SW¼26	31S	32E
Cinnabar, Rhyolite, Granite.	SW¼26	31S	32E
Cinnabar, Rhyolite, Granite.	NE¼27	31S	32E

La Liebre Ranch Quadrangle 7½'

Garnet, Magnetite, Hematite, Limonite, Limestone, Granite Cassiterite.	SW¼25	9N	17W
Cassiterite, Limonite, Magnetite, Tourmaline, Limestone, Granite.	NW¼SW¼30	9N	17W

Lebec Quadrangle 7½'

Cassiterite, Magnetite, Garnet, Epidote, Scheelite, Limestone, Granite.	NE¼SE¼34	9N	18W
Magnetite, Garnet, Epidote, Cassiterite, Limestone, Granite.	SW¼34	9N	18W
Sphalerite, Limestone, Granite.	SE¼23	9N	18W
Magnetite, Ludwigite, Arsenopyrite, Molybdenite, Cassiterite, Magnetite.	NE¼23	9N	18W
Cuprite, Malachite, Chrysocolla, Jarosite, Gypsum, Chalcedony, Zoisite, Arsenopyrite, Galena, Powellite, Strontianite, Cassiterite, Magnetite, Scheelite, Molybdenite, Tourmaline, Phlogopite, Pyrite, Epidote, Garnet, Apatite, Calcite, Opal, native Copper.	SW¼25	9N	18W

Pleito Hills Quadrangle 7½:

Psilomelane, Quartz Mica Schist.	center 12	9N	21W
Stibnite, Quartz, Quartz Diorite.	10	9N	21W
Stibnite, Quartz, Granite.	SW¼11	9N	21W
Stibnite, Calcite, Pyrite, Arsenopyrite, Quartz Diorite.	9,10	9N	21W

Ridgecrest Quadrangle 15'

LODE GOLD PROPERTIES

Gold, Limonite, Quartz, Pyrite, Copper minerals.	NW¼29	27S	40E
Chalcopyrite, Copper Oxides, Granodiorite.	7,8	28S	40E
Gold, Quartz.	NE¼33	27S	40E
Gold, Quartz, Limonite.	SE¼22,NW¼26	27S	40E
Gold, Malachite, Quartz, Limonite.	NW¼26	27S	40E

	SECTION	T.	R.
Gold, Limonite, Copper Oxides.	NW¼34	27S	40E
Gold, Pyrite, Quartz.	SW¼NW¼29	27S	40E
Gold, Quartz.	SW¼26	27S	40E
Gold, Limonite, Copper Oxides.	S½29	27S	40E
Gold, Quartz, Pyrite, Chalcopyrite.	NE corner NW¼22	27S	40E
Gold, Quartz, Bornite, Chalcopyrite, Limonite, Galena.	center W½26	27S	40E
Bentonite (pink and white), Sandstone, Tuff, Volcanics.	16,17	28S	40E
Clay and Tuff.	W½NW¼7	28S	40E
Calcite.	SE¼,NE¼12	28S	39E
Wollastonite, Diopside, Garnet (grossularite).	SE¼SW¼12	28S	39E

Rio Bravo Ranch Quadrangle 7½'

Fossil shark teeth, Petrified Wood.	14,15	28S	29E
Gypsum.	20,21	29S	30E

Rosamond Quadrangle 15'

Magnesite, Limestone, Dolomite, Chert, Shale, Tuff, Bentonite, Clay.	NE¼11	10N	11W
Uranium minerals, Andesite.	N½S½10	9N	13W
Gold, Quartz Rhyolite.	NE¼15	9N	13W
Gold, Quartz Rhyolite.	S½11,N½14,NE¼15,SE¼10	9N	13W
Agate, Jasper, Opal, Petrified Wood.	SE¼26	10N	13W
Autunite.	SW¼25	10N	13W
Autunite, Uranophane.	center 36	10N	13W

Saltdale NW Quadrangle 7½'

Agate, Calcite Geodes, Apatite, Cassiterite, Chalcedony, Chloropal, Copper minerals, Coprolites, Dendrites, Epidote, Jasper, Opal (fire, moss, resin, milky), Petrified Wood (palm root, osage orange, black fig, white fig, conifers), Zeolites.	4,5,6,7,8,9,16,17,18	29S	38E
Pumicite.	SW¼5,NW¼8	29S	38E
Pumice.	4,5,8	29S	38E
Perlite.	SE¼8,W½9,NW¼17	29S	38E
Tuff, Bentonite.	SE¼17	29S	38E
Bentonite.	NE¼SW¼20	29S	38E
Bentonite.	NW¼NE¼30	29S	38E
Bentonite.	SE¼NE¼30,SW¼NW¼29	29S	38E
Opal (common and fire Opal), in Basalt flows as Amygdules.	E½13	29S	37E
	and NW¼18	29S	38E
Pumice.	31,32	28S	38E
Pumice.	NE¼4	29S	38E
Placer Gold.	SW¼34	28S	38E
Placer Gold.	SW¼SE¼33	28S	38E
Placer Gold.	NE¼NW¼3	29S	38E
Placer Gold.	NE¼3	29S	38E
Placer Gold.	NW¼SE¼3	29S	38E
Placer Gold.	SW¼NE¼3	29S	38E
Placer Gold.	SW¼SW¼3	29S	38E
Placer Gold.	SE¼SW¼3	29S	38E
Placer Gold.	SW¼NE¼8	29S	38E
Copper minerals, Quartz, Quartz Diorite.	center N½15	29S	38E
Malachite.	NE¼NW¼26	29S	38E

Tehachapi N.E. Quadrangle 7½'

	SECTION	T.	R.
Agate (sagenite, banded, clouded, plume, moss, lace), Chalcedony, Chrysoprase, Jasper, mammalian Fossils, Opal, Quartz clusters. This material is in Sandstone and Slates.	26,35,36	31S	34E

White River Quadrangle 7½'

Scheelite, Garnet, Epidote, Tactite, Hornblende Quartz Diorite.	SE¼2	25S	29E
Scheelite, Garnet, Tactite, Granite.	NW¼SE¼2	25S	29E
Scheelite, Garnet, Diopside, Calcite, Limonite.	NE¼SE¼2	25S	29E

Woody Quadrangle 7½'

Limonite, Azurite, Malachite, Chalcopyrite, Chalcocite, Hornblende Granodiorite. and	NE¼3 NW¼2	26S	29E
Magnetite, Garnet, Schist, Quartzite.	NW¼10	26S	29E

LAKE COUNTY

Clearlake Oaks Quadrangle 7½'

Pyrite, Sulfur, Cinnabar, Metacinnabar, Posepnyte, Opal (blue in Andesite).	6	13N	7W

Detert Reservoir Quadrangle 7½'

Cinnabar, Curtisite, Dolomite (well crystalized), Mercury (native).	23	10N	7W
Cinnabar.	NE¼NE¼22	10N	7W
Cinnabar.	NW¼NW¼23	10N	7W
Cinnabar.	near center SW¼24	10N	7W
Chromite.	3	10N	6W

Kelseyville Quadrangle 15' or 7½'

Obsidian occurs in abundance on Mount Konocti.

Lake Pillsbury Quadrangle 15'

Psilomelane (large deposit).	10	16N	10W

Lower Lake Quadrangle 15'

Gay-Lussite, Glauberite, Halite, Northupite, Pirssonite, Teepleite, Thermonatrite, Trona.	Borax Lake 7	13N	7W
Cinnabar, Marcasite, Hematite, Metacinnabar.	16	12N	6W
Chromite.	7	13N	6W
Chrysotile, Serpentine, Picrolite.	NE¼3	12N	6W

Morgan Valley Quadrangle 15'

	SECTION	T.	R.
Cinnabar, Montroydite, Tiemannite, Petroleum.	3	11N	5W

Mount St. Helena Quadrangle 7½'

	SECTION	T.	R.
Curtisite, Cinnabar, Marcasite, Tiemannite.	1	10N	8W
Cinnabar, Curtisite.	1	10N	8W
Cinnabar, Mercury (native).	1	10N	8W
Cinnabar, Mercury (native), Glaucophane.	1	10N	8W
Cinnabar.	17	10N	7W
Cinnabar, Metacinnabar, native Mercury, Millerite, Posepnyte.	16	10N	7W

Whispering Pines Quadrangle 7½'

	SECTION	T.	R.
Azurite, Malachite, Chalcopyrite, Aragonite, Gabbro, Diabase.	19	11N	7W
Cordierite (purple), Quartz crystals in Andesite.	SE¼SE¼20	12N	7W
Chrysotile, Serpentine.	NW¼32	12N	7W
Chrysotile, fibers to ½" long in Serpentine.	NE¼4	11N	7W
Chromite, Serpentine.	NE¼4	11N	7W
Chromite.	2	11N	8W
Chromite.	NE¼29	11N	7W
Chromite.	14	11N	8W

Willow Springs Quadrangle 7½'

	SECTION	T.	R.
Cinnabar, Epsomite, Marcasite, Metacinnabar.	32	14N	5W

LOS ANGELES COUNTY

Acton Quadrangle 7½'

	SECTION	T.	R.
Gold, Chalcocite, Cuprite, Bornite.	NE¼27	5N	13W
Gold.	E½27	5N	13W
Gold.	NW¼SE¼31	4N	12W
Copper minerals, Gold, Silver, Quartz; Diorite, Anorthosite.	NW¼SW¼11	4N	13W
Bornite, Malachite, Gold, Silver.	1	4N	13W
Feldspar (white Anorthosite).	NE corner 33	4N	13W
Orthoclase (pink, in Granite).	center 31	5N	12W
Jasper (red, blue).	28	5N	12W

Adobe Mountain Quadrangle 7½'

	SECTION	T.	R.
Autunite, fracture coatings in Granite.	26	7N	8W

Agua Dulce Quadrangle 7½'

	SECTION	T.	R.
Anorthosite.	8,9,10,15,16,17,26,28	4N	14W
Anorthosite.	33	4N	13W
Chalcedony, Opal.	28	5N	13W
Gold, Pyrite, Chalcopyrite.	20	4N	14W
Gold, Quartz, Granite.	28	5N	14W

Agua Dulce Quadrangle 7½' continued

	SECTION	T.	R.
Colemanite, Howlite, Probertite, Ulexite, Veatchite.	27,28,29,30,31,32,33	5N	14W
Graphite, Schist.	28	5N	14W
Ilmenite, Magnetite.	21	4N	14W
Ilmenite, Magnetite.	30	4N	13W
Columbite, small crystals in Pegmatite, head of Rattlesnake Canyon.	SW¼36	4N	14W

Burbank Quadrangle 7½'

	SECTION	T.	R.
Apophyllite, Natrolite, Analcime, Prehnite in Pacific Electric quarry, Brush Canyon.	35	1N	14W

Chilao Flat Quadrangle 7½'

	SECTION	T.	R.
Gold, Malachite, Limonite, Chalcopyrite.	N½13	3N	12W
Gold.	SE¼NE¼1	3N	12W
Gold, Pyrite, Marcasite, Chalcopyrite.	12,13	3N	12W
Ilmenite, Magnetite.	11,13,14,24,25	3N	12W

Glendora Quadrangle 7½'

	SECTION	T.	R.
Barite, large outcrop, west fork San Dimas Canyon	23	1N	9W
Gold.	NW¼NW¼30	2N	8W
Placer Gold.	SW¼NW¼30	2N	8W
Galena, Pyrite, Gold, Silver.	NW¼12	1N	10W

Green Valley Quadrangle 7½'

	SECTION	T.	R.
Graphite, Bouquet Canyon.	11,12	6N	15W
Magnesite.	11,12	6N	15W

Mint Canyon Quadrangle 7½'

	SECTION	T.	R.
Placer Gold.	26,29	5N	15W
Gypsum.	29,30	5N	14W
Ilmenite, Magnetite.	36	4N	15W

Mount San Antonio Quadrangle 7½'

	SECTION	T.	R.
Lode Gold.	SW¼NE¼8	2N	8W
Lode Gold.	NE¼NW¼10	2N	8W
Lode Gold.	NW¼2	2N	8W
Lode Gold.	SW¼NW¼24	3N	8W
Lode Gold.	NE¼5	2N	8W

Neenach School Quadrangle 7½'

	SECTION	T.	R.
Gold (lode).	W½26,NE¼27,NW¼NE¼34	8N	16W

Newhall Quadrangle 7½'

	SECTION	T.	R.
Placer Gold.	S½1,11,12	4N	16W

Pasadena Quadrangle 7½'

	SECTION	T.	R.
Graphite, large deposit in Verdugo Hills.	4	1N	13W

Ritter Ridge Quadrangle 7½'

Lode Gold.	N½23	5N	13W
Lode Gold.	NE¼23	5N	13W
Lode Gold.	NE¼NW¼21	5N	13W
Lode Gold, Pyrite, Chalcopyrite, Sylvanite.	NE¼NE¼22	5N	13W
Rhodonite, Psilomelane, Spessartite, Quartzite, Mica Schist.	NE¼NE¼30	6N	12W
Rhodonite, Psilomelane, Quartzite, Mica Schist.	NW¼NW¼24	6N	13W

San Fernando Quadrangle 7½'

Tremolite.	16	3N	15W
Gold, Quartz; Gabbro, Norite.	N½SE¼1	3N	15W
Placer Gold.	5	3N	15W
Placer Gold.	SW¼NW¼3	3N	15W
Dolomite.	S½SW¼7,18	3N	14W

Sleepy Valley Quadrangle 7½'

Lode Gold.	SW¼21	6N	14W
Lode Gold.	SE¼13	5N	14W
Clinochlore, Clinozoisite, Tourmaline.	center 2	5N	14W
Soapstone, Schist.	SE¼8	5N	13W

Sunland Quadrangle 7½'

Gold, Quartz; Pyrite, Chalcopyrite, Gabbro, Norite.	12	3N	14W
Gold, Quartz, Ilmenite, Magnetite.	4	3N	14W
Gold, Quartz; Granite.	28	3N	14W
Placer Gold.	27	3N	14W
Graphite.	16,17,28	3N	14W
Ilmenite, Magnetite.	2,3,4,8,11,12	3N	14W
Annabergite, Chalcopyrite, Pyrrhotite, Galena, Sphalerite, Quartz; Gabbro-norite.	10,11	3N	14W
Blue Quartz in graphic Granite.	NE¼6	3N	13W
Allanite, Zircon, Apatite, in Pacoima Canyon.	17	3N	13W

MADERA COUNTY

Daulton Quadrangle 7½'

Daulton mine, Andalusite crystals to 3″ in Kyanite Schist, Azurite, Sphalerite, Chalcopyrite.	E½35	9S	18E

Raymond Quadrangle 7½'

Cobaltite (Cubes and Pyritohedrons), Pyrrhotite, Epidote, Chalcopyrite, Pyrite, Schist, Gneiss.	SE¼13	9S	18E
Connellite (radiating groups of blue-green Acicular crystals in Schist), Azurite, Pyrrhotite, Chalcopyrite.	34	8S	18E

Yosemite Quadrangle 15'

	SECTION	T.	R.
Magnetite.	1,12	5S	22E
Galena, Pyrite, Sphalerite.	9,10	5S	22E
Magnetite, Chalcopyrite, Sphalerite, Galena, Pyrite, Quartzite. (SW slope of Mt. Raymond).	9,10	5S	22E
Galena, large cubes, Magnetite in Metamorphics and Granitics.	10	5S	22E

MARIPOSA COUNTY

Bear Valley Quadrangle 7½'

Gold, (specimens to 50 lbs. been found here), Arsenopyrite, Pyrite, Chalcopyrite, Tetrahedrite, Galena, Quartz; Calcite, Limonite, Greenstone.	E½29	4S	18E
Gold, Quartz; Greenstone.	SE¼30	4S	18E
Gold (specimen), Quartz; Greenstone.	29,32	4S	18E
Gold, Pyrite, Quartz.	12,13	5S	17E
Gold, Quartz; Slate.	11	5S	17E
Gold, Quartz; Slate, Greenstone.	SE¼28NE¼23	4S	17E
Gold, Pyrite, Quartz; Slate.	11	5S	17E
Gold, Quartz; Greenstone.	30	4S	18E
Specimen Gold, Pyrite, Chalcopyrite, Arsenopyrite, Galena, Quartz; Greenstone.	29	4S	18E
Gold, Pyrite, Arsenopyrite, Galena, Niccolite, Millerite, Garnierite, Quartz; Slate, Serpentine.	8,9,16,17	4S	17E
Gold, Pyrite, Chalcopyrite, Galena, Quartz; Greenstone.	29,31,32	4S	18E
Gold, Pyrite, Chalcopyrite, Galena, Quartz; Greenstone.	32	4S	18E

Ben Hur Quadrangle 7½'

Azurite, Malachite, Chalcocite, Cuprite, native Copper, Chalcopyrite, Pyrrhotite.	3,10	8S	18E

Buckhorn Peak Quadrangle 7½'

Gold Pyrite, Galena, Sphalerite, Tetrahedrite, Quartz; Granite.	NW¼7	3S	18E
Gold, Pyrite, Chalcopyrite, Sphalerite, Galena, Quartz; Slate, Schist, Greenstone.	25	2S	17E
Gold, Calcite, Quartz; Slate, Greenstone.	28,33	3S	17E
Gold, Tetrahedrite, Pyrite.	11	3S	17E
Gold, Tetrahedrite, Galena, Arsenopyrite, Quartz; Slate.	1,2	3S	17E
Gold, Pyrite, Chalcopyrite, Arsenopyrite, Galena, Sphalerite, blue and white Quartz; Slate.	NE¼23	2S	17E
Gold, Galena, Sphalerite, Pyrite, Slate, Schist, Quartz.	25,26	2S	17E
Gold, Quartz; Slate.	center 11	3S	17E
Specimen Gold Ore, Galena, Chalcopyrite, Pyrite, blue and white Quartz.	30,31	2S	18E
Gold, Pyrite, Galena, Sphalerite, Tetrahedrite, Quartz; Slate.	15,16	3S	17E
Gold, Quartz; Albitite, Slate, Schist.	34	3S	17E
Limestone.	19,20,29,30	2S	18E

Coulterville Quadrangle 7½'

	SECTION	T.	R.
Chromite, Serpentine.	NE¼29	2S	16E
Chromite, Serpentine.	SW¼27	2S	16E
Chromite, Serpentine.	NE¼22	3S	16E
Pyrite, Chalcopyrite, Malachite, Quartz; Greenstone.	29,30,32	3S	16E
Gold, Galena, Pyrite, Chalcopyrite, Quartz; Ankerite, Mariposite, Serpentine, Slate.	NE¼22,NW¼23	3S	16E
Specimen Gold, Pyrite, Quartz; Serpentine, Slate.	NW¼19	3S	17E
Gold, Pyrite, Quartz-ankerite-mariposite rock, Serpentine.	E¼33	2S	16E
Gold, Quartz-ankerite-mariposite rock.	28	2S	16E
Gold, Galena, Pyrite, Quartz; Greenstone.	35	3S	16E
Gold, Pyrite, Quartz; Ankerite-mariposite rock, Slate, Greenstone.	3	3S	16E
Gold, Pyrite, Quartz-ankerite-mariposite rock, Quartz; Slate.	4.9,10	3S	16E
Gold, Quartz-ankerite-mariposite rock, limonite, Slate, Schist, Serpentine.	3,10,11	3S	16E
Gold, Pyrite, Argentiferous Galena, Quartz-ankerite-mariposite rock, Serpentine, Slate.	36	3S	16E
Gold, Pyrite, Chalcopyrite, Covellite, Quartz.	9,10	3S	16E
Gold, Pyrite, Chalcopyrite, Galena, Quartz-ankerite-mariposite rock (to 100' thick), Serpentine, Slate.	13,14	3S	16E
Cinnabar, Calcite, Sulfur, Greenstone.	15,16	3S	16E
Talc (white, 75' wide), Flyaway Gulch near Hwy. 49.	31	3S	17E

Coulterville-Groveland Quadrangles 7½'

	SECTION	T.	R.
Gold, Pyrite, Chalcopyrite, Quartz-mariposite-ankerite rock, to 200' thick, Limonite, Slate, Serpentine.	19,20,29	2S	16E

Coulterville-Hornitos Quadrangles 7½'

		SECTION	T.	R.
Gold, blue Quartz; Chert, Greenstone.		32,33	3S	16E
	and	4	4S	16E

El Portal Quadrangle 7½'

	SECTION	T.	R.
Barite.	18,19	3S	20E
Gold, Pyrite, Galena, Arsenopyrite, milky and glassy Quartz.	31,32	3S	20E
Gold.	22,26,27	3S	19E

Feliciana Mountain Quadrangle 7½'

		SECTION	T.	R.
Gold, Quartz; Slate, Greenstone.		SW¼13	4S	18E
Gold, Pyrite, Slate, Quartz; Greenstone.		center 27	4S	18E
Gold, Galena, Chalcopyrite, Pyrite, Quartz; Slate, Phyllite.	and	7,8	4S	19E
		12,13	4S	18E
Gold (rich pockets), glassy blue Quartz; Chalcopyrite, Quartz; Granite.		27,34	4S	18E
Specimen Gold,		27	4S	18E
Gold, Quartz; Schist, Serpentine.		12	5S	18E
Gold, glassy and milky Quartz; Pyrite.		17,20	4S	19E
Limestone.		N½NE¼11	4S	18E

150

Hornitos Quadrangle 7½'

	SECTION	T.	R.
Azurite, Chalcocite, Malachite, Pyrite, Chalcopyrite, Quartz; Greenstone.	4,9,10	4S	16E
Gold, Pyrite, Chalcopyrite, Quartz crystals, Slate, Greenstone, Schist.	2	5S	16E
Gold, blue Quartz.	3,4	4S	16E
Gold, Pyrite, Chalcopyrite, Galena, Greenstone.	NW¼24	4S	16E
Gold, Quartz; Basalt, Greenstone, Slate, Chert. and	NW¼4	4S	16E
	SW¼33	3S	16E
Gold, Quartz; Greenstone.	SW¼19	4S	17E
Galena, Sphalerite, Pyrite, Arsenopyrite, Proustite, Argentite, Barite, Quartz; Greenstone.	35,36	4S	16E
Gold, Pyrite, Limonite, Quartz; Slate, Greenstone, Schist.	2,11	5S	16E
Gold, Pyrite, Quartz; Schist, Gneiss, Hornfels.	10	5S	16E
Gold, Sphalerite, Galena, Pyrite, Quartz; Greenstone.	14,15,23	4S	16E
Gold, blue Quartz; Greenstone.	center 10	4S	16E
Gold, Pyrite, Chalcopyrite, Galena, Sphalerite, Arsenopyrite, Quartz; Hornfels, Slate.	28	4S	16E
Gold, Pyrite, Chalcopyrite, Quartz-ankerite-mariposite rock, Schist, Hornfels.	4,5	5S	16E

Illinois Hill Quadrangle 7½'

	SECTION	T.	R.
Azurite, Malachite, Chalcopyrite, Slate, Mica-andalusite Schist, Hornfels. and	32	7S	18E
	5,8,9	8S	18E
Chalcopyrite, Pyrite, Pyrrhotite, Quartz-mica-chiastolite Schist.	NE¼31	7S	18E
Azurite, Malachite, Chrysocolla, Chalcopyrite, Pyrite, Sphalerite, Pyrrhotite, Andalusite-schist.	NW¼12	7S	17E
Muscovite-quartz Schist (100' wide, 1 mile long).	1,2	7S	17E
Quartz vein, Slate.	14	7S	17E

Indian Gulch Quadrangle 7½'

	SECTION	T.	R.
Gold, Pyrite, Chalcopyrite, Galena, Sphalerite, Quartz; Volcanics.	21,28	5S	16E
Gold, Pyrite, Quartz; Greenstone, Schist, Hornfels.	16,21	5S	16E
Sphalerite, Pyrite, Chalcopyrite, Galena, Arsenopyrite, Quartz; Granodiorite.	19	5S	17E
Andalusite, pink crystals. (On Indian Gulch, Planada Ranch road 1¼ miles SW of 3 Buttes).	SW¼17	6S	16E
Slate.	16	6S	16E
Pyrophyllite, crystallized rosettes, golden-yellow with Quartz (on 3 Buttes).	8,16,17	6S	16E
Serpentine (Bastite).	8,16,17	6S	16E

Jawbone Ridge Quadrangle 7½'

	SECTION	T.	R.
Specimen Gold (in black Quartzite).	NW¼15,NE¼16	2S	17E

Kinsley Quadrangle 7½'

	SECTION	T.	R.
Gold, Pyrite, Galena, milky and glassy Quartz.	34	3S	18E

	SECTION	T.	R.
Gold, Pyrite, Galena, Quartz; Slate, Schist.	NE¼23	3S	18E
Limestone (gray to black).	7,18	3S	19E

Mariposa Quadrangle 7½'

	SECTION	T.	R.
Argentite, Proustite, Pyrargyrite, Cerargyrite, native Silver, Pyrite, Galena, Quartz; Granite.	8,9,16,17	6S	19E
Gold, Pyrite, Galena, Sphalerite. and	SW¼3	6S	18E
	NW¼10	6S	18E
Gold, Pyrite, Arsenopyrite, Quartz.	23,24	5S	18E
Gold, Galena, Pyrite, Arsenopyrite, Argentite, Proustite, Pyrargyrite, native Silver.	8,9	6S	19E

Merced Falls Quadrangle 7½'

	SECTION	T.	R.
Psilomelane, Pyrolusite, Rhodochrosite, Chert.	NE¼14	4S	15E
Sphalerite, Pyrite, Chalcopyrite, Galena, Barite, Quartz; Schist.	9,10	4S	15E
Azurite, Malachite, Sphalerite, Pyrite, Galena, Barite, Quartz; Metavolcanics.	N½30	4S	16E
Tetrahedrite, Sphalerite, Pyrite, Galena, Barite, Sericite, Calcite, Quartz.	19,30	4S	16E

MENDOCINO COUNTY

Boonville Quadrangle 15'

	SECTION	T.	R.
Sandstone (yellow-gray, suitable for garden rock or building stone).	16	15N	13W

Covelo Quadrangle 15'

	SECTION	T.	R.
Rhodochrosite.	SE¼SW¼31	23N	11W
Jade.	20,21	24N	11W

Eden Valley Quadrangle 15'

	SECTION	T.	R.
Bementite, Inesite, Neotocite, Rhodochrosite.	SW¼NE¼31	20N	11W

Hopland Quadrangle 15'

	SECTION	T.	R.
Cinnabar, Platinum, Gold, (placer deposit).	SE corner 21	13N	11W
Cinnabar, Serpentine.	NE¼6	12N	11W

Laytonville Quadrangle 15'

	SECTION	T.	R.
Glaucophane Schist, Lawsonite, Stilpnomelane, Riebeckite, in quarry 5.1 miles north of Longvale on U.S. 101.			
Sphene, Lawsonite, Zoisite, at Syke rock 3 miles east of Longvale on road to Covelo.			
Coal.	SE corner 2	21N	13W
Limestone (pink and yellow-gray).	E½ and NW¼36	22N	15W

Leggett Quadrangle 15'

	SECTION	T.	R.
Chromite.	center N½NW¼19	24N	16W
Chromite.	SE¼NW¼5	23N	15W

Ornbaum Valley Quadrangle 15'

		SECTION	T.	R.
Azurite, Chalcopyrite, Tenorite, Tetrahedrite.	and	SE corner 17	12N	13W
		NE corner 20		
Copper (native).		2,3	15N	11W

Point Arena Quadrangle 7½'

Bituminous Sandstone, Diatomaceous Shale, in sea cliffs 1 mile west of Point Arena.

Redwood Valley Quadrangle 7½'

	SECTION	T.	R.
Bementite, Jasper, Psilomelane, Rhodochrosite.	near center 22	17N	12W
Psilomelane, red Chert.	3,10	17N	12W
Psilomelane.	N½15	17N	12W

Ukiah Quadrangle 15'

	SECTION	T.	R.
Sandstone (yellow-gray, suitable for garden rock or build-ing stone).	1	14N	13W

Willits Quadrangle 15'

	SECTION	T.	R.
Limestone (travertine).	center 26	17N	13W

MODOC COUNTY

Davis Creek Quadrangle 15'

Agates, abundant on shore of the south end of Goose Lake.

Willow Ranch Quadrangle 15'

	SECTION	T.	R.
Azurite, Cuprite, native Copper, Limonite, Malachite.	18,19	45N	15E

MONO COUNTY

Benton Quadrangle 15'

	SECTION	T.	R.
Blind Spring Hill Mining District: Many Quartz veins. The following minerals have been found here, Stromeyerite, native Silver, Malachite, Azurite, Galena, Pyrite, Chalcopyrite, Chalcocite, Covellite, Tetrahedrite, Cerussite, Siderite, Anglesite, Cervantite, Kermesite, Massicot, Minium, Pyrargyrite, Stephanite, Stibnite.	section 18	2S	32E

Casa Diablo Mountain Quadrangle 15'

	SECTION	T.	R.
Scheelite, Tactite (Tactite is usually dark colored, medium to coarse grained, composed of one or more of the following minerals; dark-green Pyroxene, dark-green Amphibole, red-brown Garnet, Epidote and Quartz).			
Scheelite, Tactite.	14	3S	31E
Scheelite, Hornfels, Calcareous rocks, Alaskaite.	26	3S	31E
Scheelite, Tactite, Marble, Granodiorite.	10	3S	31E
Powellite, Molybdenite, Scheelite (minor), Tactite.	23	3S	31E
Scheelite, Tactite.	1	3S	30E
Diorite-gabbro, Gold, Pyrite, Galena, Chalcopyrite, Sphalerite, Quartz.	18	3S	31E
Quartz; Granodiorite, Galena, Chalcopyrite, Azurite, Malachite, Gold, Silver.	2	4S	31E
Quartz; Granite, Pyrite, Chalcopyrite, Galena, Gold.	21	4S	31E
Quartz; Granodiorite, Pyrite, Gold, Silver.	8	3S	31E
Quartz; Sericite-andalusite Hornfels, Pyrite, Galena, Gold, Silver.	15	3S	31E
Quartz; Gold, Mica Schist, Pyrite, Galena, Chalcopyrite.	33	3S	31E
Quartz; Hornfels, Rhyolite, Pyrite, Chalcopyrite, Gold, Silver.	28	3S	31E
Gold, Silver, Lead, Hornfels, Diorite, Rhyolite, Quartz.	33	3S	31E
Sphalerite, Pyrite, Galena, Granodiorite, Quartz; Gold, Silver.	3	3S	31E
Alaskaite, Pyrite, Galena, Quartz; Gold, Silver.	6	3S	31E
Magnetite, Hematite, Talc, Epidote-garnet Tactite.	2	3S	31E
Pumice.	35	4S	29E

Glass Mountain Quadrangle 15'

Obsidian, at Glass Mountain.	2S	30E

Mono Craters Quadrangle 15'

Obsidian at Mono Craters.

MONTEREY COUNTY

Alder Peak Quadrangle 7½'

Chromite, Kammererite, Uvarovite (green Garnet), Serpentine.	SW¼29	23S	6E

Bryson Quadrangle 7½'

Diatomite.	18	24S	9E

Burro Mountain Quadrangle 7½'

Chrysotile, Serpentine.	SE¼SW¼2,SE¼3	24S	6E
Chromite, Serpentine.	NW¼26	24S	6E
Chromite, Serpentine.	N½27	24S	6E
Cinnabar, Metacinnabar, Pyrite, Calcite, Sandstone.	SE¼28	24S	6E

154

Cape San Martin Quadrangle 7½'

	SECTION	T.	R.
Chrysotile, Serpentine.	30,31,NW¼32	23S	5E
Nephrite Jade in Schist and in the beach Sands and Gravels south of Plaskett Creek.	and W½19	23S	5E
	NE¼31	23S	5E

The Dark Hole Quadrangle 7½'

	SECTION	T.	R.
Chrysotile, Serpentine, Talc.	30	23S	16E
Azurite, Malachite, Serpentine.	21	23S	15E
Chalcocite, Serpentine.	26	23S	15E
Magnesite, small lenses in Serpentine.	28	23S	15E
Magnesite, small lenses in Serpentine.	26	23S	15E
Cinnabar, Silica Carbonate rock, Serpentine.	NE¼30	23S	16E

Gonzales Quadrangle 7½'

	SECTION	T.	R.
Feldspar, in Pegmatite and coarse Granite.	SE¼28	15S	5E

Lopez Point Quadrangle 7½'

	SECTION	T.	R.
Rhodonite (pink, gem variety), in boulders at mouth of Limekiln Creek.	22	22S	4E

Parkfield Quadrangle 7½'

	SECTION	T.	R.
Cinnabar, Silica-carbonate rock, Serpentine.	E½2	23S	14E
Cinnabar, Silica-carbonate rock, Serpentine.	W½1	23S	14E
Cinnabar, Silica-carbonate rock, Serpentine.	NE¼2	23S	14E

Priest Valley Quadrangle 15'

	SECTION	T.	R.
Coal.	17,21	20S	12E
Coal.	14	22S	13E
Jasper, Chalcedony (white, blue, black, takes high polish, private property).	SW¼16	22S	13E

San Ardo Quadrangle 15'

	SECTION	T.	R.
Chromite (boulders), in Cow Creek at Hwy 198, also Uvarovite (green Garnet).	SW¼9	20S	11E

San Juan Batista Quadrangle 7½'

	SECTION	T.	R.
Barite (in Limestone and Dolomite).	SE¼34	13S	4E

Soberanes Point Quadrangle 7½'

	SECTION	T.	R.
Coal.	E½1	17S	1W

Stockdale Mountain Quadrangle 7½'

	SECTION	T.	R.
"Sand Calcite crystals." (Cholame Hills).	14,23	23S	13E

Sycamore Flat Quadrangle 7½'

	SECTION	T.	R.
Cinnabar, Calcite, Sandstone, Granodiorite.	SW¼31	18S	5E

Thompson Canyon Quadrangle 7½'

Diatomite.	28,33,34	19S	7E
Diatomite.	13,14,24	20S	7E

Villa Creek Quadrangle 7½'

Chromite (float in soil), Serpentine.	NW¼3	24S	5E
Stibnite.	W½1	24S	5E

NAPA COUNTY

Aetna Springs Quadrangle 7½'

Chalcopyrite, Serpentine.	17	10N	5W
Manganiferous Chert, Greenstone.	NE¼31	10N	5W
Manganese minerals.	18	10N	5W
Cinnabar, Metacinnabar, Millerite.	2,3	9N	6W

Calistoga Quadrangle 15'

Pyrargyrite, Proustite, Argentite, Arsenopyrite, Dewey-lite, Galena, Gypsum (good crystals), Marcasite, Melanterite.	24	9N	7W
Manganiferous Iron Ore.	3	9N	6W

Capell Quadrangle 7½'

Chrysotile, Serpentine.	SE¼4,SW¼3	7N	3W

Detert Reservoir Quandrangle 7½'

Argentite, Cerargyrite, Gold, Quartz crystals.	SE¼SW¼2	9N	7W
Cinnabar, Epsomite, Calomel, Metacinnabar, Millerite.	NE¼33	10N	6W
Cinnabar.	NW¼4	10N	6W
Cinnabar, Silica-carbonate rock.	32,33	10N	6W
Cinnabar.	S½34	10N	6W

Knoxville Quadrangle 7½'

Aragotite, Barite, Botroygen (red, small crystals), Calomel, Cinnabar, Coquimbite (yellow-green), Curtisite, Epsomite, Fibroferrite, Hohmannite (in Opal), Marcasite, Melanterite, Metacinnabar, Mirabilite, Opal, Pyrolusite, Redingtonite (pale purple), Stibnite, Sulfur, Voltaite (black cubic crystals), Knoxvillite.	6,7	11N	4W
Cinnabar, Jamesonite, Pyrolusite, Stibnite, banded silicified Tuff.	1	11N	5W
Chromite.	SW¼SE¼18	11N	4W

	SECTION	T.	R.
Manganese minerals, Chert, Greenstone.	32	11N	4W
Copper minerals.	1	11N	5W

Lake Berryessa Quadrangle 15' or 7½'

	SECTION	T.	R.
Ammonite fossils (Upper Jurassic).	near center E½29	8N	3W

From oil prospect tunnel near the Hwy. in bluff on east side of Capell Creek.

Napa Quadrangle 7½'

	SECTION	T.	R.
Pumice.	24,25	6N	4W

St. Helena Quadrangle 15'

	SECTION	T.	R.
Chromite.	32,36	10N	5W
Magnesite.	2	9N	5W
Magnesite (green).	28	8N	4W
Manganiferous Chert, Greenstone.	SE¼20	9N	4W
Obsidian.	23	8N	6W

NEVADA COUNTY

Alleghany Quadrangle 7½'

LODE GOLD:

	SECTION	T.	R.
Slate.	8	18N	11E
Slate, Granite, Granodiorite, Pyrite, Arsenopyrite, Galena, Chalcopyrite, some blue Quartz.	21,22,27,28,33	18N	11E
Slate, Sulfides.	8,17	18N	11E
Amphibolite, specimen Gold Ore from here was associated with Arsenopyrite.	15	18N	10E
Barite, White to creamy, massive.	NW¼19	18N	11E

Dutch Flat Quadrangle 7½'

	SECTION	T.	R.
Barite, vari-colored, pink, gray, black.	24	16N	10E

Emmigrant Gap Quadrangle 15'

LODE GOLD:

	SECTION	T.	R.
Diabase Porphyry.	6	18N	13E
Granite, Slate, Pyrite, Galena, Chalcopyrite.	21	18N	11E
Pyrite, Arsenopyrite, Sphalerite, Quartz veins to 45' thick.	27	18N	13E
Granite, Slate, light blue Quartz; Galena, Silver.	15,16	18N	11E
Quartz Porphyry, Sulfides.	9	18N	12E
Granite.	26,27,34	18N	11E
Pyrite, Galena, Sphalerite.	35	18N	11E

Grass Valley Quadrangle 7½'

LODE GOLD: Generally in Quartz veins, associated rocks and minerals also listed.

	SECTION	T.	R.
Pyrite, Chalcopyrite, Galena.	2,11	15N	8E

	SECTION	T.	R.
Amphibolite, Diabase, Gabbro, Diorite, Sulfides.	5	15N	8E
Amphibolite, Gabbro, Pyrite.	20,29,30	16N	8E
Granodiorite.	11	15N	8E
Granodiorite, Diabase, Galena, Pyrite.	1	15N	8E
Amphibolite, Pyrite, specimen Gold came from here.	24,25	16N	8E
Amphibolite, Galena, Pyrite, Chalcopyrite.	25,36	16N	8E
Granodiorite, Diabase, Pyrite, Galena.	1,2	15N	8E
Slate, Granodiorite.	17	16N	8E
Serpentine, Slate, Pyrite, Chalcopyrite, Galena.	27	16N	8E
Diabase Porphyry.	26	16N	8E
Granodiorite, Diabase, Pyrite, Galena, Chalcopyrite.	2,3	15N	8E
Granodiorite, Slate.	29	16N	8E
Serpentine, Mariposite, Pyrite.	25,26	16N	8E
Volcanics, Slate, Diabase.	6	15N	9E
Granodiorite, Sulfides.	11,15	15N	8E
Diabase.	1,12	15N	8E
Slate, Sulfides, some specimen Gold.	34	16N	8E
Amphibolite, Diorite, Gabbro, 5-10% Sulfides, gulches in the area were rich with placer Gold eroded from the veins.	31	16N	8E
Chromite, Serpentine.	21	16N	8E
Chromite, Serpentine.	26	16N	8E
Chromite, Serpentine.	21	16N	8E
Chromite, Serpentine.	4	15N	8E
Chromite, Serpentine.	25	16N	8E

Lake Combie Quadrangle 7½'

Stibnite.	SW¼25	15N	8E
Chromite, Serpentine.	5	14N	8E
LODE GOLD:			
Diabase, Slate, Calcite, Chalcopyrite.	20,29	14N	8E

Nevada City Quadrangle 7½'

LODE GOLD:			
Granodiorite.	12	16N	8E
Slate, Granodiorite, Pyrite, Galena, Chalcopyrite, Sphalerite.	2,11,13,14	16N	8E
Diorite, Aplite, Slate, Pyrite, Galena, Sphalerite.	3	16N	8E
Granodiorite, Limonite, Sulfides.	36	17N	8E
CHROMITE:			
Chromite, Serpentine.	SW¼SE¼11	16N	8E
Chromite, Serpentine.	E½SW¼11	16N	8E

North Bloomfield Quadrangle 7½'

LODE GOLD:			
Granodiorite, Slate.	9	16N	9E
Granodiorite, Slate, Pyrite, Arsenopyrite, Galena.	10	16N	9E
Granodiorite, Stibnite, some specimen Gold from here.	9	16N	9E
Diorite, Molybdenite, Tetrahedrite.	16	16N	9E
Granodiorite, some rich placer specimens came from this area.	11	16N	9E

Rough & Ready Quadrangle 7½'

	SECTION	T.	R.
Amphibolite, Diabase, Gabbro, Diorite, Sulfides.	6	15N	8E
Amphibolite, Gabbro, specimen Ore was found here.	25,30	16N	7E
Granodiorite, Sulfides.	36	17N	8E
CHROMITE:			
Chromite, Serpentine.	6	15N	8E

Smartville Quadrangle 7½'

	SECTION	T.	R.
COPPER:			
Pyrite, Chalcopyrite, Galena, Sphalerite, Epidote, Calcite, Quartz.	13	15N	6E
Malachite, Bornite, Chalcopyrite, Pyrite, Quartz.	12	15N	6E
Chalcopyrite, Pyrite.	25,27	15N	6E

Washington Quadrangle 7½'

	SECTION	T.	R.
LODE GOLD:			
Schist, Serpentine, Pyrite, Chalcopyrite.	2	17N	10E
Serpentine, Slate, Chromite, Ankerite, Mariposite, specimen Gold from here.	12,13	17N	10E
Serpentine, Slate, Ankerite, Dolomite.	1	17N	10E
Schist, Slate, Sulfides.	14,23	16N	10E
Slate, Sulfides.	9	17N	11E
ASBESTOS:			
Chrysotile in Serpentine.	2,11	17N	10E
CHROMITE:			
Chromite, Serpentine.	1	17N	10E

PLACER COUNTY

Auburn Quadrangle 7½'

	SECTION	T.	R.
Gold, Pyrite, Galena, Sulfides, assays $10-15 ton.	E½SE¼18	12N	8E
Gold, Quartz; Pyrite, Chalcopyrite, Ore in small rich shoots but generally low grade. Vein is in Amphibolite Schist.	17	12N	8E
Gold, Silver, Quartz; Pyrite, Galena, Argentite, Granodiorite, ($7-8 Ore).	NW¼17	12N	8E
Gold, Quartz; Amphibolite Schist. Rich Ore mined in the the 1870's, two weeks run produced $50,000. ½ mile NE Ophir.	8	12N	8E
Gold, Quartz; Amphibolite Schist, rich pocket mine, yielded $150,000.	29	13N	8E
Gold, Quartz; Pyrite, Chalcopyrite, Galena, Greenstone, some good pockets.	NW¼30	13N	8E
Gold, Quartz; vein 1,000' long in Amphibolite Schist, good Ore from shallow workings.	17	12N	8E
Gold, Silver, Pyrite, Galena, Granodiorite, Schist, some specimen Ore but averaged about $8 ton. One shoot produced $90,000.	7,8	12N	8E
Sphalerite, yellow and transparent.	NE¼17	12N	8E
Gold, Quartz; electrum (Gold and Silver), Granodiorite, Schist, pocket mine (produced $180,000.)	17	12N	8E

Blue Canyon Quadrangle 7½'

	SECTION	T.	R.
Gold, 3 veins in Blue Canyon slate, low grade. South of Bear River.	3	16N	11E
Gold, Quartz; Blue Canyon slate, 1½ miles SE of Blue Canyon.	14	16N	11E

Camp Far West Quadrangle 7½'

	SECTION	T.	R.
Gold, Silver, Copper, Porphyry, Amphibolite Schist.	S½27	14N	6E

Chicago Park Quadrangle 7½'

	SECTION	T.	R.
Gold, Silver, Sulfide lens in slate, some good Ore.	SE¼SE¼13	15N	9E

Colfax Quadrangle 7½'

	SECTION	T.	R.
Gold, Quartz; Pyrite, Limonite, Schist.	24,25	14N	9E
Gold, Quartz; Diabase, Gabbro, (0.6 oz. Gold).	S½33	15N	9E
Gold, Pyrite, Slate, was good producer.	SW¼35	14N	9E
Gold, Quartz; some good assays.	SW¼23	14N	9E
Gold, Quartz; Sulfides, Diabase walls, $20 Ore (rich pockets produced over $2,000,000).	33,34	15N	9E
Gold, Quartz; vein at contact of Serpentine and Calaveras formation. In Codfish Canyon.	3	13N	9E
Gold, Quartz; Mudstone, Graywacke, fine Gold reported. and	W½25 E½26	14N	9E
Gold, Quartz; abundant Sulfides, Pyrite, Arsenopyrite, Tetrahedrite, Conglomerate, Slate, Quartzite.	17	14N	9E
Placer Gold, drift mine, was rich in coarse Gold.	SE¼5	14N	10E
Chrysotile, Serpentine.	SE¼35	15N	9E
Tremolite, Serpentine.	NE¼2	14N	9E
Limestone, 400' long and 200' thick, dark-gray veined with white and black Calcite. Along SE bank of Bear River.	NW corner 4	14N	9E

Duncan Peak Quadrangle 7½'

	SECTION	T.	R.
Gold, Quartz; Pyrite, Galena, Blue Canyon formation; Slate, Quartzite, Greenstone. $34 Ore.	5	15N	13E
Gold, Quartz; igneous dike contains coarse Pyrite in Blue Canyon formation. Near head of Antone Canyon.	4	15N	13E

Foresthill Quadrangle 7½'

	SECTION	T.	R.
Placer Gold, on divide between first and second Brushy Canyons.	N½27	14N	10E
Placer Gold, Gravel average $6 ton.	3,4	14N	10E
Placer Gold, yielded $1,000,000.	27,33,34	15N	10E
Drift Gold mine, cemented Gravels average $7 ton, Gravel 150' above bedrock produced much Gold.	23,24	14N	10E
Placer Gold, yielded $5,000,000.	21	14N	11E
Gold, Quartz; Slate, basic dikes and sills carry abundant Pyrite, on slope of the north side of the middle fork of the American River.	33	14N	11E

160

	SECTION	T.	R.
Gold, Ankerite vein in Serpentine, (Gold, $53 a ton).	30,31	14N	11E
Gold, Ankerite, Serpentine, $18 ton.	30	14N	11E
Gold, Quartz; in Ladys canyon near Mosquito ridge, Quartz in Volcanics and Serpentine, small fortune taken out. Some crystallized Gold pockets in this area.	and SE¼30 SW¼29	14N 14N	11E 11E
Gold, 3' Quartz vein, on west bank of the north fork of Shirttail Canyon upstream from the junction with Snail Canyon, some good assays.	25	15N	10E
Gold, Quartz lode at contact of Serpentine intrusion, vein 3-4' wide, high grade in small bunches along the hanging wall. (In Volcano Canyon).	31	14N	11E
Chromite, massive lenses in Serpentine, on NW side of Volcano Canyon.	N½30	14N	11E
Tremolite Asbestos in Serpentine, NW corner of Roach Hill.	E½28	15N	10E
Chrysotile, Serpentine.	S½33	15N	10E
Pyrite, crystals and lenses of Pyrite abundant in Slate and Greenstone, west central part of section 33 close to Mosquito Ridge road.	33	14N	11E
Chrysotile, long fibers in Serpentine.	28,33	15N	10E
Gold, Quartz.	13,14	14N	10E
Gold, Quartz; some pockets of crystallized Gold. In Lady Canyon.	31,32	15N	11E

Gold Hill Quadrangle 7½'

	SECTION	T.	R.
Gold, Quartz; Sulfides, Granodiorite, produced $350,000.	and 12 7	12N 12N	7E 8E
Gold, Sulfides, Granodiorite.	12	12N	7E
Gold, Quartz; Granodiorite, produced $6,000.	SW¼NW¼12	12N	7E
Gold, Silver, Sulfides, vein been traced 8,000' in Granodiorite and Amphibolite Schist. ½ mile SW of the town of Ophir.	18	12N	8E
Gold, glassy Quartz; Stibnite, Pyrite, Galena, Granodiorite, Diorite dike. ½ mile NW Ophir.	7	12N	8E
Gold, Quartz; Amphibolite, Granodiorite.	SW¼SE¼7	12N	8E
Azurite, Malachite, native Copper.	9	13N	7E

Lake Combie Quadrangle 7½'

	SECTION	T.	R.
Chalcopyrite, Pyrite.	4	13N	8E

Lincoln Quadrangle 7½'

	SECTION	T.	R.
Native Copper.	24	13N	6E

Michigan Bluff Quadrangle 7½'

	SECTION	T.	R.
Gold, Quartz seams.	22	14N	11E
Gold, Quartz. Produced a few thousand dollars.	29	15N	12E

Gold, Quartz; Ankerite, Mariposite, Graphite Schist. High grade Ore in bunches, also specimen Ore. This area extends 2 miles along a dike of Serpentine and its contact with Schists. Located in Volcano Canyon 1 mile north of the Middle Fork of the American River.

Placerville Quadrangle 7½'

	SECTION	T.	R.
Gold, Quartz; Slate ($20 Ore).	center SW¼31	10N	11E
Gold, Quartz; Slate, Greenstone.	S½SW¼31	10N	11E
Gold, Quartz; Slate.	SW¼SE¼30	10N	11E
Gold, Quartz.	NW¼SW¼29	10N	11E
Gold, Quartz; Slate.	N½NW¼29	10N	11E
Limestone.	27,28	10N	11E
Placer Gold.	NE¼16	10N	11E
Drift Gold mine ($3.25 yard).	NE¼SE¼17	10N	11E
Drift Gold mine.	center 17	10N	11E
Gold, Quartz.	E½18	10N	11E
Gold, Quartz; Slate.	center N½6	10N	11E
Gold, Quartz; Slate, 3% Pyrite, ($3-6.50 Ore).	NW¼8	10N	11E
Gold, Pyrite, Calcite, Talc, Schist, Slate, some rich free Gold pockets at contacts of vein and country rock.	SE¼21	10N	10E
Gold, Quartz; Slate.	NW¼27	10N	10E
Gold, Slate, Quartz.	NE¼1	9N	10E
Gold, Quartz; Quartz Porphyry.	N½NE¼1	9N	10E
Gold, Quartz.	SW¼SE¼3	9N	10E
Gold, Quartz; Diorite Porphyry, ($4 to $25 Ore).	SW corner 11	9N	10E
Gold, Quartz Porphyry, Greenstone, Pyrite, Arsenopy-rite, some high grade produced.	NW¼SW¼11	9N	10E
Gold, Quartz; Granodiorite.	NW¼11	9N	10E
Gold, Quartz.	E½NW¼11	9N	10E
Gold, Quartz; Slate, Diabase.	SE¼SW¼11	9N	10E
Gold, Quartz; Slate, small rich shoots.	SE¼SE¼11	9N	10E
Gold, Quartz; Slate, Sulfides, (best Ore $30).	NW¼12	9N	10E
Gold, Quartz; Slate.	SW¼NE¼12	9N	10E
Gold, Quartz; Slate.	N½NE¼12	9N	10E
Gold, Quartz; Slate.	SE¼NW¼13	9N	10E
Rhodonite, Manganese Oxides, Chert, Schist.	S½NE¼13	9N	10E
Gold, Quartz; Slate, Greenstone, Mariposite, Ankerite.	NE¼SE¼13	9N	10E

Rocklin Quadrangle 7½'

Gold, Quartz; Sulfides, Granodiorite, $17 Ore, best Ore was associated with Sphalerite.	35,36	12N	7E

Royal Gorge Quadrangle 7½'

Gold, Quartz; Diabase Porphyry, good surface Ore, lower grade with depth and increasing Sulfides.	32	16N	14E

Westville Quadrangle 7½'

Gold, Quartz; Slate, Schist, low grade Ore. North of the mouth of Humbug Creek.	3	15N	12E
Gold, Quartz; Blue Canyon Slate.	34,35	16N	11E
Gold, Quartz; Sulfides, Slate, igneous dike. Vein average 4' wide, $9-21 Ore. Was a large producer.	3,4,10	15N	11E
Gold, Quartz; Sulfides, Slate, dike rocks. Produced $300,000. Ore ran about $7. Located on Texas Ridge.	4	15N	11E
Gold, Quartz; Slate, igneous dike, ($3-5 ton, some higher).	4	15N	11E

PLUMAS COUNTY

Almanor Quadrangle 15'

	SECTION	T.	R.
LODE GOLD:			
Slate, Greenstone, Pyrite, Arsenopyrite, some rich pocket Gold.	9	26N	8E
Slate, Serpentine, Limestone, Sulfides.	17,18	25N	8E
Slate, Arsenopyrite, nearby Rich Gulch yielded $9 million in the early days.	1,12	25N	7E
Slate, Serpentine, Schist, Sulfides.	36	27N	8E
Slate, Serpentine, Sulfides.	12	25N	7E
Slate, Schist, Sulfides.	15	26N	8E
Slate, Andesite.	29,30	26N	9E
Slate.	16	26N	8E
Serpentine, Andesite, Limonite, Sulfides.	26,35	27N	8E
Slate, Andesite, Quartzite, Greenstone.	29,30	26N	9E
Quartzite, Schist, Slate, Calcite, Sulfides, some large pieces of angular Gold were found in the Gravels in this area.	9	25N	8E
Slate, Andesite, Sulfides.	5	26N	8E
Slate, Calcite, Sulfides (Ore, maximum $14 a ton).	2	25N	7E
PLACER GOLD:			
On Soda Ravine, tributary to Mosquito Creek, creek Gravel carried smooth coarse Gold and rough Quartz Gold.	28	26N	7E
GOLD DRIFT MINES: Gold mined from Gravels by underground methods.			
Gravels ran $10 a yard.	8,17	26N	8E
Rose Quartz boulders, Gold ran $4.50 per square foot of bedrock.	2	25N	8E
Rich surface placers here in the past, also Lode Gold in the area.	18	26N	8E
Limestone.	6,7,8,16,17,21,28	25N	8E
Barite, large lenses in Slate.	5	26N	8E
Barite.	32	27N	8E

Blairsden Quadrangle 15'

	SECTION	T.	R.
LODE GOLD:			
Andesite, Slate, Limonite, Chalcocite, Chalcopyrite, Manganese Oxides.	25,26	25N	11E
COPPER:			
Tetrahedrite, Bornite, Chalcopyrite (to 7% Copper).	7	24N	12E
Azurite.	1,11,12	24N	11E
Tridymite, crystals in Andesite (on Smith Peak road).	11	23N	13E

Blue Nose Mountain Quadrangle 7½'

	SECTION	T.	R.
LODE GOLD:			
Slate, Sulfides, some assays to $1,700 a ton.	5	22N	11E
Slate, Limonite, Arsenopyrite.	10,15	22N	10E
Augite Porphyry (about $50 ton).	32	23N	11E
and	5	22N	11E
Slate, abundant Arsenopyrite ($25 Ore).	9	22N	10E
Slate, Porphyry, Sulfides, rose Quartz; free Gold in glassy Quartz; Arsenopyrite.	3	22N	10E

163

Bucks Lake Quadrangle 15'

Lode Gold, associated with Quartz veins and generally associated with one or more of the following Sulfides, Pyrite, Arsenopyrite, Galena, Sphalerite, Chalcopyrite. The wall rocks enclosing the vein are generally included in the following lists.

	SECTION	T.	R.
Diorite, Porphyry, Sulfides.	15	22N	8E
Granite, Diorite, Pyrite.	30	23N	7E
Serpentine, Slate, some coarse surface Gold has been mined here.	10	23N	7E
Diorite Porphyry, Mica Schist, Galena, Chalcopyrite.	35	23N	8E
Quartzite, Slate, Sulfides.	34	25N	8E
Schist, Dolomite, Limonite, Chalcopyrite, some rich pockets of Gold were mined here.	33	24N	8E
Slate, Galena, Chalcopyrite.	5,7	22N	7E
Dolomite, Chalcedony, Manganese Oxides. Rich free Gold was mined here 200' below the surface.	23	24N	8E
Quartzite, Slate, Sulfides.	29,30	25N	9E
Siliceous Dolomite.	29	24N	8E
Diorite, Slate, Schist, Galena, Pyrite, rich surface pockets mined here.	35	23N	8E
Granite, Sulfides.	4,5	23N	7E
Granite.	26	24N	7E
Granite, Sulfides.	28,33	24N	7E
Slate, Schist, Serpentine, Sulfides, some rich pockets.	5,6	24N	8E
Granite, Diorite, glassy Quartz crystals; Sulfides.	30,31	23N	7E
Diorite, Galena, Chalcopyrite, some surface Ore ran over $100 a ton.	30	23N	7E

Chilcoot Quadrangle 15'

LODE GOLD:

	SECTION	T.	R.
Granite, Malachite, Azurite, Chalcopyrite, Bornite, Chalcocite, Graphite, Molybdenite (to 6% Copper).	25	24N	16E

Greenville Quadrangle 15'

LODE GOLD:

	SECTION	T.	R.
Porphyry, conglomerate, Calcite, Copper minerals.	25	27N	10E
Porphyry, Limestone.	24	25N	10E
and	19	25N	11E
Granite, Andesite, Slate, Calcite, Pyrite, Chalcopyrite.	1,2,3,10,11,14	27N	10E
Slate, Granodiorite, Serpentine, Rhyolite, some rich pockets of Gold.	14,23	26N	9E
Granodiorite, Rhyolite, Sulfides.	11	26N	9E
Rhyolite, Granodiorite, Serpentine, Limonite, Manganese Oxides, Sulfides.	9,10,15,16	26N	9E
Slate, Serpentine, Rhyolite, Pyrite.	24	26N	9E
Andesite, Sandstone, Bornite, some 10% Copper Ore.	6	25N	11E
Granodiorite, Andesite, Sulfides.	12	27N	10E
Granodiorite, Andesite, Calcite, Limonite, Bornite, Malachite, Azurite, some Silver to 15 oz.; Copper to 48%.	1,12,13	27N	10E
Slate, Greenstone, Sulfides, Azurite (to 10%).	3	25N	9E
Rhyolite, Sulfides.	10,11	26N	9E
Andesite, Barite, Malachite, Azurite.	32	27N	11E
Sandstone, Slate, Serpentine, Malachite, Azurite, some solid lenses of Nickel bearing Pyrrhotite, Copper to 12%.	2	25N	10E

164

	SECTION	T.	R.
Augite Porphyry, Sulfides.	25	25N	10E
Slate, Porphyry, Sulfides.	32,33	26N	9E
Quartz Porphyry, Pyrite.	10,15	26N	9E
Felsite Porphyry, Schist, Pyrolusite, Malachite, Azurite, Bornite, Chalcocite.	7	26N	11E
Granodiorite.	32,33	26N	10E
Rhyolite.	13	26N	9E
Granodiorite, Rhyolite, Limonite.	11,14	26N	9E
LODE GOLD:			
Rhyolite, Diorite, Pyrite (Pyrite concentrates ran over $100 a ton). Ore averaged $20-30 a ton.	10,11	26N	9E
Rhyolite, rich pocket Gold from the surface to over 50' associated with finely disseminated Galena. Vein strikes N32W, dip vertical.	23	26N	9E
Braunite, Piemontite (abundant).	27	26N	9E
Tetrahedrite (Argentiferous).	24	27N	10E
COPPER:			
Granodiorite, Norite, Chalcocite, Covellite, Bornite, Limonite, Malachite, Chrysocolla.	4	27N	11E
Schist, Bornite, Malachite, Azurite.	32,33	26N	9E

Kettle Rock Quadrangle 15'

	SECTION	T.	R.
LODE GOLD:			
Andesite, Schist, Bornite.	23,24	25N	11E
Granodiorite, Slate, Limestone.	2	25N	11E
Andesite, Porphyry, Chalcopyrite, some Silver.	14	26N	11E
Granodiorite, Slate, Limestone; Malachite, Azurite, some solid masses of Chalcopyrite and Bornite in Slate and Limestone.	3	25N	11E
Granodiorite, Limestone; Bornite, Chalcocite, some rich Silver Ore, (to 160 oz.).	31	26N	12E
Andesite, Schist, Slate, Sulfides, Chalcocite (contained good Silver and Gold values).	23	25N	11E
Andesite, Slate, Schist, Calcite, Tetrahedrite, Limonite and Manganese Oxides contained pockets of Gold.	14	25N	11E
Andesite, Hematite, Copper Ores (to 4%).	24	26N	11E
Andesite, Schist, Copper Sulfides, Silver to 43 oz.	14,15	25N	11E
Meta-andesite, free Gold values to $700 ton, Silver to 20 oz.; Copper to 6%; Bornite, Tetrahedrite.	15,22	25N	11E
Andesite, Slate, Chalcopyrite.	13,14	25N	11E
COPPER:			
Bornite, Malachite, Azurite.	15	25N	11E

Milford Quadrangle 15'

	SECTION	T.	R.
COPPER:			
Diorite, Schist, Limonite, Chalcopyrite, Bornite, Magnetite.	21,28	26N	15E

Onion Valley Quadrangle 7½'

	SECTION	T.	R.
LODE GOLD:			
Schist, Serpentine.	13,14	23N	9E

	SECTION	T.	R.
Serpentine, Slate, Schist, Arsenopyrite, Pyrite.	30	23N	10E
Serpentine, Schist, Mariposite.	24	23N	9E
Slate, Kaolin (about $18 Ore).	20	23N	10E
Schist, Slate, Serpentine, Limonite (outcrop will pan free Gold).	11	23N	9E
CHROMITE:			
Chromite, Serpentine.	14	23N	9E

Pulga Quadrangle 15'

	SECTION	T.	R.
LODE GOLD:			
Granite, Pyrite.	25,30	23N	6E
Granite, Porphyry, Chalcopyrite.	26	23N	6E
Sulfides.	25	23N	6E
Granite, Sulfides.	25	23N	6E
Slate.	12	22N	6E
Granite, Sulfides, rich specimen Ore was found here, one small shoot produced $20,000.	24	23N	6E

Quincy Quadrangle 7½'

	SECTION	T.	R.
LODE GOLD:			
Slate, Pyrite, Manganese Oxides.	3	24N	9E
Slate, Pyrite.	10	24N	9E
Slate, Basalt, Pyrite.	25,26	24N	9E
Slate, Pyrite (Ore averaged about $20 ton).	34	25N	9E
Quartzite, Slate, Pyrite.	34	25N	9E
GOLD DRIFT MINES:			
Gold in Gravels on bedrock as high as $4 a square foot.	10	24N	9E

RIVERSIDE COUNTY

Big Maria Mountains Quadrangle 15'

	SECTION	T.	R.
Malachite, Azurite, Limestone, Diorite.	17,18	4S	22E

Chuckwalla Mountains Quadrangle 15'

	SECTION	T.	R.
Gold, Malachite, Azurite, Pyrite, Quartz; Granite.	31,32	6S	16E
Gold, Quartz; Granite, some high grade Ore.	33	6S	15E
Gold, Quartz; Pyrite, Granite, Porphyry, some good Ore.	5	7S	15E
Scheelite, Granite, Limestone.	32	6S	16E
Scheelite, Epidote, Garnet, Diorite, Schist, large Scheelite crystals (½" or more) in Diorite dike.	28	7S	15E

Corona Quadrangle 15'

	SECTION	T.	R.
Stibnite, in veins on the ridge SE of Mabey Canyon, a few large boulders in overburden.	8	4S	7W

Dale Lake Quadrangle 15'

	SECTION	T.	R.
Malachite, Azurite, Quartz; Granite, Schist.	9	2S	1E

Hemet Quadrangle 15'

	SECTION	T.	R.
Kunzite, beryl, black, pink and green tourmaline, rose Quartz; in Pegmatite dike in Granite.	32,33	6S	2E
Beryl, yellow and pale green, Columbite.	NW¼SW¼33	6S	2E
Andalusite, large pink crystals in Pegmatite dike, beryl and rose Quartz.	29	6S	2E
Monazite, rose Quartz.	20	7S	2E

Idyllwild Quadrangle 15'

	SECTION	T.	R.
Smoky Quartz crystals in Pegmatite near Tripp Flats.	2	7S	2E

Midland Quadrangle 15'

	SECTION	T.	R.
Chrysocolla, Malachite, Azurite, Bornite, Granite, Schist.	2,3	4S	20E
Chrysocolla, Malachite, Azurite, Bornite, Granite, Schist.	27,34,35	3S	20E
Chalcocite, Cuprite, Malachite, Azurite, Quartz-Calcite, Schist, Granite.	29,30	4S	20E
Psilomelane, Quartz; Porphyry.	13,14	4S	19E
Manganite, Pyrolusite, Psilomelane, Limestone.	8	4S	21E
Fluorite, Quartzite, Schist.	27	3S	20E

Murrieta Quadrangle 7½'

	SECTION	T.	R.
Chrysocolla, Cuprite, Chalcopyrite, Pyrite, Gold, Silver, Schist, Granite.	25	6S	4W
Magnesite, veins in Serpentine. and	NW¼30	5S	1W
	NW¼31	5S	1W

Palen Mountains Quadrangle 15'

	SECTION	T.	R.
Fluorspar, Malachite, Azurite, Diorite, Limestone.	4	3S	18E
Gypsum, Limestone, Granite.	2,3,4,9,10,11	3S	18E

Palm Desert Quadrangle 15'

	SECTION	T.	R.
Scheelite, Garnet, Epidote, Quartz; Granite, Schist.	20	7S	5E
Scheelite, Garnet, Epidote.	28	7S	5E
Scheelite, Garnet, Epidote, Granite, Limestone.	2	8S	6E
Scheelite, Garnet, Epidote, Limestone, Granite, ½ mile south of Pinyon Flat.	11	7S	5E
Amphibole Asbestos in Serpentine, north of Pinyon Flat.	32,35	6S	5E
Amphibole Asbestos in Olivene-hornblende rock.	29	6S	5E

Pinto Basin Quadrangle 15'

	SECTION	T.	R.
Gold, Quartz. $15 Ore.	15,16	2S	12E
Gold, Chalcopyrite, Pyrite, Limonite, Hematite, Limestone; Quartz Diorite, (Ore average $10).	27	3S	13E
Gold, Quartz; Granite, Ore shoots ran $25-40 a ton.	5	3S	12E

San Jacinto Quadrangle 7½'

	SECTION	T.	R.
Corundum, large crystals.	5	4S	1E

Vidal Quadrangle 15'

	SECTION	T.	R.
Gold, Malachite, Azurite, Chalcopyrite, Quartz; Granite, Schist. (0.4 oz. Gold, 1-3% Copper).	25,26	1S	23E
Chrysocolla, Gold, Calcite, Barite, Schist, Limestone. (1,500' vein).	35,36	1S	23E
Copper, Gold, Silver, Limonite, Manganese Dioxides, Diabase, Limestone, Schist. (10-$35 Ore).	36	1S	24E
Scheelite.	25,36	1S	23E

SAN BENITO COUNTY

Hernandez Valley Quadrangle 15'

	SECTION	T.	R.
Chalcopyrite, at Lewis Creek.	2,3,4	19S	10E
Coal.	20,21	17S	10E
Gypsum.	15	18S	9E
Gypsum.	11,32	18S	10E
Gypsum.	5	19S	10E
Cinnabar.	36	18S	11E

New Idria Quadrangle 15'

	SECTION	T.	R.
Chrysotile, Serpentine, on Picacho Creek.	near center 25	18S	11E
Chromite, Serpentine.	5	18S	12E
Uvarovite, Kammererite, Serpentine.	SW¼21	18S	12E
Benitoite, blue (rare gem variety).	NW¼25	18S	12E
CINNABAR: Generally in Silica-carbonate rock, Opal or Siliceous veins in Serpentine. Deposits are often found along the contacts between Serpentine and Sandstones and Shales of the Franciscan formation.			
Cinnabar, Serpentine, Silica-carbonate rock.	NW¼13,14	18S	11E
Cinnabar, Serpentine, Silica-carbonate rock.	NE¼5	18S	12E
Cinnabar.	31	18S	12E
Cinnabar.	2,11,12,18	18S	12E
Cinnabar.	11,12	18S	11E
Cinnabar, Pyrite, black Shale.	SW¼32	18S	12E
Cinnabar, (New Idria mine).	and 28,29,32,33	17S	12E
	3,4	18S	12E
Cinnabar.	31	18S	12E
Cinnabar, Pyrite, Silica-carbonate rock, Serpentine.	19,20	18S	12E
Cinnabar.	31	17S	12E
Analcime, crystals in seams of Barkevikite Syenite.	25,26	18S	12E
Natrolite, large crystals in Serpentine (near headwaters of San Benito Creek).	29	18S	12E
Natrolite, well formed crystals (on clear creek).	12	18S	11E
Magnesite, Serpentine.	SE¼35	17S	11E
Pectolite, radiating masses in veins in Basalt.	32	18S	12E

Panoche Valley Quadrangle 15'

	SECTION	T.	R.
Cinnabar, on Bitter Water Creek.	25	15S	9E
Cinnabar.	31	15S	10E

	SECTION	T.	R.
Cinnabar.	6	16S	10E
Cinnabar.	12	15S	9E
Cinnabar, low grade, 1-2 lb. Ore in Sandstone.	1,2,11,12	16S	10E
Cinnabar.	7	15S	10E
Cinnabar.	12	15S	9E
Cinnabar.	12,13	15S	9E
Cinnabar.	7,8	15S	10E
Turquoise, in veins in Glauconite Schist.	33	14S	10E
Metacinnabar, Kaolinised Sandstone.	5,6	15S	10E

Quien Sabe Quadrangle 15'

	SECTION	T.	R.
Stibnite, Cinnabar, Pyrite, Siliceous veins in Basalt and Andesite.	5,8	12S	7E

San Benito Quadrangle 15'

	SECTION	T.	R.
Bentonite.	30,33	15S	7E
Cinnabar (in Serpentine), on Tres Pinos Creek.	3,4,9	15S	8E

SAN BERNADINO COUNTY

Avawatz Pass Quadrangle 15'

	SECTION	T.	R.
Celestite, Gypsum.	17 and	18N	5E 6E
Gypsum, Halite.	15,22	18N	5E
Oolite, Pisolite (blue, gray, black).	N½2	18N	5E
Vari-colored Rhyolite.	N½1	18N	5E

Bagdad Quadrangle 15'

	SECTION	T.	R.
Hematite, Magnetite, Limestone, Granite.	7,18	6N	12E
Malachite, Azurite, Quartz Porphyry.	18	7N	11E
Copper minerals, Quartz, Granite.	7	7N	11E
Lode Gold, Silver, Malachite, Chrysocolla.	23	7N	11E
Lode Gold, Copper Minerals.	29,30	7N	11E
Volcanic cinders.	16	6N	10E
Perlite.	32	8N	10E
Perlite.	8,9,10	7N	11E
Chalcedony roses.	SE¼29	8N	10E
Chalcedony, Jasper.	13	7N	9E
Apache tears (Obsidian).	16	6N	11E

Baker Quadrangle 15'

	SECTION	T.	R.
Gold, Silver, Galena, Quartz, Schist, Granite.	25	15N	9E
Chalcopyrite, Limestone, Diorite.	21	15N	7E
Cerargyrite, native Silver, Cerussite, Galena, Limestone.	2	16N	8E
Chrysocolla, Malachite, Cerussite, Galena, Chalcopyrite.	27	14N	7E
Silver, Galena.	6	16N	9E
Copper minerals, Gold, Silver, Quartz, Granite.	25	14N	7E
Copper minerals, Gold, Silver, Galena, Quartz, Granite.	23,24,25,26	14N	8E

	SECTION	T.	R.
Turquoise.	31	16N	10E
Malachite, Chrysocolla, Galena, Chalcopyrite, Cerussite.	35	14N	7E

Bannock Quadrangle 15'

	SECTION	T.	R.
Copper minerals, Granite, Schist.	24	10N	20E
Copper minerals.	36	10N	21E
Magnesite, Dolomite, Tuff, Shale.	15,22	8N	21E

Barstow Quadrangle 15'

	SECTION	T.	R.
Marble (banded, blue-black and white).	N½3	6N	2W
Marble (white, green, black, pink, purple).	SE¼2,NE¼11	6N	2W
Magnesite.	NW¼3	6N	2W
Magnetite.	NE¼4	6N	2W
Barite, Chalcocite, Chalcopyrite, Chrysocolla, Chalcedony, Malachite, black Opal, Brochantite, Jarosite.	NW¼SE¼8	6N	2W
Gold, Silver, Pyrite, Limonite, Chalcopyrite, Brochantite, Pyrolusite, Dacite, Felsite, Quartz Monzonite Porphyry.	SW¼4,SE¼5	6N	2W
Gold, Silver, Quartz; Pyrite, Galena, Chalcopyrite, Dacite, Andesite.	SE¼27	7N	4W
Hematite variety: Specularite.	SW¼21	7N	2W
Hematite variety: Specularite.	NW¼28	7N	2W
Marble, Epidote, Garnet, Actinolite, Hematite variety: Specularite.	W½28	7N	2W
Pyrite, Chalcopyrite, Galena, Sphalerite, Cerussite, Anglesite, Limonite, Calcite, Barite, Felsite, Quartz Latite, Granite, Gneiss.	SE¼7	10N	2W
Barite.	N½9	10N	2W
Cerargyrite, Silver (native), Argentite, Pyrite, Barite, Jasper.	NE¼13	10N	2W
Hematite variety: Specularite.	N½20,21	10N	1W
Magnetite, Hematite variety: Specularite, Lazulite.	1	7N	3W
Pyrophyllite.	NE¼25	7N	3W
Rutile, Quartzite.	SE¼SW¼21	9N	3W
Dolomite.	SW¼12	9N	4W
Tremolite (pink and yellow).	36	9N	4W
Clay.	SE¼36	9N	4W
Marl.	SE¼8	8N	4W
Gold, Pyrite, Quartz; Andesite, Dacite.	SW corner 3	6N	4W
Gold, Pyrite, Chalcopyrite, Andesite, Quartz.	NW corner 10	6N	4W
Gold, Pyrite, Quartz; Schist.	S½NW¼17	6N	4W
Cerussite, Galena, Sphalerite, Gold, Silver, Limestone, Schist.	N½NE¼17	6N	4W
Chalcopyrite, Magnetite, Malachite, Chrysocolla.	NE¼15	6N	4W
Jarosite, Limonite, Galena, Pyrite, Sphalerite, Gold, Silver.	SW¼31	7N	5W
Magnesite.	SW¼3	9N	6W

Broadwell Lake Quadrangle 15'

	SECTION	T.	R.
Lace, plume Agate, Chalcedony.	4,5,9,16	8N	7E

(Broadwell Lake Quadrangle 15' cont.)

	SECTION	T.	R.
Celestite.	29,30	8N	7E
Chrysocolla, Malachite, Cuprite, Bornite, Hematite.	23	9N	7E
Psilomelane, Jasper, Calcite, Hematite, Rhyolite.	22,23	8N	7E

Cadiz Quadrangle 15'

	SECTION	T.	R.
Gold, Silver.	26	7N	13E
Magnetite, Limestone.	24	6N	12E
Magnetite, Hematite, Garnet, Epidote, Calcite, Serpentine, Limestone, Granite.	17,18,19,20,21	6N	14E

Cady Mountains Quadrangle 15'

	SECTION	T.	R.
Manganese minerals, Granite, Limestone.	28	11N	6E
Pyrolusite, Psilomelane, Andesite.	10	8N	6E
Cyrtolite, Betafite, Orthoclase, Magnetite, Pegmatite in Quartz Monzonite.	15	9N	6E
Fluorite, Siderite, Calcite, Andesite, Basalt.	7	10N	6E
Clay (Hectorite).	31	9N	5E
Montmorillonite.	2,6,27	8N	6E
Agate, Jasper, Chalcedony, Opal.	16	8N	5E

Cave Mountain Quadrangle 15'

	SECTION	T.	R.
Magnetite, Limonite, Limestone, Gneiss, Schist, Quartzite.	11,12	11N	6E
Magnesite (white, pink), conglomerate.	21	11N	6E
Various types of Agate, Jasp-agate, green Opalite, Chalcedony, Calcite.	18,19,20,30,31,32	11N	6E
Agate, Petrified Wood, vari-colored Jasper.	21,28	12N	5E

Clark Mountain Quadrangle 15'

	SECTION	T.	R.
Gold, Chalcopyrite, Sphalerite, Galena, Marcasite, Rhyolite, Granite.	10,14	17N	13E
Galena, Sphalerite, Copper minerals, Silver, Limestone, Granite.	31	17N	13E
Sphalerite, Galena, Chalcopyrite, Gold, Silver, Quartz, Limestone, Shale, Quartz Monzonite.	30	17N	13E
Carnotite, Copper Oxides, Jasper, Quartz, Chert, Phyllite.	10	17N	12E
Copper minerals, Galena, Silver, Gold, Limestone.	9	17N	13E
Scheelite, Wolframite, Quartz, Schist, Granite.	10	17N	13E

Colton Well Quadrangle 15'

	SECTION	T.	R.
Scheelite, Garnet Limestone, Schist, Granite.	14,23	8N	15E
Galena, Cerussite, Silver.	9	10N	14E
Argentiferous Galena, Limestone.	9	10N	14E
Galena, Cerussite, Cerargyrite, Monzonite.	31	10N	14E
Cerussite, Galena, Limestone.	21	10N	14E
Galena, Copper minerals, Silver.	32	10N	14E
Chalcopyrite, Galena, Gold, Silver, Quartz, Andesite, Quartz Monzonite.	20	9N	14E

Crescent Peak Quadrangle 15'

	SECTION	T.	R.
Kaolinite.	13,24	14N	17E
Gold, Pyrite, Marcasite, Galena, Chalcopyrite, Quartz, Limonite, Gneiss, Schist, Quartzite.	23	14N	16E
Perlite, Chalcedony Geodes.	28,29	15N	18E

Cucamonga Peak Quadrangle 7½'

	SECTION	T.	R.
Garnet, Epidote, Sphalerite, Limestone, Granite.	25	2N	7W
Sphalerite, Galena, Cerussite, Limestone.	29,32	2N	6W
Lazurite, Mica-diopside Schist.	NE¼6	1N	7W

Daggett Quadrangle 15'

	SECTION	T.	R.
Azurite, Malachite, Gold, Quartz Monzonite.	9,10	8N	1E
Barite, Schist, Dolomite.	3	10N	1W
Barite, Quartzite, Schist.	NE¼27,21,22,28	10N	1W
Cerussite, Galena, Cerargyrite, Limonite, Pyrolusite, Barite, Quartz; Andesite Porphyry, Volcanic Tuff.	36	10N	1W
Barite (bladed), Andesite.	5	10N	1E
Cerussite, Cerargyrite, Barite, Limonite, Pyrolusite, Quartz.	NW¼8	10N	1E
Embolite, Cerargyrite, Cerussite, Azurite, Chrysocolla, Barite, Jasper, Silver, Quartz; Rhyolite Tuff.	10,11,14,15,23	10N	1E
Galena, Sphalerite, Cerussite, Chalcopyrite, Cerargyrite, Barite, Limonite, Pyrolusite, Gold, Silver, Volcanic Tuffs, Flows and Breccias, Sandstone, Shale.	SE¼16,15,21	10N	1E
Bentonite.	17	10N	1E
Petrified Wood.	18,19	10N	2E
Agate (various types).	13	9N	2E
		9N	1E

Dale Lake Quadrangle 15'

	SECTION	T.	R.
Galena, Cerussite, Pyrargyrite, Polybasite, Cerargyrite, Stephanite, Diorite, Granodiorite.	11,14	1S	12E
Gold, Galena, Quartz, Andesite Porphyry.	21,22,27,28	1S	12E
Magnetite, Hematite, Epidote, Garnet, Calcite, Granite.	20,29	1S	13E
Gold, Limonite, Copper minerals, Quartz, Granodiorite.	36	1S	12E

Danby Quadrangle 15'

	SECTION	T.	R.
Hematite, Magnetite.	11,12	5N	15E
Pumicite.	13	5N	15E

Essex Quadrangle 15'

	SECTION	T.	R.
Lead, Silver.	3,10,11	5N	17E
Scheelite, Epidote, Limestone; Schist.	4	5N	17E
Epidote, Scheelite, Garnet, Limestone; Schist, Granite.	6,8,9	5N	17E
Arsenopyrite, Galena, Pyrite, Sphalerite, Quartz, Granite.	19,20	6N	17E
Argentite, Cerussite, Cerargyrite, Chalcopyrite, Galena, Quartz; Granite.	25,30	6N	17E
Scheelite, Garnet, Epidote.	28	6N	17E

Flynn Quadrangle 15'

	SECTION	T.	R.
Argentiferous Galena, Limestone.	9	10N	14E
Magnetite, Hematite, Limonite, Calcite, Serpentine, Pyrite.	25,36	10N	13E
Perlite.	22	8N	13E

Halloran Springs Quadrangle 15'

Gold, Azurite, Cerussite, Quartz; Quartz Monzonite.	8	15N	10E
Azurite, Malachite, Silver.	17	15N	10E
Calcite, Gold, Siderite, Limonite, Pyrite, Chalcopyrite, Quartz Monzonite.	16,17,20	15N	11E
Turquoise, Alunite, Quartz; Granite.	32,33	16N	11E
Turquoise, Alunite, Quartz; Granite.	32,33	16N	10E
Turquoise, Alunite, Quartz; Granite.	31	16N	10E
Turquoise, Alunite, Quartz; Granite.	36	16N	9E
Turquoise, Alunite, Quartz; Granite.	4	15N	11E

Ivanpah Quadrangle 15'

Gold, Silver, Copper minerals, Galena.	11,12,13,14	12N	15E
Auriferous Pyrite, Galena, Chalcopyrite, Quartz; Granite.	18	12N	15E
Fluorite (purple).	8	14N	14E
Cerussite, Galena, Chalcopyrite, Limestone.	3,10,15	15N	14E
Wolframite, Quartz; Pegmatite.	23	14N	15E
Wolframite, Quartz; Pegmatite in Granite.	25,36	14N	15E
Hubnerite, Wolframite, Pegmatite.	32	14N	15E
Molybdenite, Wolframite, Hubnerite.	35	14N	15E
Cerussite, Galena, Chalcopyrite, Limestone.	3,10,15	15N	14E
Malachite, Azurite.	14	14N	15E
Zinc, Copper minerals.	4	15N	14E
Chalcopyrite, Malachite, Azurite, Limestone; Granite.	9	15N	14E
Magnesite, Limestone.	15,16	15N	14E
Scheelite, Chalcopyrite, Galena, Gold, Silver, Limestone; Quartz Monzonite.	19,30	15N	14E
Magnesite.	15,16,21,22	15N	14E
Lead, Silver, Gold, Copper minerals, Dolomite.	19,30	15N	14E
Pyrite, Gold, Copper minerals, Lead, Quartz; Granite Gneiss.	2	14N	16E
Chalcopyrite, Galena, Gold, Quartzite; Schist, Gneiss.	2,3	14N	16E
Scheelite, Fluorite, Quartz; Limestone; Granite.	17	14N	16E
Scheelite, Ferberite, Fluorite, Copper, Lead, Zinc, Silver, Dolomite, Quartz Monzonite.	29	14N	16E
Scheelite, Copper minerals, Zinc, Dolomite, Quartz Monzonite.	30	14N	16E
Malachite, Azurite, Quartz.	31,32	14N	16E
Hubnerite, Stibnite, Sphalerite, Chalcopyrite, Galena, Quartz; Rhodochrosite, Quartzite.	33,34	14N	16E
Hydrozincite, Smithsonite, Cerussite, Galena, Sphalerite, Limestone.	4	15½N	14E

Kelso Quadrangle 15'

Gold, Silver, Galena, Copper minerals.	35	13N	12E

	SECTION	T.	R.
Hematite, Magnetite.			
Gold, Galena, Sphalerite, Copper minerals, Diorite.	13,14	12N	12E
Gold, Wolframite, Chalcopyrite, Pyrite, Granite.	3	11N	14E
Scheelite, Galena, Chalcopyrite, Sphalerite.	5	11N	14E
Gold, Silver, Pyrite, Galena, Quartz, Gneiss.	7	11N	14E
Cerussite, Cerargyrite, Galena, Limestone.	9	11N	14E
	34	11N	14E

Kerens Quadrangle 15'

	SECTION	T.	R.
Marble Onyx.	8	8N	10E
Gold, Silver, Copper minerals.	31,32	8N	11E

Kingston Peak Quadrangle 15'

	SECTION	T.	R.
Galena, Silver, Gneiss, Quartzite.	17	17N	10E
Cerussite, Galena, Cerargyrite, Quartz, Garnet-biotite Schist.	14	17N	11E
Azurite, Malachite, Cerussite, Cerargyrite, Gold.	15,16	17N	11E
Malachite, Azurite, Chrysocolla, Dolomite, Quartz Monzonite.	4	16N	10E

Lane Mountain Quadrangle 15'

	SECTION	T.	R.
Agate (moss and plume).	22	11N	1W
Scheelite, Quartz, Granite.	32	31S	47E
Limonite, Manganese Oxides, Gold, Quartz, Granite.	18	12N	1E
Gold, Copper minerals.	29	12N	1E
Barite, Tremolite, Marble.	SE¼8	11N	1E
Placer Gold.	20,21,28,29	32S	47E

Lanfair Valley Quadrangle 15'

	SECTION	T.	R.
Malachite, Pyrite, Limonite, Chalcopyrite, Gold, Silver, Granite, Quartz Diorite, Gabbro.	2,10,11,15	11N	17E
Opal (red and green), Agate, Chalcedony, Petrified Wood.	and 31,32	12N	17E
	5,6	11N	17E
Gold, Silver, Galena, Cerussite, Volcanics.	18	11N	17E
Vanadinite, Cuprodescloizite, Gold, Silver, Galena, Cerussite, Quartz, Granite.	15,22	11N	18E

Lavic Quadrangle 15'

	SECTION	T.	R.
Argentite, Galena, Chalcopyrite, Pyrite, Barite, Calcite, Wulfenite, Cerargyrite, Cerussite, Quartz, Quartz Porphyry.	and 25,26	7N	5E
	31	7N	6E
Volcanic Cinders.	32	8N	6E
Vari-colored Jasper.	11,12	7N	6E

Leach Lake Quadrangle 15'

	SECTION	T.	R.
Barite, Celestite, Shale.	23	18N	3E
Hematite, Pyrolusite, Psilomelane, Limestone.	16	18N	3E

	SECTION	T.	R.
Manganese Oxides.	18	18N	3E
Smoky Quartz crystals.	30	19N	4E

Lead Mountain Quadrangle 15'

	SECTION	T.	R.
Hematite, Arsenopyrite, Chalcopyrite, Quartz, Granite.	18,19	4N	12E
Celestite.	S½6	4N	12E

Lucerne Valley Quadrangle 15'

	SECTION	T.	R.
Pitchblende, Pyrite, Galena, Limestone.	4	2N	1E
Wulfenite, Cerussite, Galena, Limestone.	12	3N	1E
Gold, Hematite, Quartz Monzonite.	20	3N	1E
Sphalerite, Limonite, Pyrite, Chalcopyrite, Galena.	22,23,27	3N	1E
Gold, Quartz; Schist, Quartzite.	25,36	3N	1E
Argentiferous Galena.	30	3N	1E
Quartzite (white, red, orange, lavender).	6,7	2N	2E
Cerargyrite, Azurite, Galena, Limestone.	3,4	3N	2E
Galena, Chalcopyrite.	8	3N	2E
Cerussite, Azurite, Malachite, Galena, Limonite, Limestone; Granite.	19	3N	2E
Chalcopyrite, Galena.	21	3N	2E
Molybdenite (fluorescent), Garnet, Epidote.	NE¼32	3N	2E
Cerargyrite, Galena, Chalcopyrite, Limestone.	33,34	4N	2E

Ludlow Quadrangle 15'

	SECTION	T.	R.
Gold, Silver, Rhyolite.	32	7N	8E
Specular Hematite, Gold, Dacite Porphyry.	33	7N	8E
Chrysocolla, Azurite, Malachite, Galena, Cerussite, Chalcopyrite, Monzonite, Rhyolite.	7,8	6N	8E
Gold, Silver, Limonite.	18	6N	8E
Obsidian.	S½3,4	7N	7E
Barite.	30	8N	8E

Mescal Range Quadrangle 15'

	SECTION	T.	R.
Scheelite, Galena.	16	16N	12E
Cassiterite, Scheelite, Hematite, Magnetite, Pyrite, Chalcopyrite, Azurite, Malachite, Limestone; Quartz Monzonite.	24	15N	13E
Azurite, Garnet, Gold, Limonite.	25	15N	13E
Scheelite, Chrysocolla, Azurite, Malachite, Limestone; Quartz Monzonite.	18,19	15N	14E
Galena, Sphalerite, Chalcopyrite, Limonite, Pyrolusite, Cerussite, Smithsonite, Adamite, Duftite, Limestone; Granite.	7,8,17,18	16N	13E
Cerussite, Chalcopyrite, Galena, Limestone; Marble, Diorite Porphyry.	8,17	16N	13E
Gold, Quartz; Dolomitic Limestone.	24	16N	13E
Sandstone (lavender, red, yellow).	25	16N	13E
Stibnite, Quartz; Calcite, Granite Gneiss.	18	16N	14E
Azurite, Chalcopyrite, Limestone; Porphyry.	1	16N	12E

	SECTION	T.	R.
Cerussite, Malachite, Azurite, Galena, Chalcopyrite, Limestone; Monzonite.			
Calcite, Limonite, Cerussite, Malachite.	6	16N	12E
	35	16N	12E

Mid Hills Quadrangle 15'

	SECTION	T.	R.
Embolite, Argentite, Cerargyrite, Galena, Diorite, Granite.			
Hubnerite, Quartz.	11	13N	14E
Galena, Cerussite, Limestone.	33,34	13N	16E
Wolframite, Hubnerite.	34	11N	14E
	5	11N	14E

Old Dad Mountain Quadrangle 15'

	SECTION	T.	R.
Gold, Magnetite, Pyrite, Chalcopyrite, Marcasite, Quartz, Schist, Gneiss, Granite.	22,23	13N	10E
Chrysotile, Limestone, Serpentine.	14,15	12N	9E
Bentonite.	10	12N	11E
Galena, Dolomite.	35	12N	10E
Gold, Pyrite, Quartzite, Schist, Dolomite.	23,26	13N	10E
Magnetite, Hematite.	10,11	12N	10E
Gold, Quartzite, red and orange Sandstone.	26,27	13N	10E
Uranium minerals in Limestone.	8	13N	10E

Old Woman Springs Quadrangle 15'

	SECTION	T.	R.
Scheelite, Barite, Limestone, Schist.	11,13,14	2N	2E
Quartzite (white, red, orange, lavender).	1,12	2N	1E

Opal Mountain Quadrangle 15'

	SECTION	T.	R.
Gold, Malachite, Azurite, Chrysocolla, Cuprite, Argentite, Cinnabar, Quartz, Granite.	8,9	11N	1W
Pumice.	7,8,17,18	32S	46E
Opal (red, orange, green), Geodes, Jasp-agate.	1	32S	44E
Opal (red, orange, green), Geodes, Jasp-agate.	6,7	32S	45E

Ord Mountain Quadrangle 15'

	SECTION	T.	R.
Fluorite, Granite, Quartz.	1	6N	1W
Magnesite, Dolomitic Limestone.	15	6N	1W
Scheelite, Quartz; Amphibolite.	4	6N	1E
Fluorite, Quartz; Granite.	7,8	6N	1E
Travertine.	SE¼3	7N	1E
Galena, Sphalerite, Pyrite, Marcasite.	11	7N	1E
Azurite, Malachite, Bornite, Chalcopyrite, Andesite.	SE¼SE¼12	7N	1E
Hematite, Limonite, Chrysocolla, Scheelite.	E½NE¼12	7N	1E
Azurite, Barite, Bornite, Chalcocite, Chalcopyrite, Chrysocolla, Galena, Malachite, Pyrite.	12,13,24	7N	1E

Pilot Knob Quadrangle 15'

	SECTION	T.	R.
"Myrickite" (Cinnabar in Chalcedony).	4	30S	46E

176

	SECTION	T.	R.
Azurite, Malachite.	SE¼24	7N	1E
Magnetite, Epidote. center of boundary between SW¼5,SE¼6		7N	2E
Scheelite, Garnet, Epidote, Volcanics.	E½SE¼7	7N	2E
Azurite, Malachite, Bornite, Chalcopyrite.	SW¼SW¼7	7N	2E
Chalcopyrite, Chrysocolla, Pyrite.	W½SW¼30	7N	2E
Chrysocolla, Chalcopyrite, Chalcocite, Molybdenite, Powellite.	S½SE¼31	7N	2E
Placer Gold.	W½W½11	7N	1E

Red Pass Lake Quadrangle 15'

Hematite, Magnetite, Limestone, Sandstone.	18,19	15N	7E
Hematite, Magnetite, Limestone.	11,12,13,14	15N	6E
Galena, Sphalerite, Chalcopyrite, Quartzite.	26	16N	6E

Rodman Mountains Quadrangle 15'

Azurite, Malachite, Bornite, Chalcopyrite.	17	7N	3E
Magnetite, Hematite, Pyrite, Limonite, Diopside, Calcite, Epidote.	12	5N	4E
Magnetite, Hematite, Diopside, Epidote, Garnet, Calcite, Dolomite, Granite.	27,28	6N	4E
Marcasite.	25	6N	2E
Vari-colored Rhyolite.	10,11	6N	2E

Silurian Hills Quadrangle 15'

Silver, Galena.	24	17N	8E
Gold, Silver, Galena, Copper minerals, Dolomite, Quartzite, Granite.	26,27	17N	8E
Gold, Silver, Copper minerals, Cerussite.	26	18N	8E
Vari-colored Petrified Wood.	1 thru 18	19N	8E

Turtle Mountains Quadrangle 15'

Chrysocolla.	32	2N	21E

SAN DIEGO COUNTY

Alpine Quadrangle 7½'

Lavender Dumortierite, Sillimanite, Quartz.	N½NW¼NE¼9	16S	2E

Borrego Mountain SE Quadrangle 7½'

Gypsum.	N½NE¼36 and SE¼25	13S	8E

Boucher Hill Quadrangle 7½'

Blue, yellow-green Beryl.	center S½19	10S	1E

El Cajon Mountain Quadrangle 7½'

	SECTION	T.	R.
Copper Oxides, Malachite, Azurite, Pyrite, Chalcopyrite, Limonite, Schist.	11	14S	1E

Escondido Quadrangle 7½'

	SECTION	T.	R.
Pyrophyllite, Volcanics.	NE¼19	13S	2W

Fonts Point Quadrangle 7½'

		SECTION	T.	R.
Optical Calcite, Gypsum, common Calcite, Sandstone, conglomerate.		NW¼SE¼14	10S	8E
	and	S½SW¼14	10S	8E
	and	S½15	10S	8E

Hot Springs Mountain Quadrangle 7½'

	SECTION	T.	R.
Black Tourmaline.	NE¼NE¼28	9S	4E

Jacumba Quadrangle 7½'

	SECTION	T.	R.
Beryl, green Muscovite.	NW¼NE¼2	17S	7E

Mesa Grande Quadrangle 7½'

GEM MINERALS: Associated with Pegmatite dikes.

	SECTION	T.	R.
Spodumene, pink Beryl, blue-green Tourmaline (also pink), some large Quartz crystals.	E½NE¼SW¼13	11S	1E
Pink and green Tourmaline, Spodumene, Topaz.	SE¼SW¼17	11S	2E
Tourmaline, Beryl, Quartz; Perthite, Clevelandite, Albite, Muscovite, Lepidolite, Garnet.	NE¼NW¼20	11S	2E
Amber and wine colored Tourmaline, Garnet, Beryl.	SE¼NE¼19	11S	2E
Blue, green, purple Tourmaline, blue Beryl.	N½N½NE¼19	11S	2E
Colorless and pink Beryl, dark blue and green Tourmaline, Muscovite, Lepidolite.	W½SW¼18	11S	2E
Vari-colored Tourmaline.	SE¼SW¼17	11S	2E
Rose colored Quartz.	W½NW¼SW¼19	11S	2E

Palomar Observatory Quadrangle 7½'

		SECTION	T.	R.
Green and blue Tourmaline, pink and blue Beryl, blue Topaz.	and	NW¼SW¼3	10S	2E
		S½SW¼3		
Blue Tourmaline, Topaz.		S½NW¼10	10S	2E

Pechanga Quadrangle 7½'

GEM MINERALS:

		SECTION	T.	R.
Spodumene, Tourmaline, pink Beryl.	and	E½SW¼SE¼14	9S	2W
		SE¼SE¼14		
Pink Tourmaline, red Garnet, Lepidolite, Rubellite.		SE¼15	9S	2W
Green Tourmaline, pink Lepidolite.		E½SE¼15	9S	2W
Spodumene, Beryl, Quartz.		S½24	9S	2W
Spodumene (Kunzite), green and pink Beryl, pale yellow Quartz; Tourmaline, Molybdenite, large clear Feldspar crystals, pink Beryl.		N½SE¼24	9S	2W

	SECTION	T.	R.
Smoky and colorless Quartz crystals (to 100 lbs.), pink, green and blue-green Spodumene.	SE¼24	9S	2W
Pink Spodumene (Kunzite).	W½SE¼24	9S	2W

Ramona Quadrangle 7½'

GEM MINERALS:

	SECTION	T.	R.
Pink Beryl.	NW¼NW¼8	13S	2E
Smoky Quartz crystals; Tourmaline, Topaz, orange Spessartine.	NE¼SE¼8	13S	2E
Garnet, Tourmaline, Muscovite, Beryl.	W½SW¼SW¼9	13S	2E

Rancho Santa Fe Quadrangle 7½'

	SECTION	T.	R.
Malachite, Chalcopyrite, Pyrite, Limonite, Volcanics. and	SE¼32	12S	3W
	SW¼SW¼33	12S	3W
Malachite, Chalcopyrite, Pyrite, Volcanics.	NE¼NE¼5	13S	3W
Pyrophyllite, Volcanics.	center 23 and S½S½3	13S	3W

Warner Springs Quadrangle 7½'

	SECTION	T.	R.
Black Tourmaline (to 9" long), grass green, blue, colorless, pink Tourmaline.	NE¼14	10S	3E

Warners Ranch Quadrangle 7½'

	SECTION	T.	R.
Quartz, rose colored and white.	E½NE¼SE¼24	11S	1E

SAN LUIS OBISPO COUNTY

Cypress Mountain Quadrangle 7½'

	SECTION	T.	R.
Stibnite, Quartz; Sandstone.	SW¼SW¼2	27S	9E
Cinnabar.	1,2	27S	9E
Cinnabar.	13	27S	9E
Cinnabar.	21	27S	10E
Cinnabar.	29	27S	10E
Cinnabar.	17	27S	10E
Cinnabar, altered Serpentine.	22	27S	10E
Cinnabar.	7	27S	10E
Cinnabar.	24	27S	9E

Lime Mountain Quadrangle 7½'

	SECTION	T.	R.
Limestone.	18,19	26S	10E
Limestone.	15	26S	9E
Cinnabar, Marcasite, Millerite, Sandstone, Shale, Quartz; Chalcedony.	33	26S	10E
Cinnabar, Serpentine, Sandstone.	SW¼NW¼7	27S	10E
Cinnabar, Sandstone.	15,21	27S	9E
Cinnabar.	32	26S	10E

Lopez Mountain Quadrangle 7½'

	SECTION	T.	R.
Dolomite, upper end of Little Falls Canyon.	13	30S	13E

Nipomo Quadrangle 15'

Onyx Marble.	9,16	31S	15E
Cinnabar, Calcite, Sandstone.	32	32S	16E

San Luis Obispo Quadrangle 7½'

Chromite, Serpentine.	E½29	29S	12E
Chromite, Serpentine.	32,33,34	29S	12E
Chromite, Serpentine.	SW¼SE¼33	29S	12E

SANTA CLARA COUNTY

Los Gatos Quadrangle 7½'

Azurite, Chalcopyrite, Malachite, Pyrrhotite, Serpentine.	NW¼SW¼10	9S	1W
Cinnabar, in Silica-carbonate rock in Serpentine.	30	8S	1E

Morgan Hill Quadrangle 7½'

Gold, in red Garnets of the Eclogite at Coyote Creek 6 miles north of San Martin.

Chromite, Serpentine.	S½24	8S	2E
Chromite,	E½23	8S	2E
Chromite,	S½13	8S	2E

Mount Boardman Quadrangle 7½'

Bementite, Rhodochrosite, Chert.	NW¼27	6S	5E
Rhodochrosite, white Chert.	NW¼30	6S	5E
Manganese Oxides, Chert.	SE¼28	6S	5E
Manganese.	NE¼28	6S	5E
Manganese.	SW¼28	6S	5E
Manganese.	NE¼32	6S	5E
Manganese.	NW¼32	6S	5E
Magnesite, Serpentine.	SW¼12,NE¼13	6S	4E
Magnesite, Serpentine.	1	6S	4E
Rhodochrosite, Chert.	NW¼12	6S	4E

Quien Sabe Quadrangle 15'

Cinnabar in Silica-carbonate rock in Serpentine.	center 19	11S	7E
Cinnabar, Quartz veins in Basalt.	SE¼5	12S	7E
Cinnabar, Siliceous zones in Tuff Breccia.	NE¼5	12S	7E
Cinnabar, in Quartz.	32	11S	7E

Santa Teresa Hills Quadrangle 7½'

Cinnabar, New Almaden mine.	3	9S	1E
Cinnabar.	24	8S	1E

180

SHASTA COUNTY

Bollibokka Mountain Quadrangle 15'

	SECTION	T.	R.
Barite.	33	36N	3W
Barite.	29	34N	3W

Dunsmuir Quadrangle 15'

	SECTION	T.	R.
Barite, Limestone, Slate.	18,19	38N	3W
Chromite, Serpentine.	2	38N	4W
Chromite, Serpentine.	22	37N	5W
Molybdenite (considerable deposit), in dike in Peridotite, on Boulder Creek.	33	37N	5W

French Gulch Quadrangle 15'

	SECTION	T.	R.
Pyrite, Chalcopyrite, Sphalerite, Limonite, Rhyolite, Tuff.	11,12,13,14	33N	6W
Azurite, native Copper, Copper Sulfides.	6	32N	7W
Gold, Pyrite, Galena, Quartz, Slate, conglomerate.	12,13	33N	7W
Gold, Quartz, Pyrite, Diorite.	7,18	31N	6W
Gold, Slate, Andesite.	4	35N	6W
Gold, Quartz, Slate, Sandstone, conglomerate, produced $3-5 million.	18	33N	6W
Pyrite, Limonite, Rhyolite.	23,24	33N	6W
Gold, Quartz, some rich pockets, (average $14-20 ton).	2,11	31N	6W
Gold, Quartz, Slate, ($15 Ore), produced $½ million.	9,10	33N	7W
Gold, Quartz, Sulfides, Slate, Diorite Porphyry.	19	33N	7W
Gold, Quartz, produced over $1 million.	6,7,8,17,18	33N	7W
Argentite, native Silver, Freibergite, Stephanite, produced over $1 million.	17,18 19,20	31N	6W
Pyrite, abundant.	NE¼34	33N	6W

Lamoine Quadrangle 15'

	SECTION	T.	R.
Barite, veins in Gabbro.	2	34N	4W
Barite, vein to 8' wide.	35	35N	4W
Pyritic Copper Ore, Rhyolite.	28,29,30,33	34N	5W
Magnetite.	26	34N	4W

Shasta Dam Quadrangle 7½'

	SECTION	T.	R.
Pyrite, Limonite, Gold, Silver, Rhyolite, Tuff and Breccia.	7	33N	5W
Pyrite, Chalcopyrite, Sphalerite, Gold, Silver, Rhyolite.	28	33N	5W

SIERRA COUNTY

Alleghany Quadrangle 7½'

LODE GOLD:

	SECTION	T.	R.
Serpentine, Jasper, Arsenopyrite.	2,3,5,8	18N	10E
Schist, Diabase, Serpentine, Arsenopyrite, Pyrite.	4	18N	10E
and	33	19N	10E

	SECTION	T.	R.
Schist, Serpentine.	35	19N	10E
Serpentine, Amphibolite, Mariposite, Arsenopyrite, (Ore ran $70-$80 a ton).	34,35	19N	10E
Serpentine, Amphibolite, Sulfides.	11	18N	10E
Schist, Serpentine, Arsenopyrite (shoots to $45 a ton).	35	19N	10E
Schist, Diorite, Pyrite, Arsenopyrite.	4	18N	10E
Serpentine, Talc Schist, Arsenopyrite.	26	19N	10E
Serpentine, Schist, some specimen Ore was mined here.	2,3	18N	10E
Quartzite, Slate, Arsenopyrite, Pyrite.	25,26	20N	10E
Amphibolite, Sulfides, rare Gold in small crystals on Pyrite.	34	19N	10E
Granite, Schist, Pyrite, Arsenopyrite, one area 15' x 21' produced $1,000,000.	33 and 4	19N 18N	10E 10E
Amphibolite, Serpentine, rich shoots were mined at vein intersections.	2	18N	10E
Slate, Porphyry.	28	19N	10E
Serpentine, Schist, Mariposite, rich specimen Ore in quantity was taken from here, rich Ore was associated with Arsenopyrite.	27,34	19N	10E

GOLD DRIFT MINES:

	SECTION	T.	R.
Rich Ore was mined from the Gravels here.	2	18N	10E
Numerous nuggets were mined here.	15,16,21,22	19N	10E

Downieville Quadrangle 7½'

LODE GOLD: In Quartz veins, associated minerals and enclosing wall rocks also listed below.

	SECTION	T.	R.
Rich Ore was mined here.	2	19N	10E
High grade producer.	W½SW¼26	20N	10E
Slate, Porphyry, Arsenopyrite.	25,36	20N	10E
Slate, Porphyry, Arsenopyrite, Galena.	20	19N	11E
Slate, Granite.	9	19N	11E
Sulfides.	1	19N	10E
Slate, Porphyry, Arsenopyrite.	8	19N	11E
Porphyry, Sulfides.	20	19N	10E
Slate, Serpentine.	22,23,26,27	20N	10E
Rich pockets of Gold and Arsenopyrite were found here near vein intersections.	2,3	19N	10E
Manganese Oxides.	1	19N	10E
Serpentine, Porphyry, Arsenopyrite.	22	20N	10E
Schist, Diorite, Arsenopyrite, Marcasite, Pyrite, (some rich Silver Ore was mined here).	15,16,21,22	19N	10E

GOLD DRIFT MINES: Gold bearing Gravels mined by underground methods.

	SECTION	T.	R.
Nuggets from 1-45 ounces recovered here in the early days, one weighed 200 ounces. This nugget was found in a intervolcanic channel (in Gravels sandwiched between Basalt flows).	10,11,14,15	19N	10E
Numerous nuggets were mined from the Gravels here, the largest was 9 ounces.	15	19N	10E

Mount Filmore Quadrangle 7½'

LODE GOLD:

	SECTION	T.	R.
Serpentine, Slate, Mariposite, Sulfides.	10	21N	10E

	SECTION	T.	R.
Slate, Porphyry, Sulfides.	34	22N	10E
Serpentine, Slate, Pyrite.	3	21N	10E
COPPER:			
Cuprite, Malachite, Azurite, Pyrite, vein up to 50' wide.	10	21N	10E

Pike Quadrangle 7½'

	SECTION	T.	R.
LODE GOLD:			
Serpentine, Sulfides (Ore average $30 a ton).	29,32	19N	10E
GOLD DRIFT MINE:			
Rich pockets were mined here.	31,32	19N	10E
One pocket yielded $75,000.	29	19N	10E

Sierra City Quadrangle 15'

	SECTION	T.	R.
LODE GOLD:			
Slate, Porphyry, Arsenopyrite.	21	19N	11E
Slate, Porphyry, Pyrite, Galena, Limonite.	30	20N	12E
Quartz Porphyry, Schist, $500,000 taken from one pocket 15' below the surface.	2,9,10,11	21N	11E
Slate, Porphyry.	7	19N	12E
Diorite, Porphyry, Sulfides.	21,22	20N	12E
Slate, Porphyry.	28	20N	12E
Slate, Porphyry.	6	19N	12E
Augite Porphyry, Sulfides.	21,26	21N	12E
Greenstone, Serpentine, Quartz Porphyry, Sulfides.	29	20N	12E
Some rich pockets were mined here.	26,27	20N	12E
Slate, Porphyry, Sulfides (some very good Ore).	24	21N	11E
COPPER:			
Native Copper.	11	20N	12E
Malachite, Azurite, Chalcopyrite.	30	20N	13E
Chalcopyrite, Bornite.	19	20N	12E
Magnetite, (Sierra Iron mine).	11,12	21N	11E

SISKIYOU COUNTY

China Mountain Quadrangle 15'

	SECTION	T.	R.
Chrysotile, Serpentine.	16,17,20	42N	6W
Chromite, Serpentine.	1	41N	7W
Chromite, Serpentine.	35	42N	7W
Chalcopyrite, Pyrite, Serpentine, Quartz.	20	40N	7W
Gold, Quartz, Granodiorite, Chalcopyrite.	14	41N	7W
Galena, Sphalerite, Andesite.	NE¼29	41N	7W
Chalcopyrite, Pyrite, Serpentine.	12	40N	8W

Condrey Mountain Quadrangle 15'

	SECTION	T.	R.
Gold, Quartz, black Shale.	6	45N	9W
Gold.	1	45N	10W
Cinnabar, Hornblende Schist.	15,16	46N	10W
Cinnabar (coarse crystalline aggregates), Metacinnabar.	34	48N	9W
Cinnabar.	22	46N	10W

Dwinnell Reservoir Quadrangle 15'

	SECTION	T.	R.
Molybdenite, Chalcopyrite, Pyrite, Quartz.	W½25	43N	4W

Etna Quadrangle 15'

	SECTION	T.	R.
Chromite, Serpentine.	1	41N	9W
Chromite, Serpentine.	N½19	42N	8W
Bornite, Chalcocite, Chalcopyrite, Quartz, Diorite, Serpentine.	36	40N	9W
Malachite, Azurite, Shale.	SW¼23	41N	9W
Gold (to $200 a ton), Quartz, Serpentine, Porphyry, Limonite.	2	40N	9W
Pyrite, Andesite, Limonite.	2	40N	9W
Limestone.	9,20,29,32,33	41N	8W

Fort Jones Quadrangle 15'

	SECTION	T.	R.
Chromite, Serpentine.	21	48N	9W
Gold, Quartz; Andesite, (some rich specimens associated with Pyrite and Galena).	27	45N	8W

Happy Camp Quadrangle 15'

	SECTION	T.	R.
Malachite, Chalcopyrite, Sphalerite, Pyrite, Andesite.	31	16N	8E
Chalcopyrite, Pyrite, Schist.	13,14,23	17N	7E
Gold (placer) average $ .20 a yard.	27,28	16N	7E
Idocrase ("Californite"), on Indian Creek (south fork, 10½ miles north of Happy Camp, also on O'Meara Creek.)	7	17N	7E

Hornbrook Quadrangle 15'

	SECTION	T.	R.
Gold, Quartz; Granodiorite, Pyrite, Chalcopyrite.	26	48N	8W
Quartz,Greenstone, fine cubes of Pyrite.	8	45N	7W
Cinnabar, native Mercury.	13,14,24	47N	8W
Highly fossiliferous black Sandstone.	NE¼26	46N	6W

Medicine Lake Quadrangle 15'

Obsidian at Glass Mountain, 4 miles NE of Medicine Lake, one of the largest deposits of Obsidian in the U.S.

Preston Peak Quadrangle 15'

	SECTION	T.	R.
Chromite, Serpentine.	S½15	17N	5E
Chromite, Serpentine.	W½32	17N	5E

Salmon Mountain Quadrangle 15'

	SECTION	T.	R.
Gold, Quartz, (100 oz. recovered from 30 tons of sorted Ore).	1,2	9N	7E

Sawyers Bar Quadrangle 15'

	SECTION	T.	R.
Gold, Quartz; ($10 Ore).	10	39N	11W
Gold, Quartz; produced $3,000,000.	13	39N	12W
Gold, Quartz.	7	39N	11W
Gold, placer, $ .25 to $1.00 a yard.	33	40N	11W

Scott Bar Quadrangle 15'

Chromite, Serpentine.	30	45N	10W
Chromite, Serpentine.	25	45N	11W
Gold (some rich Gold pockets were mined here), Pyrite, Galena, Quartz; Mica Schist.	16	45N	10W

Seiad Valley Quadrangle 15'

Chromite, Serpentine.	11	46N	11W
Chromite, Serpentine.	27,34	46N	11W
Chromite, Serpentine.	15	46N	11W
Chromite, Serpentine.	7,17,18,19,20	47N	11W
Copper Sulfides.	3	47N	11W
Chalcopyrite, Pyrite, Gold, Silver.	34	48N	11W
Graphite, Sandstone, Andesite.	12	47N	12W
Cinnabar in Hornblende Schist on west bank of Horse Creek, where the bridge crosses the Klamath River.	15,16	46N	10W

Ukonom Lake Quadrangle 15'

Gold, massive Pyrite, Limonite.	4,5	15N	7E
Gold, Quartz, ($17. Ore).	32	15N	7E

Weed Quadrangle 15'

Chrysotile, Serpentine.	8	41N	5W
Chromite, Serpentine.	35	39N	4W

Yreka Quadrangle 15'

Chromite, Serpentine.	24	44N	8W
Chromite, Serpentine.	9	44N	8W
Chromite, Serpentine.	25	44N	8W
Chromite, Serpentine.	26	45N	8W
Limestone.	4	44N	7W
Limestone.	4,5,6,7,8	42N	6W
Limestone.	35,36	43N	8W
Limestone.	1,7,12	42N	7W

SONOMA COUNTY

Asti Quadrangle 7½'

Magnesite.	N½NW¼15	11N	10W
Magnesite.	NE¼NE¼15	11N	10W
Chromite.	NW¼NE¼31	11N	10W
Limestone.	NE¼NW¼32	11N	9W

Cazadero Quadrangle 7½'

	SECTION	T.	R.
Aragonite.	SW¼NE¼18	8N	11W
Chromite.	NE¼SW¼21	9N	11W
Magnesite.	NW¼SW¼31	9N	10W
Magnesite.	NE corner 20	9N	11W
Magnesite.	16,17,21	9N	11W
Magnesite.	SE¼NW¼6	8N	10W

Cotati Quadrangle 7½'

Perlite.	NE¼NE¼7	6N	7W

Duncan Mills Quadrangle 7½'

Copper minerals.	SE¼NW¼17	7N	10W
Cinnabar.	SW¼NE¼17	7N	10W
Chromite.	NE¼NW¼27	7N	10W

Fort Ross Quadrangle 7½'

Rhodochrosite, Bementite.	15	8N	12W
Chromite.	NE¼SW¼13	9N	12W

Geyserville Quadrangle 7½'

Copper minerals.	center NW¼5	9N	10W
and	SE¼NE¼4	9N	10W
Cinnabar.	SW¼NW¼8	8N	10W
Cinnabar.	common corner 8,9,16,17	8N	10W

Guerneville Quadrangle 7½'

Graphite.	NE¼NE¼14	9N	10W
Copper minerals.	SW¼NW¼22	9N	10W
Limestone.	SE¼NE¼23	9N	10W

Healdsburg Quadrangle 15'

Lawsonite (good green crystals on highway ½ mile south of Cazadero).	21	8N	10W
Manganese minerals.	center 6	8N	8W
Magnesite.	31	9N	10W

Jimtown Quadrangle 7½'

Cinnabar.	center 20	10N	8W
Cinnabar.	NW¼NW¼4	10N	8W
Cinnabar.	NE corner 5	10N	8W
Cinnabar.	NW¼NE¼5	10N	8W

Kelseyville Quadrangle 15'

Azurite, Chalcopyrite.	33,34	12N	9W
Magnesite.	32	12N	10W

Kenwood Quadrangle 7½'

	SECTION	T.	R.
Coal.	center of section line common to 3 and 10	6N	6W
Perlite.	NW¼NE¼35	7N	7W
Manganese minerals.	SW¼NW¼1	7N	7W
Opal (small, precious) in white Clay and Rhyolite.	SE¼SW¼3	6N	6W

Mark West Springs Quadrangle 7½'

Manganese minerals.	SE¼SW¼27	8N	7W
Coal.	NE¼NW¼27	8N	7W
Diatomite.	SE¼NW¼10	8N	8W

Mount St. Helena Quadrangle 7½'

Cinnabar.	SE¼NW¼9	9N	7W
Cinnabar.	SE¼NE¼25	10N	8W
Cinnabar.	center N½NE¼10	10N	8W
Cinnabar.	SE¼NE¼10	10N	8W
Cinnabar.	NW¼NE¼11	10N	8W
Cinnabar.	center E½NW¼11	10N	8W
Cinnabar.	NW¼SE¼11	10N	8W
Cinnabar.	SE corner 4	10N	8W
Chromite.	NE¼NW¼10	10N	8W
Manganese minerals.	NE¼SE¼9	10N	8W
and	NW¼SE¼10	10N	8W

Rutherford Quadrangle 7½'

Coal.	SE¼NE¼2	6N	6W
Perlite.	NW¼NE¼11	6N	6W
Cinnabar.	NE¼24	7N	6W

Santa Rosa Quadrangle 15'

Hisingerite, Tridymite, Augite Andesite.	NE¼10	7N	7W
Kaolinite (fire Clay).	3	6N	6W
Coal.	SE¼NW¼31	7N	7W
Perlite.	SE¼SW¼15	7N	7W

Skaggs Springs Quadrangle 7½'

Cinnabar, Orpiment, Curtisite, Realgar.	SE¼SE¼24	10N	11W
Chromite.	SE¼NW¼13	10N	11W

The Geysers Quadrangle 7½'

Cinnabar.	center NW¼31	11N	8W
Cinnabar.	NE¼NW¼32	11N	8W
Cinnabar, Metacinnabar.	SW¼NE¼32	11N	8W
Cinnabar.	SW¼33	11N	8W
Cinnabar.	SE¼32	11N	8W
Cinnabar.	center 14	11N	9W
Cinnabar.	NW¼NW¼23	11N	9W

	SECTION	T.	R.
Cinnabar.	SW¼SW¼24	11N	9W
Cinnabar.	SW¼SE¼32	11N	8W
Cinnabar.	center E½SE¼10	11N	9W
Cinnabar.	SW¼SW¼3	11N	9W
Chromite.	SE¼SW¼15	11N	9W

TEHAMA COUNTY

Colyear Springs Quadrangle 15'

Ammonite fossils, Lower Cretaceous, also Buchia (Pelecypods). On north side of Cottonwood Creek just SW of the loop in the stream.	NW¼NW¼12	26N	8W
Ammonites, Lower Cretaceous. On north side of Cottonwood Creek about 400' due west of the previous locality.			
Ammonites, Lower Cretaceous. 300' west and 650' south. On east bank of Cottonwood Creek.	NE corner 11	26N	8W
Ammonites, Lower Cretaceous. 1,050' E. and 1.900' N. of SW corner 20		25N	6W
Ammonites, Upper Jurassic. South side of Middle Fork of Elder Creek, 10' east of junction with small tributary from west.	SE¼NE¼SW¼SE¼19	25N	6W
Ammonites and Buchia fossils, Upper Jurassic. Located 30' east of previous locale on Middle Fork of Elder Creek.			
Chromite, Uvarovite, Kammererite, (large deposit of Chromite) north fork of Elder Creek.	16	25N	7W
Copper, native.	4	25N	7W
Wollastonite.	16	25N	7W

Manton Buttes Quadrangle 15'

Opal, Stalactites and Stalagmites in a Lava tunnel on the north side of Inskip Hill.		29N	1W

Paskenta Quadrangle 15'

Bementite, Rhodochrosite, Chert.	17	23N	7W

Yolla Bolly Quadrangle 15'

Chalcopyrite, Pyrite, Diabase.	25	27N	9W
Manganese Oxides, Schist.	1,2,11	26N	10W
Bementite.	NE¼8	27N	9W

TRINITY COUNTY

Black Rock Mountain Quadrangle 15'

Rhodochrosite, Chert.	NW corner 33	27N	10W
Rhodochrosite, Chert.	center 9	26N	12W
Asbestos (Chrysotile), Serpentine.	SW¼SW¼33	26N	12W
Bementite, Rhodochrosite, Chert, Rhodonite.	9	26N	12W
Copper (native), Barite, Hausmannite, Azurite.	NW¼17	26N	12W

Bonanza King Quadrangle 15'

	SECTION	T.	R.
Asbestos (Tremolite), found in Serpentine.	center N½19	38N	6W
Chromite found in Serpentine.	SW¼11	38N	6W
Chromite found in Serpentine.	center N½14	38N	6W
Chromite found in Serpentine.	NE corner 14	38N	6W
Chromite found in Serpentine.	SW¼SE¼15	38N	6W
Cinnabar found in Hornblende Diorite.	SW¼22	38N	6W
Cinnabar found in Serpentine, Diorite.	SE corner 15	38N	6W
Cinnabar found in Serpentine.	SE¼NE¼14	38N	6W
Placer Gold.	NW¼26	39N	7W
Lode Gold, Quartz.	NE¼25	39N	8W
Magnetite.	2,3,34,35	38N	7W
Lode Gold found in Gabbro, Serpentine.	center S½32	38N	7W
Lode Gold found in Basalt.	NW¼13	37N	8W
Placer Gold.	SW¼19	37N	7W
Lode Gold, Pyrite, Calcite, Quartz Limonite, Manganese Oxides.	SE corner 8	37N	7W
Lode Gold found in Andesite. center of section line between 10,15		37N	7W
Lode Gold.	NE¼NW¼13	37N	7W
Malachite, Pyrite, Limonite, Cinnabar.	SE¼NW¼16	37N	7W
Lode Gold, Quartz found in Granodiorite, Serpentine.	NW¼NW¼17	37N	7W
Lode Gold.	NE¼SE¼18	37N	7W
Lode Gold, Pyrite, Chalcopyrite.	NW¼NW¼21	37N	7W

Chanchelulla Peak Quadrangle 15'

		T.	R.
Magnetite.	SE¼NE¼4	30N	10W
Lode Gold, Quartz.found in Serpentine.	NW¼NE¼12	30N	10W

Coffee Creek Quadrangle 15'

		T.	R.
Lode Gold, Quartz.	SW¼SW¼23	38N	9W
Placer Gold.	SE¼SE¼26	38N	9W
Placer Gold.	NE¼NE¼31	38N	9W
Placer Gold.	SE¼SE¼33	38N	9W
Placer Gold.	NE¼35	38N	9W
Lode Gold, Quartz found in Granodiorite, Serpentine.	center S½34	38N	8W
Lode Gold, Quartz.	NW¼4	37N	8W
Lode Gold, Quartz, Sylvanite, Galena, Pyrite found in Granodiorite.	NW¼4	37N	8W

Dubakella Mountain Quadrangle 15'

		T.	R.
Chromite found in Serpentine.	center S½34	31N	12W
Chromite found in Serpentine.	SW corner 22	30N	12W
Braunite, Rhodonite, Bementite, Rhodochrosite found in Chert.	SW¼SE¼26	30N	12W
Chromite found in Serpentine.	SW¼SE¼32	30N	12W
Chromite found in Serpentine.	NE¼NW¼9	29N	11W
Chromite found in Serpentine.	center SW¼11	29N	11W
Chromite found in Serpentine.	NW corner 14	29N	11W
Chromite found in Serpentine.	SE corner 35	29N	11W
Rhodonite (pink), found in Chert.	NE¼SE¼9	28N	11W
Manganese Oxides found in Chert.	SW¼SW¼16	28N	11W
Manganese Oxides found in Chert.	center SW¼24	28N	11W
Chromite found in Serpentine.			

French Gulch Quadrangle 15'

	SECTION	T.	R.
Lode Gold, Quartz found in Diorite, Greenstone.	SE¼SE¼2	33N	8W
Lode Gold, Quartz, Limonite.	NW¼NW¼11	33N	8W
Lode Gold, Quartz, Galena, Pyrite found in Slate.	NE¼SW¼11	33N	8W
Lode Gold, Quartz, found in Diorite, Slate.	center E½11	33N	8W
Lode Gold, Quartz, Galena, Pyrite found in Diorite, Slate.	NE corner 14	33N	8W
Lode Gold, Quartz, Limonite found in Diorite, Slate.	SW¼NW¼13	33N	8W
Lode Gold, Quartz found in Diorite, Slate.	SE¼NE¼13	33N	8W

Hayfork Quadrangle 15'

Placer Gold.	SE¼SE¼7	33N	10W
Placer Gold.	center NE¼19	33N	10W
Placer Gold.	NW¼NE¼30	33N	10W
Placer Gold.	NE¼NW¼5	32N	10W
Lode Gold, Quartz.	SW corner 3	33N	11W
Placer Gold.	SW¼SW¼8	31N	11W
Lode Gold, Quartz,Arsenopyrite, Galena, Pyrite found in Slate.	SE¼SW¼17	31N	11W
Lode Gold.	center N½NE¼20	31N	11W
Lode Gold, Quartz found in Slate, Chert.	SW¼SW¼21	31N	11W
Lode Gold.	NE¼NW¼27	31N	11W

Helena Quadrangle 15'

Lode Gold.	NE corner 9	35N	11W
Lode Gold, Quartz found in Slate.	NW¼NW¼14	35N	11W
Lode Gold.	center N½32	35N	11W
Lode Gold, Quartz, Galena, Sphalerite, Pyrite.	center NW¼33	35N	11W
Lode Gold, Quartz.	center W½33	35N	11W
Lode Gold, Chalcopyrite, Pyrite.	SW¼21	35N	10W
Lode Gold, Quartz found in Slate, Granodiorite.	SE corner 28	35N	10W
Placer Gold.	NE corner 31	35N	10W
Lode Gold, Quartz found in Schist, Diorite.	SE corner 32	35N	10W
Lode Gold, Quartz found in Diorite.	NE¼33	35N	10W
Lode Gold found in Slate.	SW¼4	34N	11W
Placer Gold.	NE¼SE¼1	34N	11W
Placer Gold.	SE¼NW¼9	34N	11W
Placer Gold.	NE corner 13	34N	11W
Placer Gold.	NW¼24	34N	11W
Placer Gold.	center 29	34N	11W
Placer Gold.	NW corner 34	34N	11W
Placer Gold.	SE¼35	34N	11W
Copper (native).	27,28,34	34N	11W

Hyampon Quadrangle 15'

Placer Gold.	SE¼NW¼5	33N	12W
Placer Gold.	center NE¼6	33N	12W
Chromite found in Serpentine.	SE¼SW¼30	31N	12W
Chromite found in Serpentine.	NE¼SW¼10	2N	7E
Chromite found in Serpentine.	NW¼NW¼10	2N	7E
Chromite found in Serpentine.	NW¼SE¼10	2N	7E

Ironside Mountain Quadrangle 15'

	SECTION	T.	R.
Lode Gold, Quartz, Copper.	NE¼NE¼29	7N	7E
Lode Gold, Quartz, Bornite, Chalcopyrite, Azurite, Malachite found in Granodiorite.	center 28	7N	7E
Lode Gold.	NE¼NE¼32	7N	7E
Barite.	SE¼SE¼32	7N	7E
Lode Gold, Quartz.	SW¼34	7N	7E
Placer Gold.	NW¼NE¼25	7N	7E
Placer Gold.	SW¼NW¼29	5N	8E
Placer Gold.	SW¼SW¼29	5N	8E

Kettenpom Quadrangle 15'

Chalcopyrite, Bornite, Cubanite, Pyrrhotite, Pyrite, Arsenopyrite, Galena, Sphalerite.	9,10,15	5S	6E

Pickett Peak Quadrangle 15'

Copper (native), Malachite, Cuprite, Bornite.	center 36	1N	7E
Inesite, Bementite, Rhodochrosite.	NW¼23	1S	6E

Trinity Dam Quadrangle 15'

Lode Gold, Quartz found in Diorite.	center 15	35N	10W
Placer Gold.	NE¼NE¼34	35N	9W
Lode Gold, Quartz, Hematite, Limonite.	center 13	34N	9W
Placer Gold.	NE corner 27	34N	9W
Placer Gold.	NW¼16	34N	9W
Lode Gold found in Schist, Slate, Volcanics.	SE¼NE¼31	34N	9W
Placer Gold.	NW¼NE¼20	35N	8W
Placer Gold.	SW¼NW¼27	35N	8W
Placer Gold.	SW corner 28	35N	8W
Placer Gold.	center 33	35N	8W
Lode Gold, Quartz found in Slate.	NW¼SE¼10	34N	8W
Lode Gold.	NE¼NE¼19	34N	8W
Placer Gold.	center 33	34N	8W

Weaverville Quadrangle 15'

Lode Gold.	center of south section line of 3	33N	8W
Placer Gold.	NE corner 6	33N	8W
Placer Gold.	NE corner 8	33N	8W
Placer Gold.	SE¼8	33N	8W
Lode Gold, Quartz, Arsenopyrite, Galena, Pyrite.	center of south section line of 3	33N	8W
Placer Gold.	NE corner 6	33N	8W
Placer Gold.	NW and SW corners of 8,5	33N	8W
Placer Gold.	NW¼20	33N	8W
Placer Gold.	SW¼29	32N	8W
Placer Gold.	NE¼SE¼32	32N	8W
Placer Gold.	SW¼7	33N	9W
Placer Gold.	SE¼SW¼20	33N	9W
Placer Gold.	SW¼SW¼31	33N	9W
Placer Gold.	NE¼NE¼6	32N	9W
Placer Gold.	center N½SW¼18	32N	9W

	SECTION	T.	R.
Lode Gold, Quartz.	NW¼SE¼14	32N	9W
Lode Gold, Galena, Sphalerite.	NW¼NE¼23	32N	9W
Lignite.	NW¼NW¼32	32N	9W
Placer Gold.	SE¼SW¼3	33N	10W
Placer Gold.	At intersection of 13,14,23,24	33N	10W
Placer Gold.	NE¼SW¼1	32N	10W

TULARE COUNTY

California Hot Springs Quadrangle 15'

	SECTION	T.	R.
Scheelite (well formed crystals), Diopside, Calcite, Quartz; Wollastonite, Epidote, Garnet, Granodiorite,Hornfels, Quartzite, Limestone.	N½35	23S	30E
Limestone.	2,3,10,11,14	23S	30E

Camp Nelson Quadrangle 15'

	SECTION	T.	R.
Native Copper, Bornite, middle fork of the Tule River.	30	19S	31E
Chalcopyrite, Pyrrhotite, north fork of the middle fork of the Tule River.	30,32	19S	31E
Barite.	SW¼33	20S	31E

Frazier Valley Quadrangle 7½'

	SECTION	T.	R.
Limestone, blue-gray to black, Schist and Granite walls, 1 mile out-crop.	SE¼6	20S	28E

Kaweah Quadrangle 15'

	SECTION	T.	R.
Scheelite, Garnet, Epidote, Granite, Limestone.	NW¼30	18S	28E
Scheelite, Garnet, Calcite, Epidote, Biotite-hornblende Granodiorite, Limestone.	SE¼SE¼25	17S	28E
Scheelite, Granodiorite, Limestone.	SW¼12	21S	29E
and extreme	NW¼13	21S	29E
Scheelite, Garnet, Epidote, Diopside, Wollastonite, Hornblende-biotite Granodiorite, Limestone.	SE¼27	18S	29E
Scheelite, Hedenbergite, Pyrrhotite, Hornblende-biotite Granodiorite, Limestone.	NW¼31	19S	29E
Scheelite, Garnet, Epidote, Quartzite, Hornfels, Granodiorite, Limestone.	NE¼11	19S	28E
Barite, Slate, Quartzite, Limestone.	SW¼33	20S	31E
Gabbro-diorite (black, takes a good polish).	NW¼29	21S	29E
Pyrolusite, glassy Quartz; Hematite, Limonite, Granite.	33	19S	29E
Feldspar (massive out-crop).	23,24,25	17S	29E
Limestone, blue-gray to black, astride 3 rivers—Garfield Big trees road, ½ mile SE 3 rivers.	SW¼25	17S	28E

Miramonte Quadrangle 7½'

	SECTION	T.	R.
Scheelite (large crystals in Garnet Gangue), Granodiorite, Limestone.	SW¼2	15S	26E
Massive blue Calcite, Scheelite, Garnet, Epidote.	N½11	15S	26E

	SECTION	T.	R.
Limestone.	N½SW¼30	17S	29E
Cordierite, Andalusite, Quartz; Biotite, Orthoclase, in Metamorphics on the north side of the south fork of the Kaweah River ½ mile SE. 3 rivers between sections 25,36		17S	28E

Lamont Peak Quadrangle 15'

	SECTION	T.	R.
Barite, reached by road from Inyo County.	34,35	23S	36E
and	2	24S	36E

Lindsay Quadrangle 7½'

	SECTION	T.	R.
Azurite, Malachite, Jarosite, Serpentine, Gabbro.	SE¼SE¼3	20S	27E
Chrysoprase, laterized Serpentine.	SW¼NW¼5	20S	27E
and	N½NE¼17	20S	27E

Rocky Hill Quadrangle 7½'

	SECTION	T.	R.
Chromite, Serpentinized Dunite.	NW¼20	19S	27E
Chromite, Dunite.	SE¼22	19S	27E
Chromite, Talc, Magnesite, Serpentine.	SE¼NW¼16	19S	27E
Chromite, Serpentine.	SW¼17	19S	27E
and	NW¼20	19S	27E
Azurite, Malachite, Pyrrhotite, Talc, Chalcopyrite, Hematite, Andesite, Granite Gneiss.	NE¼SW¼33	18S	27E
Feldspar.	SW¼15	18S	27E

Success Dam Quadrangle 7½'

	SECTION	T.	R.
Variegated and light gray Limestone.	SE¼13	21S	28E
and	N½13	21S	28E

Tehipite Dome Quadrangle 15'

	SECTION	T.	R.
Molybdenite, Wolframite, Scheelite, Andalusite (crystals to 2″), Granite. West side of valley of Sheep Creek	NW¼34	11S	28E

Tucker Mountain Quadrangle 7½'

	SECTION	T.	R.
Graphite.	4,5	15S	26E

White River Quadrangle 15'

	SECTION	T.	R.
Yellow-green Nickeliferous Magnesite, white Magnesite, Talc, Chalcedony, Cordierite, Andalusite, Magnetite. and	SE¼SE¼21 NE¼NE¼28	22S	28E
Scheelite, Garnet, Norite, Granodiorite, Limestone.	S½SW¼17	23S	29E
Chrysoprase, Silicified Serpentine (Opal and Jasper), Magnesite, Garnierite. and	SE¼20 NE¼29	22S 22S	28E 28E

Woodlake Quadrangle 7½'

	SECTION	T.	R.
Limestone, pure white to black.	NE¼35	17S	27E

TUOLUMNE COUNTY

Chinese Camp Quadrangle 7½'

	SECTION	T.	R.
Chromite, Serpentine.	4,5,8,9	1S	14E
Magnesite, Serpentine.	E½16	1S	14E
Magnesite, Serpentine.	S½S½6	1S	14E
Magnesite, Serpentine.	SW¼6	1S	14E
Slate.	36	1S	13E

Columbia Quadrangle 15'

	SECTION	T.	R.
Gold Drift Mine, was a profitable operation on the Table Mountain Channel.	SE¼22	2N	14E
Gold, Quartz; Pyrite, Marcasite, Galena, Granodiorite.	4	2N	14E
Gold, Quartz; Pyrite, Galena, Chalcopyrite, Dolomitic Limestone; Diorite. (Gold, average $5-15 a ton).	NW¼1	2N	14E
Gold, Quartz; Schist, total production about $100,000.	4	2N	15E

Lazar pocket Gold mine, east side of Woods Creek near Browns Flat, 1½ miles north of Sonora. 1929-31, produced $11,000 in crystallized Gold specimens. Pocket worth, $5,000, mined in 1934. Pocket worth $13,000 in 1935.

	SECTION	T.	R.
Gold, Quartz; basic dikes, Slate, Limestone. (Over $100,000 from pockets).	25	2N	14E
Graphite.	E½9	2N	14E
Graphite, Sandstone; Slate, several hundred tons produced.	W½24	2N	14E
Limestone, Marble.	NE¼23	2N	14E
Limestone.	2,3	2N	14E

Columbia SE Quadrangle 7½'

		SECTION	T.	R.
Gold, important pocket producer, $700,000. Much of the Gold was beautifully crystallized in white Quartz and Talc with Petzite, Sylvanite and Pyrite.	and	S½SW¼19	2N	15E
		N½NW¼30	2N	15E

La Grange Quadrangle 7½'

	SECTION	T.	R.
Chalcocite, Pyrite, Chalcopyrite, Bornite, Arsenopyrite, Sphalerite, Quartz; Augite Porphyry, Schist.	30	2S	14E

Long Barn Quadrangle 15'

	SECTION	T.	R.
Epidote.	11,14	2N	16E
Gold, Quartz; Granodiorite, produced several million dollars.	W½10	2N	16E
Molybdenite, Epidote, Garnet, Quartz.	16,17	3N	17E

Melones Dam Quadrangle 7½'

	SECTION	T.	R.
Chromite, Serpentine, several thousand tons produced.	2	1S	13E

Moccasin Quadrangle 7½'

	SECTION	T.	R.
Bementite, Rhodochrosite, Chert.	17	2S	15E

	SECTION	T.	R.
Gold, some rich pockets in Pyritic Slate.	NE¼26	1S	15E
Gold, Quartz; Slate, Pyritic Slate, one beautiful specimen taken out in 1946 was 6" wide and 13" long and weighed 67 ounces.	E½E½26	1S	15E
Gold, Quartz, small high grade shoots.	SE¼30	1S	16E

Sonora Quadrangle 7½'

	SECTION	T.	R.
Chromite, Serpentine.	21,28	1N	14E
Malachite, Azurite, Chalcopyrite.	N½28	1N	14E
Gold, Quartz, Calcite, Amphibolite Schist. Pocket mine, two pockets yielded $11,000.	center 30	2N	14E
Gold (Bonanza mine), produced over $200,000, from small rich pockets, claim is on Gold Hill in Sonora at the head of Washington street.			
Gold, Quartz; Sulfides.	NE¼27	1N	14E
Gold, Quartz, Calcite, Amphibolite Schist, Pyrite cubes to 1" square, some larger. A thin coating of Gold sometimes found on the crystal faces.	29,30	2N	14E
Gold, Quartz, Tetradymite (Gold, $5.25 a ton).	27,35	1N	14E

Standard Quadrangle 7½'

	SECTION	T.	R.
Gold, Quartz, Pyrite, Galena, Sphalerite, Schist, Diorite.	32	2N	16E
Gold, Quartz; some good Ore.	1	1N	15E
Gold, Quartz; some good Ore.	SW¼NE¼30	2N	16E
Gold, one pocket yielded 386 oz. from two tons of Ore.	6	1N	15E
Limestone, Marble.	20,29	1N	15E
Limestone.	26,27,32,34,35	1N	15E
Limestone.	center 7	1N	15E

TO ORDER MAPS: Send your name, address, and zip code.

Denver Distribution Section

U.S. Geological Survey
Denver Federal Center, Bldg. 41
Denver, Colorado, 80225

ORDER BY

State: California
County:
Quadrangle:
Current Price: Prepayment of 75 cents
each.

For maps of National Forests in California

WRITE TO:

U.S. Forest Service
630 Sansome Street
San Francisco, California 94111

195

Bibliography

Chesterman, Charles W. 1979. *The Aududon Society Field Guild to North American Rocks and Minerals.* Knopf.

Fenton, Carroll Lane, and Mildred A. Fenton. 1940. *The Rock Book.* Doubleday, Doran and Co., New York. A good beginner's guide.

Ford, Wm. E. 1954. *Dana's Textbook of Mineralogy, 5th edition.* John Wiley and Sons, New York.

Geologic Guidebook along Highway 49—Sierran Gold Belt, by various authors. 1953. Bulletin 141, California State Division of Mines, 3rd edition.

Geologic Guidebook of the San Francisco Bay Counties, by various authors. 1951. Bulletin 154, California State Division of Mines. History, landscape, geology, fossils, minerals, industry, and routes to travel.

Geology of Southern California (a set of several books, booklets and maps by various authors). 1955. California State Division of Mines.

Henry, Darold J. and Lowell R. Gordon. 1952. *Principle California Locations, Gem Trail Journal.* Long Beach, California.

Hinds, Norman E.A. 1952. *Evolution of the California Landscape,* Bulletin 158, Calif. State Division of Mines.

Liddicont, Richard T. 1981. *Handbook of Gemstone Identification,* 11th Edition. Gemnological Publications.

Mondedor, Editor. 1985. *Simon & Schuster's Guide to Rocks and Minerals.* Simon & Schuster.

Pearl, Richard M. 1980. *Cleaning and Preserving Minerals.* 5th Edition. Earth Sciences.

Pough, Frederick H. 1976. *A Field Guide to Rocks and Minerals, 4th Edition.* Peterson Field Guide Series, Houghton Mifflin.

Robbins, Michael. 1983. *The Collector's Book of Florescent Minerals.* Van Nostrand Rhinehold.

Toulovkian, U.S. and C.V. Ho. 1981. *Physical Properties of Rocks and Minerals.* McGraw-Hill.

Index

Where an * is placed before a number, as in *66, this indicates an illustration is found on that page. A number in boldface, as in **10,** refers to the page where there is the most full description of a rock or mineral. Rare minerals that are listed only once in the book are listed in the Habitat Chart on pages 38 to 40. Rock-forming minerals are printed in boldface, as in **quartz.** See pages 115–119 for Supplementary Rocks and Minerals not listed in Index. See Quadrangle Map information, pages 119–195 and general Topography Map information in Foreword.

197

199